Language and th

LANGUAGE AND THE LEXICON

An Introduction

DAVID SINGLETON
Associate Professor of Applied Linguistics
Trinity College Dublin

A member of the Hodder Headline Group
LONDON

Co-published in the United States of America by
Oxford University Press Inc., New York

First published in Great Britain in 2000 by
Arnold, a member of the Hodder Headline Group,
338 Euston Road, London NW1 3BH

http://www.arnoldpublishers.com

Co-published in the United States of America by
Oxford University Press Inc.,
198 Madison Avenue, New York, NY10016

British Library Cataloguing in Publication Data
A catalogue record for this book is available from the British Library

Library of Congress Cataloging-in-Publication Data
A catalog record for this book is available from the Library of Congress

ISBN 0 340 73173 7 (hb)
ISBN 0 340 73174 5 (pb)

1 2 3 4 5 6 7 8 9 10

Production Editor: Anke Ueberberg
Production Controller: Bryan Eccleshall
Cover Design: Terry Griffiths

Typeset in 10/12 Sabon by Saxon Graphics Ltd, Derby

In memoriam

This book is dedicated to the memory of my much-missed friend
Andrew Corrigan, unvanquished jazzman, wordsmith *extraordinaire* and
irreplaceable companion.

Too irreverent for the clergy,
Too irrelevant for the sages,
I tinker on,
Lost in a maze of words
That hide their meanings
In a jovial host
Of irreverence
And irrelevance.

Andrew Corrigan, 'Disbelief Between', October 1973

Contents

Preface

A number of people have made valuable contributions to the process of which this book is the product. I especially need to acknowledge the absolutely indispensable assistance I received in the initial stages of planning and writing the volume from Lisa Ryan, now Research Fellow in Linguistics at University College, Dublin. Without Lisa's input, some of the early chapters might never have reached any kind of conclusion, never mind a happy one. I am also indebted to Jennifer Pariseau for using some of the time she spent teaching in Thailand in 1998–99 to collect examples in Thai, which she was then good enough to pass on to me for recycling in the pages that follow.

Various other colleagues have shown their usual generosity in agreeing to cast a critical eye over parts of the book relating to areas where their expertise easily outstrips mine. In this connection I should like to thank Nicola McLelland of the Department of Germanic Studies, Trinity College Dublin, Breffni O'Rourke of the Centre for Language and Communication Studies, Trinity College Dublin, Vera Regan of the Department of French, University College Dublin, and Carl Vogel of the Department of Computer Science, Trinity College, Dublin. A further very helpful sounding board was provided by the editorial team at Edward Arnold, and in particular by Christina Wipf Perry, to whom I am most grateful indeed not only for the unflagging encouragement she offered but also for her great sensitivity and aplomb in guiding me away from all manner of blind alleys.

At an institutional level my thanks are due to the Trinity College Dublin Arts/ESS Benefactions Fund for financial support of my research in the lexical area and to the Board of Trinity College Dublin for granting me a six-month leave of absence while I was preparing this book.

Finally, I should like most warmly to thank my wife, Emer, and my sons, Christopher and Daniel, for various kinds of help they have given me over the past two years and perhaps above all for their forbearance!

I am all too aware that, despite all the advice and assistance I have received from the above, the volume is very far from perfect and contains many faults and failings, for which I am entirely unabashed to recognize my sole responsibility. After all, in the words of the Chevalier de Boufflers, perfectibility is to perfection what time is to eternity.

Greystones, County Wicklow
February 2000

|1|

Introduction:
The lexicon – words and more

1.1 Some preliminary definitions

This book is about the lexicon. *Lexicon* is the Anglicized version of a Greek word (λεξικόν), which basically means 'dictionary', and it is the term used by linguists to refer to those aspects of a language which relate to words, otherwise known as its *lexical* aspects. *Lexicon* is based on the term *lexis* (λέξις), whose Greek meaning is 'word', but which is used as a collective expression in linguistic terminology in the sense of 'vocabulary'. The study of lexis and the lexicon is called *lexicology*.

In fact, as we shall see in the course of the next 200 pages or so, almost everything in language is related in some way or other to words. We shall also see that, conversely, the lexical dimension of language needs to be conceived of as rather more than just a list of lexical items.

1.2 Words and language

'In the beginning was the Word . . . '

This opening pronouncement of the Gospel of John in the New Testament may or may not be a true claim about the origins of the cosmos. However, if taken as a statement about where our thinking about language started from (and continues to start from) it is hard to fault.

The original version of John's Gospel was written in Greek, and in this version the term used for 'word' is *lógos* (λόγος), which, significantly enough, meant (and in Modern Greek still means) 'speech' as well as 'word'. This kind of association between the concept of word and a more general concept of speech or language is by no means confined to Greek culture. For example, to stay with the Gospel of John for just a little longer, the Latin translation of the above quotation is : '*In principio erat Verbum . . .*', where λόγος is replaced by *verbum*, an expression which, like the Greek term, was applicable to speech as well as to individual words. Thus, for example, one way of saying 'to speak in public' in Latin was *verbum in publico facere* (literally, 'word in public to make').

A similar association between 'word' and 'speech' is to be found in many other languages. For example, this dual meaning attaches to French *parole*, Italian *parola* and Spanish *palabra*. Similarly, in Japanese the term *kotoba* ('word', 'phrase', 'expression') is often abbreviated to *koto* or *goto* and is used as a suffix in expressions referring to speech such as *hitorigoto o iu* (literally, 'by-oneself-word say' = 'talk to oneself') and *negoto o iu* (literally, 'sleep-word say' = 'talk in one's sleep'); in Swedish the expression *en ordets man* (literally, 'an of-the-word man') is used to refer to a skilled speaker; and in German one way of saying 'to refuse someone permission to speak' translates literally as 'from someone the word to remove' – *einem das Wort entziehen*. In English, too, the association between the word and language in use is very much a feature of the way in which linguistic events are talked about in ordinary parlance, as the following examples illustrate:

That traffic warden wants a <u>word</u> with you.

A <u>word</u> in the right ear works wonders.

When you are free for lunch just say the <u>word</u>.

The Prime Minister's <u>words</u> have been misinterpreted by the media.

The <u>wording</u> needs to be revised.

Nor is it particularly surprising that words should loom so large in people's understanding of what language is. After all, words are vital to linguistic communication, and without them not much can be conveyed. For instance, a visitor to a Spanish-speaking country anxious to discover where the toilets are in some location or other may have a perfect command of Spanish pronunciation and sentence-structure, but will make little progress without the word *servicios* (in Spain) or *sanitarios* (in Latin America).

It needs perhaps to be added that awareness of words is not limited to literate societies. The American linguist Edward Sapir, for example, conducted a great deal of fieldwork among Native Americans in the early part of the twentieth century. His goal was the transcription and analysis of Native American languages which had not previously been described. He found that although the Native Americans he was working with were illiterate and thus unaccustomed to the concept of the written word, they nevertheless had no serious difficulty in dictating a text to him word by word, and that they were also quite capable of isolating individual words and repeating them as units.

Interestingly, a child acquiring language appears to develop an awareness of words earlier than an awareness of how sentences are formed. For example, research has shown that children in the age group 2–3½ correct themselves when they make errors with words before they start self-correcting in the area of sentence construction. Thus, examples like the first one given below will begin to appear earlier than examples like the second one cited.

you pick up . . . you take her (substitution of *take* for initial word-choice *pick up*)

The kitty cat is . . . the . . . the spider is kissing the kitty cat's back (re-ordering of elements in order to avoid the passive construction *The kitty-cat's back is being kissed by the spider*)

With regard to the specialist study of language, this too has been highly word-centred. For instance, in *phonology*, under which heading fall both the sound-structure of languages and the study of such sound-structure, a major focus of attention is the identification of sound distinctions which are significant in a particular language. Anyone with any knowledge of English, for example, is aware that in that language the broad distinction between the '*t*-sound' and the '*p*-sound' is important, whereas no such importance attaches to the distinction between an *aspirated t* (i.e. a *t*-sound pronounced with a fair amount of air being expelled) and an *unaspirated t* sound (i.e. a *t*-sound pronounced without such a voluminous expulsion of air). This last distinction is, in English, determined simply by the particular environment in which the *t*-sound occurs; thus, *aspirated t* occurs at the beginnings of words like *ten*, *tight* and *toe*, whereas *unaspirated t* occurs after the *s*-sound in words like *steer*, *sting* and *stool*. Phonologists talk about environmentally conditioned varieties of the *t*-sound in a given language as belonging to or being realizations of the /t/ *phoneme*, and label them as *allophones* of the phoneme in question. (Notice that the convention in linguistics is for phonemes to be placed between slashes – /t/ –, whereas allophones are placed between square brackets – the transcription of the aspirated allophone of /t/, for example, being [tʰ]).

To return to the role of words in all this, one of the crucial tests for phonemic distinctions is that of lexical differentiation – that is, the test of whether a particular sound distinction differentiates between words. This can be tested by use of minimal pairs – pairs of words which differ in respect of just one sound (*pin/tin*, *top/tot*, *gape/gate* etc.). Distinctions between sound segments which serve to differentiate between words in this way – such as the difference between the English *p*-sound and the English *t*-sound – are called *phonemic* distinctions, whereas distinctions between sound segments which do not differentiate between words – such as degrees of aspiration of English consonants are described as *non-phonemic*. It should be noted, incidentally, that in other languages (such as Sanskrit and its modern descendants) the distinction between aspirated and unaspirated consonants, which in English is merely allophonic, is as important in differentiating between words as the distinction between /p/ and /t/ in English.

There are other ways of studying the sounds used in human languages – ways which do not need to refer to phonemes and hence have no particular connection with lexical issues. For example, it is perfectly possible, without getting involved in questions of word differentiation and without any regard to the semantic implications of using one sound rather than another in a particular language, to study the acoustic properties of human speech (in terms of the physics of sound) or the physiological aspects of speech production (the interplay of the lips, the tongue, the vocal cords etc.). These kinds of phenomena and their investigation go under the heading of *phonetics*. The Greek root *phonē (φονή* – 'sound', 'voice'*)*, is shared by both *phonetics* and *phonology*, but whereas phonology deals with the sound systems of individual languages (and any universal organizational principles which may emerge from such investigations) – and in doing so uses lexical differentiation as an important reference point – phonetics is concerned with speech sounds without reference to linguistic system and meaning. Thus it can be said that what differentiates phonology from phonetics is an interest in lexical differentiation in the above sense.

At the grammatical level too, the distinction between two major areas of interest essentially revolves around words – although in a somewhat different manner. Grammar has traditionally been seen as having two branches – *syntax* and *morphology* – and in both cases the very definition of terms is lexically based. Thus, the term *syntax*, a derivative of the Greek word *syntaxis* (*σύνταξις* – 'putting together in order'), denotes the whole range of regularities which can be observed in the combination of sentence components (and the study of such regularities), and it turns out that these components are largely identifiable as words and groups of words. For example, the distinction between the syntax of statements in English (e.g. *John can swim.*) and the syntax of questions (e.g. *Can John swim?*) is, at least from one perspective, a distinction between different ways of ordering words. The term *morphology*, for its part, owes its origins to the Greek root *morphē (μορφή* – 'form', 'shape') and denotes the internal structure of words (and the study thereof) – that is, how words are built up out of basic units (known as *morphemes*) which may or may not be capable of standing alone as words in their own right (e.g. *un-just-ly, de-nation-al-ize, re-en-act-ment* etc.).

A third area right at the heart of linguists' interests, namely *semantics* – that is, the domain of meaning (and its investigation) – is also very much bound up with words. Although the coverage of the term *semantics* (from the Greek *sēma* (*σῆμα*) – 'sign', 'signal') extends well beyond the limits of the lexicon, and semanticists certainly do not confine their attention to the meanings of individual words, the lexical level of meaning has always been the starting point for semantic study and theorizing, and remains a focus for debate. Thus, for instance, there is continuing discussion over whether the meaning of a word like *man* should be seen as an aggregate of the relations between *man* and words such as *animal, woman, child* etc., whether it should be treated as decomposable into smaller atoms of meaning (human, male, adult etc.), whether it should be envisaged as some kind of idealized or stereotypical mental image against which actual instances of men are compared, or whether all three approaches should be integrated in some way.

1.3   What's in a word?

Although, as is clear from the above, the word is central to the way in which non-specialists and specialists alike think about language, defining what a word is poses a problem or two. To begin with, what we mean by *word* will depend very much on whether we are talking about actual occurrences of any items that might qualify or whether we are intent on grouping or classifying items in some way or other.

To illustrate this, let us begin by looking at the chorus from the Beatles' song *She Loves You*:

She loves you, yeah, yeah, yeah;

She loves you, yeah, yeah yeah;

She loves you, yeah, yeah, yeah, yeah.

How many words are there in these three lines? If we take actual occurrences of any items – word *tokens* – as the basis of our count, we shall come up with 6 words in the first line, six in the second, and seven in the third. That is 19 overall. On the other hand, if we base our count on word *types* – items with different identities – the overall figure for the entire extract will be just four (*she*, *loves*, *you* and *yeah*). Similarly, the phrase *going, going, gone* will be considered a three-word expression on a count of tokens but will be considered to contain only two words (*going* and *gone*) on a count of types.

In another sense of *word*, the sequence *going, going, gone* may be thought of as containing just one word – the verb *go*, represented by two of its forms (*going* and *gone*). This approach to the notion of the word – seeing it as a 'family' of related forms or as an abstract unit which is realized by one or other of these forms as the linguistic environment demands – calls to mind the concept of the phoneme and its allophones (see above). This linkage with the phoneme idea is expressed terminologically: the notion of the word as a family of forms or as an abstract unit is captured in the term *lexeme*, while a lexeme's concrete representatives or realizations are referred to as *word-forms*. When we want to refer to a given lexeme in, for instance, a dictionary-entry, we typically do so using just one of its various forms, and the choice of this form, known as the *citation form*, is determined by convention, which varies from culture to culture and language to language. For example, the citation form of a French verb lexeme is its infinitive form (*donner*, *sortir*, *prendre* etc.), whereas the citation form of a Modern Greek verb is the first-person singular form of the present indicative (*káno/κάνω, thélo/θέλω, akúo/ακούω* etc.).

We can also see words in different perspectives according to the particular level of linguistic classification we are applying. For example, if we look at

the English word *thinks* from the point of view of the English orthographic
(spelling) system we shall see it as a series of letters – *t* + *h* + *i* + *n*+ *k* + *s*; if we
consider it as a phonological entity we shall perceive it as a sequence of
phonemes – /ʊ/ + /ɪ/ + /n/ + /k/ + /s/ – one of which, /ʊ/, corresponds to the
letters *th* in the English writing system; if we view *thinks* in grammatical
terms, we shall focus on the fact that we have before us the third-person singular present form of a verb; and if we approach it as a carrier of meaning,
we shall be led to relate it to (among other things) the synonyms which can
replace it in different contexts, for example:

> I *think/believe* I can do it.

> The philosopher's task is to *think/cogitate*.

> I'll *think about/consider* your suggestion.

Mention of meaning brings us to the distinction which has been drawn
between what are termed *content words* (also called *full words* or *lexical
words*) and *form words* (otherwise known as *grammatical words, empty
words* or *function words*). Words described as *content words* are those
which are considered to have substantial meaning even out of context,
whereas words described as *form words* are those considered to have little or
no independent meaning and to have a largely grammatical role. Some
examples of content words are: *bucket, cheese, president*; some examples of
form words are: *a, it, of*. This distinction is not unproblematic, since many
so-called form words – such as prepositions like *around* and *towards* and
conjunctions like *although* and *whereas* – are clearly far from empty of
semantic content. In any case, we need to be careful with the idea of
'semantic content'. We have to keep in mind that it is a metaphor, and that
people not words are the sources of meanings, even if words are used as
instruments to signal such meanings. Actually, a more satisfactory way of
distinguishing between content words and form words is in terms of set
membership: grammatical words belong to classes with more or less fixed
membership (at least during any individual speaker's lifetime), while content
words belong to open classes whose membership is subject to quite rapid
change, as new terms come into being and others fall into disuse.

    In the light of all that has been said so far in this section, it is hardly sur-
prising that linguists' attempts to provide a general characterization of the
word have made reference to quite a wide variety of possible defining properties. The main lines of these different approaches are set out below.

The orthographic approach

In the orthographic approach the word is defined as a sequence of letters
bounded on either side by a blank space. This definition works up to a point
for languages using writing systems such as the Roman or Cyrillic alphabet,

but is not at all useful in relation to languages (like Chinese and Japanese) whose writing-systems do not consistently mark word-boundaries or in relation to language varieties which do not usually appear in written form (e.g. local varieties of Colloquial Arabic) or which have never been written down (e.g. many of the indigenous languages of the Americas). Also, there seems to be something rather odd about defining words in terms of the written medium given that, as we have seen, the word is in no sense a *product* of literacy, and given that, both in the history of human language and in the development of the individual, written language arrives on the scene well after spoken language. We can note further that defining words in terms of letter-sequences and spaces is very much a form-oriented, token-oriented exercise which takes absolutely no account of more abstract conceptions of the word.

The phonetic approach

Another possible way of trying to define the word is to look for some way in which words might be identifiable in terms of the way they sound – irrespective of the particular sound-systems of specific languages. It might perhaps be imagined, for example, that words are separated from each other in speech by pauses. Alas, life is not that simple! In fact, individual words can rarely be pinpointed in physical terms in the ordinary flow of speech, which is in the main a continuous burst of noise. (Anyone who needs to be convinced of this should tune to a radio station broadcasting in a totally unfamiliar language.) Indeed, the lack of phonetic independence of individual words is precisely what explains linguistic changes such as the loss from some words in English of an initial /n/ (because this was felt to belong to the preceding indefinite article, e.g. *auger* from Old English *nafu-gar*; *apron* from Old French *naperon*) and the addition of a 'stolen' /n/ in some other cases (e.g. *a newt* from *an ewt*; *a nickname* from *an eke-name*). It is, of course, true that pausing is possible between words, and that linguists in the field working on hitherto undescribed languages may sometimes be able to make use of the 'potential pause' criterion when gathering data from native speakers – as Sapir did (see above) – but, since speakers do not normally pause between words this criterion has rather limited value.

The phonological approach

At first glance a more promising approach to defining words on the basis of sound is to think in terms of the characteristics of words in particular sound-systems. For example, in some languages – English being a case in point – words tend to have only one stressed syllable, which may occur in various positions (e.g. *renew, renewable, renewability* etc.). Another instance of a word-related phonological feature is that of vowel-harmony in languages such as Estonian, Finnish, Hungarian and Turkish. In this case the nature of the vowel in the first part of a word determines the choice of vowels in what follows. This is illustrated by the following two Hungarian words : *kegy-etlen-ség-ük-ben* (literally, 'pity-less-ness-their-in' = 'in their cruelty') versus *gond-atlan-ság-uk-ban* (literally, 'care-less-ness-their-in' = 'in their careless-ness'). Also to be considered in this context is the fact that in a given language a particular phoneme or combination of phonemes may be found only rarely or not at all in a specific position in the word; for instance, in English /z/ is seldom to be found at the beginning of words and the '*ng* sound' (/ŋ/) never occurs at all in this position. One problem with phonological charac-terizations of words is that, of their very nature, they relate to specific lan-guages or, at best, to specific language-types. Also, such characterizations often have to be seen as descriptions of broad tendencies rather than as absolutely reliable; thus, with regard to stress in English, many units that are recognized as words in that language typically do not actually take stress in ordinary speech, e.g. *and, but, by, if, the* – and, on the other hand, in some groups of words which constitute fixed expressions (see below, Chapter 4) only one main stress is applied in the entire group, e.g. <u>buil</u>ding worker, <u>dan</u>cing lesson, <u>life</u>boat crew.

The semantic approach

If definitions in terms of sound have their limitations, what about definitions in terms of meaning? Might it not be possible, for example, to define words as the basic units of meaning in language? The answer to this question is unfortunately 'No'. There are admittedly individual units of meaning which are expressed in single, simple words. For example, the English words *ant*, *bottle* and *shoe* are individual and indivisible forms which convey specific individual meanings. However, the relationship between single words and particular meanings is not always quite so straightforward.

Let us consider, for instance the English word *teapot*. This is written as a single item and can be thought of as denoting a single entity, but, on the other hand, it does actually contain two elements which are words in their own right – *tea* and *pot*. Similarly, there are combinations which are not nec-essarily written as one word, such as: *public house, cricket pavilion, ice-cream kiosk* etc. Actually, if we think more carefully about the meanings of such combinations we can recognize the semantic contributions of each indi-vidual word, but the image which each combination of words first brings to mind is unquestionably that of a single building or type of building. A further obvious point to be made about the idea of words being minimum units of meaning is that there are actually units *below* the level of the word which function as semantic units. Reference has already been made to the fact that words may contain units that cannot stand alone as words in their own right. For example, the word *un-just-ly* has the word *just* as its core but also contains two elements (*un-* and *-ly*) which are vital to its meaning – *un* meaning roughly 'not' and *-ly* meaning something like 'in a . . . manner'.

The grammatical approach

The characterization of the word that seems to be least problematic is that which defines words in grammatical terms. The grammatical approach uses the criteria of 'positional mobility' and 'internal stability' . Words are said to be 'positionally mobile' in the sense that they are not fixed to specific places in a sentence. For example, in a sentence like *The cat drowsily stretched her elegant forelegs* we can re-order the words in various ways without removing or disrupting anything essential.

The cat stretched her elegant forelegs drowsily.

Drowsily the cat stretched her elegant forelegs.

Her elegant forelegs the cat drowsily stretched.

'Internal stability' refers to the fact that within words the order of morphemes remains consistent. Thus the morphemic constituents of, for example, *forelegs* (*fore + leg + s*) cannot be altered – so that *sforeleg, *slegfore, *legfores, foresleg and legsfore are not possible versions of the word in question.

Definition of the word as units which are positionally mobile but internally stable works well across languages. However, even this on the whole successful definition needs some qualification. For example, the English definite article *the* would normally be considered a word, but its positional mobility is distinctly limited. That is to say, except when it is being talked about as an object of study (as it is now), it has to be part of a noun phrase, occurring before the noun and any other elements that are included to qualify the noun; thus, *the wolf, the large wolf, the extremely large wolf* etc. Interestingly, the words that have such tight restrictions imposed on their possible positions in sentences are typically grammatical words, notably, definite articles (*the*), indefinite articles (*a, an*), prepositions (*in, on, to, from* etc.), which, as we have seen, have traditionally been regarded as lesser species of words, not 'full words'.

Defining the word: a summary

Having looked at a number of possibilities for defining the word, then, what can we say about this problem? Well, one thing is clear: there is not just one way of looking at words. We can see them as types or tokens; we can see them as lexemes or word-forms; we can see them as orthographic units, phonological units, grammatical units or semantic units. We can also make a distinction between content words and form words.

Regarding the various approaches to providing a general characterization of the word, it is clear that the grammatical approach in this connection is not only the least problematic but also the one that works best across languages. Phonetic and semantic perspectives offer little in the way of definitional criteria, but they do suggest some procedures which may be of use to the field linguist working with informants. As far as orthographic and phonological approaches are concerned, the criteria which emerge from these approaches apply in different ways and degrees to different languages.

One result of particular sets of criteria operating differently from language to language is that words in one language may have some characteristics which have little or nothing in common with the characteristics of words in another language. For example, a word in Finnish – with word-stress and vowel-harmony – is rather different from a word in French, a language in which neither word-stress nor vowel-harmony operates. This does not mean, though, that it is inappropriate to use the term *word* in a cross-linguistic context. Finnish words and French words are recognizable on the basis of other criteria – grammatical criteria, the 'potential pause' criterion etc. – which are not tied to any particular language or language-group.

1.4   The domain of the lexicon

We have seen how the word is not perhaps as easy to characterize as one might have imagined before starting to reflect on this problem. Alas, even when we have arrived at some reasonably satisfying conclusions about how to define words, we are still rather a long way from defining what the lexicon is.

As we noted earlier, *lexicon* is the Anglicized version of a Greek word meaning 'dictionary'. It may be instructive, then, in the context of a discussion of the domain of the lexicon, briefly to consider what kind of information is typically to be found in a dictionary. The following example is drawn – more or less at random – from the pages of the *Concise Oxford English Dictionary*.

> **kin** /kɪn/ *n.* & *adj.* One's relatives or family. – *predic. adj.* (of a person)
> related (*we are kin*; *he is kin to me*) (see also AKIN) □**kith and kin** see
> KITH. **near of kin** closely related by blood, or in character. **next of
> kin** see NEXT. □□**kinless** *adj.* [OE *cynn* f. Gmc]

What is interesting about such an entry is that, although the focus of the dictionary-maker is obviously on the individual word – in this specific instance on the word *kin* – a broader range of information seems inevitably to find its way into the picture. Thus, as well as information about the spelling (*kin*), sound-shape (/kɪn/) and meaning ('one's relatives or family') of the particular item in question, we are provided with information about its various grammatical roles – *n.* [= noun] *& adj.* [=adjective], some examples of how it is used as a *predic. adj.* [= predicative adjective] (*we are kin; he is kin to me*), some examples of expressions in which it occurs (*kith and kin, near of kin, next of kin*), an example of a word formed by adding a suffix to *kin* (*kinless*), and a potted history of *kin* – OE *cynn* f. Gmc [= Old English *cynn* from Germanic].

And so it is generally when one begins to look closely at any given individual word. Other issues simply cannot be kept at bay – especially issues having to do with how the word in question interacts with other elements. Take the very simple and unremarkable word *dog*, for instance. As soon as we home in on this word we have to recognize that part of its essential profile is that it is both a noun and a verb. Its grammatical categorization in these terms implies that it can appear in sentences like *We all pat the <u>dog</u>* as well as in sentences like *The President was <u>dogged</u> by misfortune*. We also have to recognize that *dog* is a participant in a wide range of frequently occurring combinations, or *collocations*, with other words, not all of which have meanings which are easily relatable to canineness – <u>*dog in the manger*</u> (= 'a person who refuses to let others have something for which he/she has no use'), <u>*dog's dinner*</u> (= 'a mess'), *raining cats and <u>dogs</u>* (= 'raining hard') etc.

One especially interesting aspect of such interaction between a word and its linguistic environment is the way in which the choice of one word may have one set of repercussions in this environment, while the choice of another word – even a word with a fairly similar meaning – may have quite a different set of repercussions. The examples below – from English, French and German respectively – illustrate this point.

We are <u>forbidden to leave</u> the building after midnight.

We are <u>prohibited from leaving</u> the building after midnight.

[choice of *forbid* entails choice of *to* + VERB; choice of *prohibit* entails choice of *from* + VERB*ing*]

Nous <u>espérons qu'elle chantera</u>.
(literally, 'We hope that she will sing.' = 'We hope she will sing.')

Nous <u>voulons qu'elle chante</u>
(literally, 'We want that she sing.' = 'We want her to sing.')

[choice of verb *espérer* entails choice of future indicative form of verb – *chantera* – in following clause; choice of verb *vouloir* entails choice of present subjunctive form of verb – *chante* – in following clause]

Sie hat <u>mir geholfen</u>.
(literally, 'She has me helped.' = 'She (has) helped me.')

Sie hat <u>mich getröstet</u>.
(literally, 'She has me comforted.' = 'She (has) comforted me.'

[choice of verb *helfen* – past participle *geholfen* – entails choice of dative form of object pronoun – *mir*; choice of verb *trösten* – past participle *getröstet* – entails choice of accusative form of object pronoun – *mich*]

This discussion of the interplay between lexis and other aspects of language continues in the chapters that follow. However, even from the foregoing brief excursion into this topic we can draw the conclusions that, on the one hand, any plausible conception of the lexicon has to be broad enough in scope to include elements other than just individual words, and that, on the other, aspects of language not customarily thought of as lexical – notably grammatical phenomena – have to be recognized as at least having a lexical dimension.

1.5   Summary

This chapter has noted the extent to which language is popularly conceived of in terms of words – even in the absence of literacy – and of the extent to which awareness of language as words features in child language development. It has also pointed to evidence of 'lexico-centricity' in the way in which linguists have traditionally approached language as an object of study. It has shown that, despite all of this, it is no easy matter to define what a word actually is, illustrating this point by reference to possible phonological, orthographic, semantic and grammatical perspectives on the problem. It has then offered some first thoughts on the proposition that words cannot be seen in isolation from other aspects of language.

With regard to the content of the remaining chapters:

- Chapter 2 continues the discussion begun in the present chapter on the relationship between lexis and syntax.
- Chapter 3 looks at the ways in which words are structured.
- Chapter 4 focuses on habitual lexical combinations – collocations.
- Chapter 5 explores various approaches to lexical semantics.
- Chapter 6 examines the relationship between the lexicon and the phonology and orthography of particular languages.
- Chapter 7 scrutinizes the ways in which the lexicon relates to social, regional and situational variation in language.
- Chapter 8 describes and exemplifies different types of lexical change in the historical development of languages.
- Chapter 9 addresses the question of what is involved in the construction of a 'internal' or 'mental' lexicon in the context of the acquisition of a language and also discusses ways in which the mental lexicon might be organized and accessed.
- Chapter 10 surveys the evolution of dictionary-making – lexicography – from its origins down to its very recent, technologically based manifestations and offers an account of how lexis has been treated in the context of language teaching.

Finally, the Conclusion draws together the threads of the various parts of the discussion in some final comments on the expanding perception of the extent and the role of the lexicon.

Sources and suggestions for further reading

See 1.2. Edward Sapir's comments on his work with Native Americans can be found on pp. 33–4 of his book *Language: an introduction to the study of speech* (New York: Harcourt Brace & World, 1921).

The source of the examples of children's self-corrections is a paper by E. V. Clark and E. Andersen entitled 'Spontaneous repairs: awareness in the process of acquiring language', which was presented at the Biennial Meeting of the Society for Research in Child Development, San Francisco, 1979. The paper is summarized and discussed in S. Brédart and J-A. Rondal, *L'analyse du langage chez l'enfant: les activités métalinguistiques* (Brussels: Pierre Mardaga, 1982).

See 1.3. The discussion of different approaches to defining the word draws heavily on the relevant sections in: R. Carter, *Vocabulary: applied linguistic perspectives* (second edition, London: Routledge, 1998); D. Cruse, *Lexical semantics* (Cambridge: Cambridge University Press, 1986); J. Lyons, *Introduction to theoretical linguistics* (Cambridge: Cambridge University Press, 1968) and S. Ullmann, *Semantics: an introduction to the science of meaning* (Oxford: Blackwell, 1962).

The examples of lexical change in the section dealing with the phonetic approach to defining the word and the Hungarian examples in the section on the phonological approach are borrowed from Ullmann.

See 1.4. The *kin* entry in the *Concise Oxford Dictionary* (eighth edition, edited by R. E. Allen, Oxford: Oxford University Press, 1991) is to be found on p. 650.

Readers in search of further reading matter on some of the issues raised in this chapter may like to consult some or all of the following:

  R. Carter, *Vocabulary: applied linguistic perspectives* (second edition, London: Routledge, 1998);
  G. Finch, *Linguistic terms and concepts* (Houndmills: Macmillan, 2000);
  H. Jackson, *Words and their meaning* (London: Longman, 1988), especially Chapter 1;
  M. Lewis, *The lexical approach* (Hove: Language Teaching Publications, 1993), especially Chapter 5;
  J. Lyons, *Linguistic semantics: an introduction* (Cambridge: Cambridge University Press, 1995), especially Chapter 2;
  F. Palmer, *Grammar* (Harmondsworth: Penguin, 1971), especially Chapter 2;

S. Pinker, *The language instinct* (New York: William Morrow & Co., 1994), especially Chapter 5;

H. G. Widdowson, *Linguistics* (Oxford: Oxford University Press, 1996), especially chapters 3, 4 and 5.

Focusing questions/topics for discussion

1. In this chapter a number of expressions were cited – expressions like *I want a <u>word</u> with you* – which show that our everyday conception of language is very much bound up with words. Think of some further examples of such expressions – in English or any other languages you know.

2. It was mentioned in the chapter in connection with phonology that lexical differentiation was one of the tests for phonemic distinctions. For example, in the 'minimal pair' *tie/dye*, the two words are differentiated by the distinction /t/ and /d/ and by that distinction alone. Which of the following pairs of words are 'minimal pairs' in which lexical differentiation similarly depends on a single phonemic distinction?

beat – peat	*role – bowl*
breath – breathe	*scope – rope*
deep – sleep	*wreath – wreathe*
dot – doll	*witch – filch*
phoney – pony	*wreck – neck*

3. We saw in the chapter that the smallest units of meaning are not words but morphemes. For example, in the word *unwise* there are two morphemes, *un* and *wise*, the second of which is a word but the first of which is not. Try to analyse the following expressions into their constituent morphemes:

antidepressant	*misfire*
bowler	*poetically*
disembarked	*resting*
encage	*unlawful*
hateful	*wedding-bells*

4. 'Positional mobility' was presented in the chapter as one of the grammatical criteria for defining words. Put together a list of English words – including both 'content words' and 'form words' – and then examine these words in the light of the 'positional mobility' criterion. Are some of the words more 'positionally mobile' than others? Are the equivalents of these words in other languages you know more or less 'positionally mobile' than the English words, or about the same?

5. It was noted in the chapter that choosing one lexical item may have one set of repercussions on other choices in the sentence in question, while choosing a different item (with a similar meaning) may have a different set of repercussions. Thus, for example: *The residents protested against the development plan* vs. *The residents objected to the development plan*. Try to think of some further instances – in English and in any other languages you know – of different lexical choices having different implications for the form of the sentence in which the relevant words are situated.

|2|

Lexis and syntax

2.1 Colligation

We saw in the previous chapter that particular syntactic patterns are associated with particular lexical items. This kind of association has sometimes been labelled *colligation* – from the Latin *cum* ('with') and *ligare* ('to tie'), the image underlying this term being that of elements being 'tied together' by, as it were, syntactic necessity.

In the past the notion of colligation has tended to be applied to a fairly restricted range of rather 'local' syntactic relationships – such as the relationship between a verb and the form of the verb that follows it (its *verbal complement*), for example:

She <u>will eat</u> chocolate tonight. [*will* + VERB]

She <u>wishes to eat</u> chocolate tonight. [*wish* + *to* + VERB]

She <u>intends to eat/intends eating</u> chocolate tonight. [*intend* + *to* + VERB/*intend* + VERB*ing*]

She <u>regrets eating</u> chocolate tonight. [*regret* + VERB*ing*]

She <u>is indulging in eating</u> chocolate tonight. [*indulge* + *in* + VERB*ing*]

She <u>is refraining from eating</u> chocolate tonight. [*refrain* + *from* + VERB*ing*]

However, the recent trend in linguistics has been towards a much wider conception of the interaction between lexicon and syntax – to the point, indeed, where it is becoming increasingly difficult to pronounce with any confidence on the question of where lexicon ends and syntax begins.

In this chapter we shall look briefly at the way in which the relationship between syntax and the lexicon has been approached in a number of different varieties of linguistics, notably computational linguistics, the 'London School', the Valency Grammar tradition, Lexical–Functional Grammar and Chomskyan linguistics.

2.2   The computational perspective

Computational linguistics refers to more or less everything that goes on at the intersection between computer science and the study of language. One dimension of computational linguistics is its interest in the relationship between what computers can do and what we humans do when we acquire and use language. Thus, some computational linguists spend their time trying to model aspects of language acquisition and processing on computers, often with very practical objectives in mind – automatic translation, speech synthesis etc. Another aspect of computational linguistics is the use of computers as an aid in the analysis of language. For example, computers are now widely used in the analysis of very large collections (*corpora* – singular *corpus*) of naturally occurring language in order to provide information about the frequency of particular items or the frequency with which certain items co-occur with certain other items. From both kinds of computational linguistics there emerges a strong sense of the difficulty of neatly separating the lexicon from syntax.

With regard to the language-modelling aspect of computational linguistics, an interesting instance of such research is the work that is being undertaken at the Laboratoire d'Automatique Documentaire et Linguistique (LADL) in Paris, where the object is to design systems which will enable computers to perform operations (such as machine translation) on texts. The systems that the LADL researchers are endeavouring to put in place have to be capable of recognizing, decoding, selecting and combining words without the online assistance of human speakers. It transpires that the principal problems which emerge from the construction of such electronic lexicons have to do with the difficulty of separating lexis and grammar.

Thus, very annoyingly, from the LADL researchers' point of view, sentences which are identical in structure and perhaps quite close in meaning do not necessarily behave identically when it comes to adjusting them in various ways, such behaviour seeming to be entirely dependent on the particular words used, for example:

Cette question <u>concerne</u> Pierre.	(Works also in the passive – in
('This question <u>concerns</u> Pierre.')	both French and English: *Pierre <u>est concerné par</u> cette question.* 'Pierre <u>is concerned by</u> this question.')
Cette question <u>regarde</u> Pierre.	(Does not work in the passive –
('This question <u>regards</u> Pierre.')	in either French or English: **Pierre <u>est regardé par</u> cette question.* '*Pierre <u>is regarded by</u> this question.')

With regard to the light shed on the lexis–syntax interface by the use of computer technology as a tool of linguistic analysis, an obvious example to cite here is the research carried out under the auspices of the Collins Birmingham University International Language Database (COBUILD), which will be discussed at greater length in Chapter 4. The relevant point to emerge from such research with reference to the present context is that there is a strong tendency for particular words or particular senses of words to be associated with particular syntactic structures. For example, the word *yield* has two main senses – 'give way/ submit/surrender' and 'produce'. It turns out that the first sense is almost always associated with uses of the word as an intransitive verb (verb without a direct object), for example:

But we did not yield then and we shall not yield now.

Love yields to business . . .

In Sweden the authorities yielded at once to the threats . . .

The second sense, on the other hand, is mostly associated with uses of the word as a noun, for example:

. . . a nuclear shell with a 15 kiloton yield . . .

. . . more fertilizer than Europe to achieve similar yields . . .

. . . Bangladesh's low annual yields . . .

A particular approach to syntax which is very widely used in computational linguistics is Head-driven Phrase Structure Grammar (HPSG). HPSG is very widely used in machine translation, especially in Europe. Its particular usefulness to computational linguists derives from the fact that it attempts to provide a totally explicit specification of how syntax operates. With regard to the lexicon, HPSG, in common with Valency Grammar and Lexical–Functional Grammar, sees words as extremely rich in grammatical information and as playing a key role in determining the syntactic shape of the sentences in which they occur. This is the sense of *head-driven* in the expression Head-driven Phrase Structure Grammar. The concept of the structure of the phrase in HPSG is that the head of a given phrase, such as a noun phrase or a verb phrase (i.e. the single word – the noun, the verb etc. – around which it is built), has attributes out of which crucial properties of the surrounding syntax are derived. For example, the lexical entry for the verb *bakes* would have to specify that it takes a subject noun, that it may also take a direct object noun and that where both a subject and a direct object are involved the relation between them is that of *agent* (doer of an action) and *patient* (undergoer of an action). Accordingly, the head of the verb phrase components of the following sentences determines the legitimacy of the nouns present in the sentence, and also determines their grammatical functions and the relations between them.

VERB PHRASE
Joanna [bakes].
HEAD
(VERB)

VERB PHRASE
Joanna [bakes bread].
HEAD
(VERB)

2.3   The 'London School' perspective

The COBUILD project took its inspiration from the work of a mid-twentieth-century British linguist, J.R. Firth, founder of the so-called 'London School' of linguistics, who took the view that the meaning of a word could be equated with the sum of its linguistic environments, and that, therefore, linguists could essentially find out what they needed to know about a word's meaning by exhaustively analysing its collocations. Firth's general approach to the study of language continues to have echoes in modern linguistics through the work of eminent heirs to the 'London School' tradition such as John Sinclair, the leading light in the COBUILD project, and Michael Halliday.

We have already begun to look at Sinclair's work and shall return to it in Chapter 4. With regard to Halliday and his followers, they see lexis and syntax not as separate entities but rather as merely different ends of the same continuum, which they label the *lexicogrammar*. In the Hallidayan perspective, a lexical distinction such as that between *man* and *woman* is seen in terms of the different environments in which they are likely to occur, just as the distinction between, for instance, a *count* or *countable* noun (e.g. *dog*) and a *mass* noun (e.g. *mud*) is seen in terms of the different syntactic frames in which these categories can occur. Thus, a count noun can occur after numerals (*She has two dogs. He drank three litres of water.*) and after quantifiers like *several* and *many* (*The child had to have several stitches. We've visited Ireland on many occasions.*), whereas a mass noun cannot occur after numerals nor after *several/many*, but can occur after a quantifier such as *much* (*There was too much mud and not enough grass for a decent game. We didn't get much enjoyment out of it.*). Similarly, *man* but not *woman* can occur in the close company of a word like *prostate* (in a sentence such as *The poor man had prostate problems.*), while *woman* but not *man* can occur in the close company of a word like *pregnant* (in a sentence such as *That woman is pregnant.*).

One argument that has been put against Halliday's contention that syntactic distinctions are not qualitatively different from lexical distinctions is that, whereas syntax is a 'purely' linguistic phenomenon, lexical distinctions are based on the nature of the real world. For example, one can argue that the fact that we do not juxtapose *man* and *pregnant* has simply to do with the limitations of male physiology. However, it also possible to argue that syntactic categories and processes are the way they are at least in part because of how things are in the world. To return to the case of the distinction between count nouns and mass nouns, for instance, it would be perfectly plausible to say that the reason why we do not normally put numerals in front of words like *mud, air, enjoyment, darkness* etc. is that the very nature of the substances or experiences to which they refer encourages a perception of them as continuous wholes rather than individual entities, a notion which receives support from the fact that across languages where the count/mass distinction exists, while there are certainly many differences in the detail of classification, the same kinds of substances and experiences tend to be referred to with mass nouns. For example, the translation-equivalents of *mud* and *air* in French (*boue, air*), German (*Schlamm, Luft*), Spanish (*barro, aire*) and Modern Greek (λασπη, αέρας) all (in those senses) normally function as mass nouns. The most sensible position would seem to be that the nature of both the lexicon and the syntax of any given language are determined by an interaction between *extra-linguistic* reality (the way things are 'outside language') and *intra-linguistic* reality (the way things are 'inside language').

2.4   The Valency Grammar perspective

Valency Grammar is particularly associated, historically, with German linguistics, but it has a wide influence on thinking about grammar generally. The term *valency* in this context derives from its application in chemistry, where a given element's valency is defined in terms of its capacity to combine with other elements. In linguistics valency refers to the number and types of bonds syntactic elements form with each other. Valency Grammar traditionally presents the verb as the fundamental or central element of the sentence and focuses on the relationship between the verb and the elements which depend on it (which are known as its arguments, expressions, complements or valents). The relevance of Valency Grammar in the present discussion is that it recognizes the shape of sentence structure as a consequence of lexical choice, that is, the choice of a particular verb with a particular valency. Some examples of verb valencies follow.

Exist, snore, vanish

Verbs like these require only a subject.

Poverty exists.

He was snoring.

The problem vanished.

In traditional terms they are labelled *intransitive*. In valency terminology they are said to be *monovalent*, having a valency of 1.

Annoy, damage, scrutinize

Verbs like these require both a subject and a direct object.

You annoy me.

The storm damaged the sea-wall.

We have scrutinized the documents.

In traditional terms they are labelled *transitive*. In valency terminology they are said to be *bivalent*, having a valency of 2.

Bestow, give, inform

Verbs like these require a subject, a direct object and one further valent.

The king bestowed a knighthood on him.

Jeremy gave the parcel to his aunt.

The police informed Jack of Jill's safe return.

In traditional terms they are labelled *ditransitive*. In valency terminology they are said to be *trivalent*, having a valency of 3.

As has been mentioned, traditionally the notion of valency has been applied to verbs. However, a number of recent approaches to grammar, which take much of their inspiration from Valency Grammar and which are grouped together under the general heading of Dependency Grammar, extend the basic valency idea to other lexical categories such as adjectives and nouns. It is clear, for example, that the valency of the adjective *tall* (which can 'stand alone' in qualifying a noun) differs from that of the adjective *susceptible* (which requires something further):

The professor is tall.

The professor is susceptible to pressure.

Similarly with the nouns *problem* and *propensity*.

He has a problem.

He has a propensity to violence.

2.5   The Lexical–Functional perspective

Lexical–Functional Grammar (LFG) developed in the 1980s as a kind of off-shoot of the Chomskyan approach to syntax – one which attempted to bring the theoretical and descriptive treatment of syntax closer to what was known about the psychological processes involved in producing and under-standing utterances. As its name suggests, Lexical–Functional Grammar places the lexicon right at the heart of its account of syntax.

In LFG every item in the lexicon is seen as coming equipped not only with indicators of how it sounds, how it is written and what it means but also with indicators of the roles of the elements to which it relates in a given sentence (its argument structure) and of the grammatical functions assigned to these roles. For example, the verbs *walk* and *stroke* can be portrayed within this framework as follows:

	(subject)		(assignment of grammatical function)
walk	(agent)		(argument structure)

	(subject)	(object)	(assignment of grammatical function)
stroke	(agent,	theme)	(argument structure)

In *walk* the argument structure consists merely of an agent argument (the role of doer of an action) which is associated with the subject of the verb, as in:

(subject of the verb *walk*)

Eric   *was walking.*

(agent – doer of the walking)

In *stroke* the argument structure consists of an agent argument (the role of doer of an action) which is associated with the subject of the verb and a patient or theme argument (the role of undergoer of the action) associated with the object of the verb, as in:

(subject of the verb *stroke*)   (object of the verb *stroke*)

Jill   *stroked*   *the cat.*

(agent – doer of the stroking)   (theme – undergoer of the stroking)

Thus, like HPSG, Valency Grammar and the various forms of Dependency Grammar, LFG presents lexical choice as the shaper of the syntax of any given sentence. A sentence is seen as involving lexical structure, constituent structure (or *c-structure*) and functional structure (or *f-structure*). Because each lexical element of a sentence is held to specify an argument structure, the lexical structure of the sentence is seen as determining its constituent structure (the component parts which make up the sentence and how these component parts relate to each other); and, because the various roles (agent, theme etc.) attached to particular lexical items are viewed as associated with grammatical functions (subject, object etc.), functional structure too is seen as dependent on lexical structure.

2.6   The Chomskyan perspective

We come finally to what would until fairly recently have been considered the most syntactic of syntactic models, namely that which is associated with the name of Noam Chomsky. In the very earliest version of the Chomskyan model the lexicon was not recognized as an autonomous component at all; words were considered to be merely the observable elements through which

syntax manifested itself – the outward signs of inward syntax – to borrow a
theological expression.

However, the evolution of Chomskyan linguistics since its beginnings in
the 1950s has consistently been in the direction of ascribing more and more
importance to the lexicon. Phenomena which had previously been represented as purely syntactic processes were by this time being treated with reference to the lexicon. A good example of this is the case of passivization. In
Chomsky's first book, *Syntactic Structures* (published 1957), syntax was represented as generated in the first place by phrase structure rules of the type:

S → NP + VP

[A SENTENCE CONSISTS OF A NOUN PHRASE AND A VERB PHRASE]

NP → (DET) + N

[A NOUN PHRASE MAY OR MAY NOT INCLUDE A DETERMINER (SUCH AS AN
ARTICLE *a*, *the*. etc.), BUT ALWAYS CONTAINS A NOUN]

The basic or *kernel* structures which were specified by the phrase structure
rules were then subject to various kinds of transformation, including passive
transformation. The passive transformation rule looked roughly like this:

ACTIVE SENTENCE				PASSIVE SENTENCE						
NP_1	+ V +	NP_2	⇒	NP_2	+	*be*	+ V +	*by*	+	NP_1
[NOUN PHRASE 1]	[VERB]	[NOUN PHRASE 2]		[NOUN PHRASE 2]			[VERB]			[NOUN PHRASE 1]

This can be exemplified as follows:

ACTIVE SENTENCE   PASSIVE SENTENCE

The man hit the ball   ⇒   *The ball was hit by the man*

NP_1 + V + NP_2 ⇒ NP_2 + *be* + V + *by* + NP_1

It later came to be recognized by Chomskyans, however, that passivization
was not something that could be dealt with simply in terms of a syntactic
generalization. Such a generalization might run something like the following: NP_2 in the active sentence moves to NP_1 position in the passivized
sentence and vice versa. This would explain how we get:

A picture was taken of Brett by the official photographer

from:

The official photographer (NP_1) *took a picture* (NP_2) *of Brett* (NP_3).

It also accounts for the questionable status of *?Brett was taken a picture of
by the official photographer*, where the noun phrase which is 'moved' to
subject position is NP_3 in the corresponding active sentence (i.e. not the
direct object). However, in some cases non-direct objects can be 'moved' to
subject position in passive sentences. For example, all three of the following

sentences are perfectly acceptable, even though in the third sentence *John* is NP_3, and does not represent the direct object of the active version of the sentence but rather the object of a preposition.

They (NP_1) *took advantage* (NP_2) *of John* (NP_3).

Advantage was taken of John.

John was taken advantage of.

The only way to explain this seemed to be in terms of a lexical restructuring rule which would allow certain whole expressions like *take advantage of* optionally to be restructured as a sort of complex transitive verb. Optional restructuring of this kind turns out to be highly idiosyncratic; thus, it works perfectly with *take care of* (e.g. *The job was taken care of*) but not so well with *take offence at* (*?The chairman's remarks were taken offence at*). Accordingly, specific lexical choice can be seen to determine the possibility or otherwise of lexical restructuring, which in turn determines the permissibility of certain kinds of passivization.

By the early 1980s the lexicon was being seen as having a crucial influence on syntactic structure. The so-called 'Projection Principle' of the 'Government and Binding' (GB) version of Chomskyan syntax current in the 1980s states that the properties of lexical entries 'project onto' the syntax of the sentence – which essentially coincides with the perspective of HPSG, Valency Grammar and LFG in the matter of the lexis–syntax interface.

The Projection Principle can be illustrated as follows. As we have seen, in early versions of Chomsky's model, the phrase structure component of the syntax fully specified the basic constituents of the sentence. Thus, for example:

S → NP + VP
[A SENTENCE CONSISTS OF A NOUN PHRASE AND A VERB PHRASE]

NP → (DET) + N
[A NOUN PHRASE MAY OR MAY NOT INCLUDE A DETERMINER (SUCH AS AN ARTICLE *a, the.* etc.), BUT ALWAYS CONTAINS A NOUN]

In this version of things the expansion of the **VP** element was:

VP → V (+ NP)
[A VERB PHRASE ALWAYS CONTAINS A VERB AND MAY OR MAY NOT INCLUDE A NOUN PHRASE]

On the other hand, the lexical entries for verbs specified whether or not they could be followed by a noun phrase. For example, the entry for a transitive verb such as *hit* would have contained the information:

[__NP]
[OCCURS IN THE ENVIRONMENT OF A FOLLOWING NOUN PHRASE]

The entry for an intransitive verb like *snooze*, on the other hand, would not have contained the specification of this particular environment.

Accordingly, there is duplication between the information provided by the phrase structure rules and that provided by the lexicon. If we take it that, as the Projection Principle states, lexical properties intervene in the shaping of syntax, then the notion of having a general statement at the syntactic level about the optionality of occurrence of a noun phrase in the verb phrase no longer makes sense, since the lexicon supplies the information for each particular verb as to whether or not it may be followed by a noun phrase.

Subsequent developments in Chomskyan linguistics went even further in a lexicalist direction. One of the major distinctive features of Chomsky's view of language is that every human being is born with a language faculty, and that it is this language faculty which enables the child to acquire language. A fundamental corollary of this view is that human languages are essentially structured along the same lines, lines which reflect the structure of the language faculty. If this were not the case, clearly, the notion of a language faculty would be unable to explain the fact that a human children will acquire any human language to which they are given adequate exposure. Chomsky labels the structural common core of languages which he posits *Universal Grammar*. According to the Chomskyan model of the 1980s, Universal Grammar consists of, on the one hand, a set of principles, applicable to all languages, and, on the other, a set of parameters, that vary from language to language within very specific limits. An example of a principle has already been given, namely the Projection Principle (see previous two paragraphs). An example of a parameter is the Head Parameter, which states, basically, that within a particular phrase (prepositional phrase, verb phrase etc.) the head of the phrase (preposition, verb etc.) occurs consistently either to the left or to the right of the other elements (the *complement*). Thus, English is said to be a 'head-first' language on the basis of data such as:

PREPOSITIONAL PHRASE

[*in Japan*]   (Preposition head to the left of its complement in a
HEAD   prepositional phrase)
(PREPOSITION)

VERB PHRASE

[*am Japanese*]   (Verb to the left of its complement in a verb phrase)

HEAD
(VERB)

Japanese, on the other hand, is said to be a 'head-last' language on the basis of data such as:

PREPOSITIONAL PHRASE

[*Nihon ni*]   (Preposition head to the right of its complement in a
         HEAD   prepositional phrase)
      (PREPOSITION)

[literally, 'Japan in']

VERB PHRASE

[*nihonjin desu*]	(Verb head to the right of its complement in a
HEAD	verb phrase)
(VERB)	

[literally, 'Japanese am']

However, towards the end of the 1980s it began to be suggested that parameters were not properties of principles, but rather properties of individual lexical items, a view known as the lexical parameterization hypothesis.

Let us look briefly at some evidence bearing on the lexical parameterization hypothesis from English and German prepositional phrases. Both English and German would be considered 'head-first' languages on the basis of the positioning of heads in prepositional (and other) phrases. For example:

ENGLISH

PREPOSITIONAL PHRASE

[*in Germany*]   (Preposition head – *in* – to the left of its complement)
HEAD
(PREPOSITION)

PREPOSITIONAL PHRASE

[*with me*]   (Preposition head – *with* – to the left of its complement)
HEAD
(PREPOSITION)

GERMAN

PREPOSITIONAL PHRASE

[*in Deutschland*]   (Preposition head – *in* – to the left of its
HEAD   complement)
(PREPOSITION)

['in Germany']

PREPOSITIONAL PHRASE

[*mit mir*]   (Preposition head – *mit* – to the left of its complement)
HEAD
(PREPOSITION)

['with me']

However, in both languages there are, in fact, prepositions which may occur to the right of their complements:

ENGLISH

PREPOSITIONAL PHRASE

[*your objection notwithstanding*]   (Preposition head – *notwithstanding*
HEAD   – to the right of its complement)
(PREPOSITION)

GERMAN

PREPOSITIONAL PHRASE

[*der Schule gegenüber*]   (Preposition head – *gegenüber* – to the right
            HEAD   of its complement)
     (PREPOSITION)

['opposite the school' –
literally, 'the school opposite']

Examples such as these last two seem to indicate that the positioning of heads of prepositional phrases is not something which is set globally for all cases within a given language, but rather, as the lexical parameterization hypothesis suggests, that such positioning is determined by the lexical properties of each particular preposition.

The lexicalizing tendency in Chomskyan linguistics reaches its logical conclusion in Chomsky's latest version of his model, the 'Minimalist Programme'. In this model the whole process of deriving a syntactic structure is represented as beginning in the lexicon, since Chomsky and his followers now accept, alongside many other schools of linguists (see earlier sections), that the particular lexical elements which are selected in any given sentence will be the principal determinants of both the content and the form of the sentence. The minimalism of the Minimalist Programme refers precisely to the fact that syntactic levels and operations are in this model reduced to an absolute minimum, with many of the most familiar features of earlier models being discarded, while the lexicon is viewed as driving the entire structure-building system. Thus, for example, instead of the syntactic rules beginning with sentence-level and then filling in what the sentence consists of, as, for example, in S → NP + VP, the minimalist model begins by building individual structures around individual lexical items and then merges these individual, lexically based structures into larger structures.

2.7   Summary

This chapter has shown that syntacticians from a very wide range of theoretical traditions view the lexicon as having a vital, determining role in the structuring of sentences. In some instances, for example 'London School' linguistics and Valency Grammar, the interpenetration of lexis and syntax was recognized from the outset; in others, for example in computational linguistics, the acknowledgment of such interpenetration was an inevitable inference arising from working with the 'nitty-gritty' of data; and in still others, for example the later Chomskyan models, increasing importance was attributed to the lexicon in respect of syntactic structure as the models in question developed in response to their perceived inadequacies. The consensus across all of the above schools (and many others) is that the syntactic shape of any sentence is very largely a function of the properties of the lexical elements out of which it is composed.

Sources and suggestions for further reading

See 2.2. The LADL examples were taken from B. Lamiroy, 'Où en sont les rapports entre les études de lexique et la syntaxe?' (*Travaux de Linguistique* 23, 1991, 133–9). The account of the lexico-syntactic findings of the COBUILD project was based on Chapter 4 of J. Sinclair, *Corpus, concordance, collocation* (Oxford: Oxford University Press, 1991).

Sources for the discussion of Head-Driven Phrase Structure Grammar were: R. D. Borsley, *Modern phrase structure grammar* (Oxford: Blackwell, 1996); C. Pollard and I. A. Sag, *Head-driven phrase structure* (Chicago: University of Chicago Press and Stanford: CSLI Publications, 1994); I. A. Sag and T. Wasow, *Syntactic theory: a formal introduction* (Stanford: CSLI Publications, in press). Also consulted in this connection was the website http://hpsg.stanford.edu/hpsg/hpsg.html.

The *bakes* example was loosely derived from R.L. Humphreys, 'Lexicon in formal grammar' (in K. Brown and J. Miller (eds), *Syntactic theory*, Oxford: Elsevier Science, 1996).

See 2.3. Discussion of M. Halliday's approach to the lexicogrammar was based on statements and arguments to be found in his very early work, such as 'Categories of the theory of grammar' (*Word* 1961, 17, 241–92), but also in his recent work – for example, *Functional grammar* (second edition, London: Edward Arnold, 1994).

The counter-argument to the Hallidayan position came from G. Sampson, in *Schools of linguistics: competition and evolution* (London: Hutchinson, 1980, p. 233).

See 2.4. The principal sources for the discussion of Valency Grammar were D. J. Allerton's book *Valency and the English verb* (London: Academic Press, 1982), and his article 'Valency grammar', in E. F. K. Koerner and R. E. Asher (eds), *Concise history of the language sciences* (Oxford: Kidlington, 1995). Material on a broad range of Dependency Grammar approaches was also consulted at the website http://ufal.mff.cuni.cz/dg/dgmain.html

See 2.5. Sources for the section on Lexical–Functional Grammar included: J. Bresnan and R. Kaplan, 'Introduction: grammars as mental representations of language', in J. Bresnan (ed.), *The mental representation of grammatical relations*, Cambridge, MA: MIT Press, 1982); S.C. Dik, *Functional Grammar* (Dordrecht: Foris, 1981); C. Neidle, 'Lexical–Functional Grammar', in K. Brown and J. Miller (eds), *Syntactic theory*, Oxford: Elsevier Science, 1996). The websites http://clwww.essex.ac.uk/LFG/ and http: //www-lfg.stanford.edu/lfg/ were also consulted.

See 2.6. The discussion of Chomskyan models drew on both editions of *Chomsky's Universal Grammar: an introduction* (first edition – authored by V. J. Cook – Oxford: Blackwell, 1988; second edition – co-authored by V. J. Cook and M. Newson – Oxford: Blackwell, 1996) and on A. Radford's books, *Transformational syntax* (Cambridge: Cambridge University Press, 1981), *Syntax: a Minimalist introduction* (Cambridge: Cambridge University Press, 1997), *Syntactic theory and the structure of English: a minimalist approach* (Cambridge: Cambridge University Press, 1997). The relevant original N. Chomsky sources were: *Syntactic structures* (The Hague: Mouton, 1957), *Lectures on Government and Binding* (Dordrecht: Foris, 1981) and *The Minimalist Program* (Cambridge, MA: MIT Press, 1995). The lexical parameterization hypothesis was the brainchild of P. Wexler and R. Manzini ('Parameters and learnability in Binding Theory', in T. Roeper and E. Williams (eds), *Parameter setting*, Dordrecht: Foris, 1987).

Readers who wish to explore syntax further might profitably begin with one or other of the following:

> L. Thomas, *Beginning syntax* (Oxford: Blackwell, 1994);
> C.L. Baker, *English syntax* (Cambridge, MA: MIT Press, 1995).

Good introductions to specifically Chomskyan syntax are provided by:

> V. J. Cook and M. Newson, *Chomsky's Universal Grammar: an introduction* (Oxford: Blackwell, 1996);
> A. Radford, *Syntax: a minimalist introduction* (Cambridge: Cambridge University Press, 1997);
> L. P. Shapiro, 'Tutorial: an introduction to syntax' (*Journal of Speech, Language and Hearing Research*, 40, 1997, 254–72).

Further discussion of the interface between the lexicon and syntax can be found in:

> R. L. Humphreys, 'Lexicon in formal grammar', in K. Brown and J. Miller (eds), *Syntactic theory*, Oxford: Elsevier Science, 1996);
> T. Stowell, 'The role of the lexicon in syntactic theory', in T. Stowell and E. Wehrli (eds), *Syntax and semantics. Volume 26. Syntax and the lexicon*, San Diego: Academic Press, 1992);
> T. Stowell and E. Wehrli, 'Introduction', in T. Stowell and E. Wehrli (eds), *Syntax and semantics. Volume 26. Syntax and the lexicon*, San Diego: Academic Press, 1992).

Focusing questions/topics for discussion

1. At the beginning of the chapter the following examples were given of different patterns of verbal complementation:

will eat [*will* + VERB];

wish to eat [*wish* + *to* + VERB];

intend to eat/intend eating [*intend* + *to* + VERB/*intend* + VERB*ing*];

regret eating [*regret* + VERB*ing*];

indulge in eating [*indulge* + *in* + VERB*ing*];

refrain from eating [*refrain* + *from* + VERB*ing*].

For each of the above cases try to find two verbs whose verbal complementation pattern parallels that of the example given (e.g. *must* follows the same pattern as *will*).

2. We saw in section 2.3 that lexical distinctions, like certain grammatical distinctions, can be seen in terms of elements with which lexical items may and may not co-occur. It is also true that co-occurrence possibilities are affected by context and by the meaning intended. Thus, with regard to the words *man* and *woman*, both of the following sentences would be unremarkable in Anglican contexts (where female as well as male priests are often encountered), but the second would be impossible in Roman Catholic or Greek Orthodox contexts (where female priests are never encountered).

The priest was a fine man.

The priest was a fine woman.

Similarly, in relation to countable and mass nouns, whereas *not many waters* would be perfectly possible in the context of a supermarket with only a limited range of brands of mineral water, *not much water* would have to be the expression used in the context of a reservoir whose water level had been affected by drought. Try to think of some other instances of contextual influence on co-occurrence possibilities.

3. In 2.4 we saw that Valency Grammar ascribes valencies to verbs according to the number of arguments they take. Thus intransitive verbs like *exist, sleep, vanish* are labelled *monovalent*, having a valency of 1, transitive verbs like *annoy, damage, scrutinize* are labelled *bivalent*, having a valency of 2, and ditransitive verbs like *give, inform, characterize* are labelled *trivalent*, having a valency of 3. Try to find five further verbs belonging to each of the above three valency categories. In performing this exercise, note the way in which some verbs have different valencies in different contexts. For instance, a normally monovalent verb like *dream* may in some contexts be bivalent (e.g. *He dreamt a strange dream*).

4. On the basis of the discussion of HPSG in 2.1 and of LFG in 2.5, identify the agent and, where applicable, the patient in each of the following sentences, and use the information so obtained to specify the argument structure of the verb in each case.

The folk-dancers slapped their thighs.

John was working.

Every February we ski in the French Alps.

Mr McVeigh sliced the tomatoes very fine.

Christopher was tuning his guitar.

5. In the account of the development of the Chomskyan model in 2.6 we encountered the notion of parameter, which was illustrated by means of the Head Parameter. Another parameter discussed by Chomskyans is the Pro-Drop Parameter, which relates to whether or not subject pronouns may be 'dropped' before verbs. Thus Spanish is said to be a pro-drop language, on the basis that, for example, *yo* ['I'] in an expression like *yo entiendo* ['I understand'] may be, and usually is, 'dropped' – so that the usual way of saying 'I understand' in Spanish is simply *entiendo*. In French, on the other hand, the *je* ['I'] of *je comprends* ['I understand'] cannot be dropped, and on the basis of this and myriad similar examples, French is said to be a non-pro-drop language. Where, then, would English stand in relation to the Pro-Drop Parameter? Is there any variation in the 'droppability' of the subject pronoun depending on context and/or on the particular verb selected?

|3|

Lexis and morphology

3.1 The inner life of words

We saw in Chapter 1 that morphology is derived from a Greek word meaning 'form' or 'shape' and that it denotes the internal structure of words (and the study thereof). A given word is not necessarily just a sequence of sounds or letters with an overall, indivisible meaning and or grammatical function; a word may be made up of a whole collection of meaningful components, of which some may in other contexts stand alone as words in their own right, and others may be used only as parts of words.

Consider, for instance the words underlined in the following sentences:

The enormous <u>fish</u> looked rather fearsome.

If you are going to dance the cancan you will need some <u>fishnet</u> stockings.

This is a story about three little <u>fishes</u>.

There's a <u>fishy</u> smell in here.

Fish is obviously a word which can stand alone in its own right. However, it can also be conjoined with other elements which can function as independent words – such as *net*. Furthermore, it can also be combined with elements which have no independent existence as words, but which clearly have meaning and function. Thus the *-es* ending in *fishes* signals that more than one fish is involved and the *-y* ending in *fishy* turns the noun *fish* into an adjective. Similarly in other languages: for example, the German translations of *fish*, *fishnet* and *fishes* are respectively *Fisch*, *Fischnetz* (*Fisch* + *Netz* – both words in their own right) and *Fische* (*Fisch* + the non-word plural ending *-e*).

The basic building blocks of meaning and grammar are not, therefore, words but rather the irreducible components out of which words are composed – that is to say, elements which cannot be further decomposed into anything relevant to their meaning or grammatical function. These irreducible entities are known as *morphemes*. In this chapter we shall examine how morphemes function, how they are customarily classified and how they relate to the lexicon.

3.2   Morphemes and allomorphs

Morphemes can be defined as the smallest elements of any language which have semantic and/or grammatical significance. As we have seen, some morphemes are also whole words – *fish*, for example, whereas others are units below the level of the word which nevertheless have their own meaning and/or grammatical function in the context of the words in which they occur, for example *-es* in *fishes*, *-y* in *fishy*.

Morphemes which can stand alone as words are known as *free morphemes* while morphemes which can only be meaningful or functional as parts of words are known as *bound morphemes*. Bound morphemes very often manifest themselves as prefixes – elements attached at the beginnings of words (e.g. *dis-* as in *disobey*) – or as suffixes – elements attached at the ends of words (e.g. *-ize* as in *idolize*). Prefixes and suffixes are known collectively as *affixes*. Other kinds of affixes to be found in the world's languages include *infixes* and *circumfixes*. Infixes are elements attached within the free morpheme bases of words; for example in Bontoc, a language of the Philippines, the infix *-um-* makes a verb out of an adjective or noun (thus, *fikas* -'strong', *fumikas* 'to be strong') . Circumfixes are elements which 'surround' the relevant base; for instance, in Chickasaw, a Native American language, the negative is formed by the alteration of the base both fore and aft (thus, *lakna* – 'it is hot', *iklakno* – 'it is not hot'). As we shall see later, bound morphemes may also sometimes be represented by nothing at all in the outer forms of words, and they may also be expressed as processes rather than or as well as additions.

Some further examples of free and bound morphemes from English and French follow.

FREE MORPHEMES		BOUND MORPHEMES
	ENGLISH	
fire	*pre-*	(as in *predispose*)
red	*-ize*	(as in *idolize*)
fast	*-ing*	(as in *sailing*)
in	*-s*	(as in *considers*)
	FRENCH	
pomme ('apple')	*ré-*	(as in *réinventer* – 'to reinvent')
jaune ('yellow')	*-ment*	(as in *poliment* – 'politely')
là ('there')	*-ions*	(as in *parlions* – '(we) talked')
sur ('on')	*-s*	(as in *vins* - 'wines')

A morpheme may be realized by different forms – its *morphemic alternants* or *allomorphs* – according to the particular environment in which it occurs.

For instance, the English past tense morpheme may be realized as /ɪd/ (as in *wanted*), as /d/ (as in *stayed*), as /t/ (as in *jumped*), and in other ways besides. An example of morphemic alternation from Italian is the case of the free morpheme *a*, which means 'to', 'at' or 'in' (depending on context). *A* is the form used before words beginning with consonants, but where the following word begins with a vowel the form *ad* is used – as is illustrated by the sentences below.

Andiamo a Milano.	('We are going to Milan')
Andiamo ad Athène.	('We are going to Athens')

A not dissimilar example from French – in this case involving a 'zero allomorph' is the way in which the bound plural morpheme attached to nouns behaves: when followed by a word beginning with a consonant it is not pronounced, whereas when followed by a vowel sound it may or may not be realized as /z/ – depending on speech style and tempo. For instance the *s* in the written form of the French word for 'cars' – *voitures* – is silent in the first of the sentences below but may be pronounced as /z/ in the second if the speech is fluent rather than halting and if the speech style is relatively formal.

Les voitures ralentissaient.	('The cars were slowing down.')
Les voitures allaient très vite.	('The cars were going very fast.')

3.3 'Lexical' morphology and inflectional morphology

Since, as we have seen, morphology in general relates to the structure of words, it would be not unreasonable to conclude that all morphology is lexical. However, many morphologists are inclined to make a distinction between morphological phenomena that have to do with word formation – to which specifically they attach the term *lexical morphology* – and aspects of morphology which have rather to do with the grammatical modification of words – which they label *inflectional morphology*. An example of lexical morphology on this definition would be the addition of the bound morpheme -*ness* to the adjective *kind* to form the abstract noun *kindness*; and an example of inflectional morphology would be the addition of the bound morpheme -*s* to the verb *run* when that verb is preceded by *he*, *she* or *it* in its present tense.

'Lexical' morphology, as defined above, can itself be seen as divisible into two further subcategories: *composition* or *compounding* on the one hand and *derivation* on the other. *Composition/compounding* is customarily applied to instances of word formation where the formation process involves free morphemes. For example, the free morpheme *light* and the free morpheme *house* combine to form the compound word *lighthouse*, which draws on the meanings of its component morphemes but which has a specific meaning all of its own. Derivation, for its part, is applied to instances of word formation in which bound morphemes play a role. For example, the word *unwise* is a different word with a different meaning from the word *wise*, and it is formed simply by the prefixing of the bound morpheme *un-* to the free morpheme *wise*. Some further examples (from English and Dutch) of words formed by composition/compounding and words formed by derivation are given below.

COMPOSITION/ COMPOUNDING	DERIVATION
	ENGLISH
teapot	*payment* (bound derivational morpheme: *-ment*)
override	*enrage* (bound derivational morpheme: *en-*)
bittersweet	*smallish* (bound derivational morpheme: *-ish*)
anyone	*swiftly* (bound derivational morpheme: *-ly*)
	DUTCH
zeeman ('seaman')	*grootheid* ('greatness'; bound derivational morpheme: *-heid*)
lichtbruin ('light brown')	*verhuizen* ('to move house'; bound derivational morphemes: *ver-*, *-en*)
eenmaal ('one time')	*katje* ('little cat', 'kitten'; bound derivational morpheme: *-je*)
welkom ('welcome')	*onwel* ('unwell'; bound derivational morpheme: *on-*)

As can be seen from these examples, bound morphemes involved in derivation may or may not change the grammatical class of the free morphemes to which they are attached. Thus, the addition of the bound derivational morpheme *-ment* to the verb *pay* yields the noun *payment* (cf. *arrange/arrangement*, *excite/excitement*, *resent/resentment*), whereas, on the other hand, the addition of the bound derivational morpheme *-ish* to the adjective small yields another, different, adjective *smallish* (cf. *grey/greyish*, *slow/slowish*, *warm/warmish*).

With regard to inflectional morphology, this can be further exemplified – again from English and Dutch – as follows.

INFLECTIONAL MORPHOLOGY

ENGLISH

trees	(as in *The trees are lovely*; bound inflectional morpheme: *-s*)

recognizes	(as in *She recognizes me*; bound inflectional morpheme: -*s*)
lifted	(as in *Jill lifted her head*; bound inflectional morpheme: -*ed*)
vaccinating	(as in *The doctor was vaccinating the ten-year-olds*; bound inflectional morpheme: -*ing*)

DUTCH

boeken	('books', as in *De boeken zijn thuis* – 'The books are at home'; bound inflectional morpheme: -*en*)
koopt	('buys', as in *Hij koopt sijn krant in de winkel* - 'He buys his newspaper in the shop'; bound inflectional morpheme -*t*)
kookte	('boiled', as in *Het water kookte* – 'The water boiled'; bound inflectional morpheme -*te*)
goede	('good', as in *Mijn vader was een goede man* – 'My father was a good man'; bound inflectional morpheme -*e*; compare *Mijn vader was goed* - 'My father was good')

As the above examples illustrate, inflectional morphemes are not involved in word formation, and they never change the actual grammatical category of the free morphemes to which they are attached. Rather, they make small adjustments to words which have important grammatical consequences – signalling, for instance, tense, person and number in verbs, and number and grammatical case in nouns. The following examples, from various languages, provide further illustration of these various roles.

Present–past distinction in German:

er lebt ('he lives') vs. *er lebte* ('he lived')

First person–second person distinction in Spanish:

regreso ('I return') vs. *regresas* ('you (sing.) return')
regresamos ('we return') vs. *regresais* ('you (plur.) return')

Singular plural distinction in French:

elle chantera ('she will sing') vs. *elles chanteront* ('they (fem.) will sing')

Singular–plural distinction in Swedish:

apelsin ('orange') vs. *apelsiner* ('oranges')

Nominative (subject case) vs. genitive (possessive case) in Modern Greek:

to neró (το νερό – 'the water') vs. *tu nerú* (του νερού – 'of the water', 'the water's')

Because of the grammatical nature of their contribution to word-structure, and because, at first sight at least, they seem to be assignable by rule rather than dependent on the particularities of lexical items, inflectional morphemes have been considered by some linguists to lie outside the domain of the lexicon and to belong rather with the grammatical rules of a language. We have seen already, with regard to syntax, that making a hard and fast distinction between lexicon and grammar is no easy task. In the case of morphology, as will become clear in the next section, such a distinction makes no sense whatsoever.

3.4   Inflectional morphemes and the lexicon

A first very basic problem about a claim that derivational morphemes are lexicon-based while inflectional morphemes are not is that it is not at all clear in some instances whether a particular morpheme is derivational or inflectional. A commonly cited illustration of this problem is the case of the positive, comparative and superlative forms of adjectives in English, exemplified below:

POSITIVE	COMPARATIVE	SUPERLATIVE
bright	*brighter*	*brightest*
dear	*dearer*	*dearest*
quick	*quicker*	*quickest*

On the one hand, this seems like a highly rule-governed pattern, and most native English speakers would probably think of, e.g. *quicker* and *quickest* as forms of *quick* rather than as different words – which seems to argue for the morphemes involved (-*er* and -*est*) being inflectional. On the other hand, the changes involved do not seem to involve fitting the adjectives to their grammatical environment in the same way that, for example, adding a plural ending to a noun does – which seems to argue for regarding the morphemes in question as derivational and as having the same kind of status as a morpheme like -*ish* (in, e.g., *quickish*).

Another problem in relation to making a hard and fast distinction between morphemes that are in the lexicon and morphemes that are supposedly excluded from it is that a particular morpheme may, in some contexts, have an inflectional role while having a derivational role in others. For example, the bound morpheme -*ing* is the marker of progressive *aspect* in English verbs. That is to say it marks a verb as referring to ongoing process or activity rather than a stable state or completed process or action, for example:

She is being awkward.

(as opposed to: *She is awkward.*)

I was working.

(as opposed to: *I worked.*)

In this kind of instance *-ing* has certainly to be seen as having an inflectional role. However, *-ing* can also be used in the formation of verbal nouns – just like derivational morphemes such as *-ion* and *-ment*, for example:

Two judges were responsible for the administering of the oath. (compare: *Two judges were responsible for the administration of the oath.*)

The deferring of the meeting had some unfortunate consequences. (compare: *The deferment of the meeting had some unfortunate consequences.*)

In this case *-ing* is clearly involved in word formation and has to be considered derivational. Are we going to say that *-ing* is sometimes supplied by the lexicon and sometimes not?

A third problem in this connection is that inflectional morphology does not conform to rules to anything like the extent that it is believed to. For example, the morphology of the pluralization of English nouns has some highly idiosyncratic features, as the examples listed below show. Indeed, there do not seem to be noticeably fewer divergences from the regular plural pattern in nouns than from the normal (derivational) pattern of adverb formation in English (ADJECTIVE + bound derivational morpheme *-ly*, for example: *dark/darkly, delicate/delicately, spiteful/spitefully* etc., but *fast/fast*). One would have thought that in both cases the lexicon would have to contain at least information as to whether a given word was subject to the normal pattern or not, and, if not, what the relevant particularities of its morphology were.

SINGULAR	PLURAL
sheep	*sheep*
wife	*wives*
man	*men*
woman	*women*
mouse	*mice*
die	*dice*
child	*children*
ox	*oxen*
phenomenon	*phenomena*
basis	*bases*

formula	*formulae* (or *formulas*)
stimulus	*stimuli*
datum	*data*
corpus	*corpora*
graffito	*graffiti*
plateau	*plateaux* (or *plateaus*)
cherub	*cherubim* (or *cherubs*)

Finally, on the question of whether or not inflectional morphemes are lexicon-based, let us consider the ways in which the addition of inflectional morphemes affects the free morphemes to which they are attached. In very many instances there is no perceptible effect at all, in spoken or written form. Thus, the addition of *-ed* to the base forms *fill, jump, stay* or *want* changes nothing in these base forms. On the other hand, as can be seen from the collection of English noun plurals above, there are plenty of other cases where noticeable alterations to the form of the free morpheme do occur. Sometimes there is just a slight change 'at the join', as it were. The plural of *wife* is a case in point; here the /f/ of the singular form is replaced by a /v/ in the plural form – *wife* (/waɪf/) → *wives* (/waɪvz/). Sometimes – especially in plurals borrowed from Greek and Latin – the last syllable of the singular form is replaced by one or more different syllables in the plural, as in: *stimulus* (/ˈstɪmjʊləs/) → *stimuli* (/ˈstɪmjʊlaɪ/). And sometimes pluralization occasions changes in the very core of the pluralized word. This is the case for *children*, where the plural is signalled not only by the attachment of the anomalous morpheme *-ren* but also by a change in the quality of the vowel sound (written *i*) in *child* from /aɪ/ in *child* to /ɪ/ in *children*. In *man – men* (/mæn/ → /mɛn/) the change in the vowel sound in the core of the word from /æ/ to /ɛ/ is the only way in which pluralization is signalled.

All of the plurals referred to in the preceding paragraph represent a challenge for linguists. As long as the morphemes they are dealing with are neatly sequential (*jump + ed, cat + s, sing + ing* etc.), and as long as the allomorphs of such morphemes resemble each other and are predictable from the phonological environment, morphologists can provide analyses which are relatively straightforward and concrete. In the cases of *wives, children, men, stimuli* and the like, however, the morpheme takes on a more abstract quality, and its allomorphs have to be treated partly or wholly in terms of processes rather than simply in terms of an added element whose variant forms are determined by phonological environment. Thus, the allomorph of the English noun plural morpheme represented in *wives* involves not only the addition of *-s* but also a process whereby the last consonant of the word changes from /f/ to /v/, which in turn means that the *-s* ending is pronounced as /z/. Similarly, in *children*, the allomorph involved is the anomalous ending *-ren* (/rən/) plus the process which changes /aɪ/ to /ɪ/ in *child*. In *man — men* and *stimulus – stimuli* only a process allomorph is involved, the changes from /æ/ to /ɛ/ and from /əs/ to /aɪ/ respectively.

It is clear, then, that inflectional morphemes are not necessarily just elements that are tacked on to free morphemes without affecting the forms of those free morphemes. Let us compare the case of inflectional morphology with that of derivational morphology in this connection. Some derivational morphemes are said to be 'neutral' in their phonological effects, that is they do not change anything in the word to which they are attached. For example, the above-mentioned adverbializing morpheme *-ly* has no impact on the forms to which it is attached; thus, the *warm* element of *warmly* is constant in both words. Similarly, 'neutral' derivational morphemes include: *-ment* (as in *pave – pavement*), *-ness* (as in *white – whiteness*) and *en-* (as in *cage – encage*). Other derivational morphemes, on the other hand, are recognized as 'non-neutral' in their impact on the free morpheme base, and are accordingly thought of as at a different level of relationship with that base and as more deeply 'lexical'. For instance, the addition of *-ic* to *meteor* changes the stress pattern of this latter; thus: <u>me</u>teor, but mete<u>or</u>ic As for the derivational morpheme *-ion*, it causes all manner of changes in the base form – sometimes occasioning a shift in stress, sometimes bringing about changes in or additions to the sound segments making up the word to which *-ion* is attached, sometimes causing both, for example:

ad<u>mire</u>	admi<u>ra</u>tion
ad<u>mit</u>	ad<u>miss</u>ion
as<u>sume</u>	as<u>sump</u>tion
di<u>vide</u>	di<u>vis</u>ion
re<u>volve</u>	revol<u>u</u>tion

To return to the case of inflectional morphemes, these can be every bit as 'non-neutral' in the above sense in relation to the words to which they are affixed as can derivational morphemes. We have seen how the English noun plural morpheme may be expressed via significant alterations in the forms of the nouns pluralized. The morpheme which marks the simple past tense (what is sometimes known as the *preterite*) in English is associated with changes in the base forms of verbs which are no less far-reaching. Thus, alongside *play – played*, *hope – hoped*, *want – wanted* etc. we have present–preterite oppositions, such as:

bear	*bore*
come	*came*
drive	*drove*
go	*went*
sing	*sang*

In sum, then, although in principle one can see the point of distinguishing between morphology which is involved in word formation and morphology which is not, it has always to be borne in mind that this distinction is by no means clear-cut. It also needs to be recognized that inflectional morphology is quirky and lexically determined in the same way that 'lexical' morphology is. Finally, it cannot be ignored that inflectional morphemes may have just as large an impact on the forms of words to which they are attached as 'lexical' morphemes. All in all, there seem to be absolutely no good grounds for suggesting that inflectional morphemes lie outside the domain of the lexicon; and to the extent that the term *lexical morphology* can be interpreted as implying that there is a morphology which is non-lexical, it needs to be treated with caution.

3.5   Summary

This chapter has explored the internal structure of words. It began by noting that the morphemes of which words are made up may be either free, that is units that may stand alone as words in their own right, or bound, that is units that can occur only as parts of words. The phenomenon of morphemic alternation – the way in which morphemes may be realized in varying ways – was also dealt with. The chapter then moved on to discuss the distinction between 'lexical' morphology – morphology involved in word formation – and inflectional morphology – morphology involved in fitting words to their grammatical environment. It was shown that the distinction between these two categories of morphology is not entirely clear-cut, that some morphemes sit astride the two categories, and that inflectional morphemes may have just as great an impact as 'lexical' morphemes on the base forms of words to which they are attached. In the light of these facts it was argued that there are no good grounds for considering one particular category of morphemes, i.e. inflectional morphemes, to lie outside the domain of the lexicon.

Sources and suggestions for further reading

The account of morphemes and allomorphs presented here draws on the broad tradition of received wisdom in morphological studies as represented in works such as: F. Katamba, *Morphology* (Basingstoke: Macmillan, 1993); J. Lyons, *Introduction to theoretical linguistics* (Cambridge: Cambridge University Press, 1968, Chapter 5); P. H. Matthews, *Morphology: an introduction to the theory of word-structure* (Cambridge: Cambridge University Press, 1974).

See 3.2. The Bontoc and Chickasaw examples in 3.1 are taken from V. Fromkin and R. Rodman, *An introduction to language* (Sixth edition, New York: Harcourt Brace, 1998, Chapter 3). The distinction between 'lexical' morphology and inflectional morphology sketched follows that to be found in P. H. Matthews, *Morphology: an introduction to the theory of word-structure* (Cambridge: Cambridge University Press, 1974). Other works adopting a similar approach include F. Katamba, *Morphology* (Basingstoke: Macmillan, 1993). The notion that inflectional morphology is grammatical rather than lexical has a long history – dating back to Bloomfield (see L. Bloomfield, *Language*, New York: Holt, 1933, 274) and beyond.

See 3.4. The ambivalence of the *-ing* morpheme is referred to by A. Akmajian, R. A. Demers, A. K. Farmer and R. M. Harnish in their book *Linguistics: an introduction to language and communication* (Cambridge, MA: MIT Press, 1990). The general difficulty of distinguishing between derivational and inflectional morphology is very widely acknowledged by linguists – even if at times a little grudgingly – see, for example, A. Spencer, *Morphological theory: an introduction to word structure in generative grammar* (Oxford: Blackwell, 1991). The concept of 'neutrality/non-neutrality' in the context of morphology is discussed by F. Katamba (*Morphology*, Basingstoke: Macmillan, 1993) and by J. Harris (*English sound structure*, Oxford: Blackwell, 1994); see also P. Kiparsky 'Word formation and the lexicon', in F. Ingemann (ed.), *Proceedings of the 1982 Mid-America Linguistics Conference*, Kansas: University of Kansas Press, 1983). The case in favour of the idea that all morphology is essentially lexically based is put by, among others, J. T. Jensen and M. Strong-Jensen (1984) 'Morphology is in the lexicon' (*Linguistic Inquiry* 15, 74–98). Arguments tending broadly in the same direction are also to be found in M. Aronoff and F. Ashen, 'Morphology and the lexicon: lexicalization and productivity', in A. Spencer and A. M. Zwicky (eds), *The handbook of morphology* (Oxford: Blackwell, 1998).

Accessible presentations of basic morphological concepts are to be found in a number of introductions to linguistics. Particularly recommended in this connection are:

> V. Fromkin and R. Rodman, *An introduction to language* (sixth edition, New York: Harcourt Brace, 1998);
> R. H. Robins, *General linguistics: an introductory survey* (London: Longman, 1989).

Among works treating morphology in greater depth and which would be suitable for more advanced reading the following is recommended (in addition to the Matthews and Katamba volumes mentioned above):

> A. Carstairs-McCarthy, *Current morphology* (London: Routledge, 1991).

For those looking for particular perspectives on morphology the following titles may be of interest:

> On the recent history of morphology: P. H. Matthews, *Grammatical theory in the United States from Bloomfield to Chomsky* (Cambridge: Cambridge University Press, 1993).

On cognitive dimensions of morphology: C. J. Hall, *Morphology and the mind: a unified approach to explanation in linguistics* (London: Routledge, 1992).

On the role of morphology in the Chomskyan framework: A. Spencer, *Morphological theory: an introduction to word structure in generative grammar* (Oxford: Blackwell, 1991).

Also to be noted is the very comprehensive work edited by A. Spencer and A. M. Zwicky, *The handbook of morphology* (Oxford: Blackwell, 1998).

Focusing questions/topics for discussion

1. In the following passage try to find five examples of free morphemes and five examples of bound morphemes.

   I wanted to go to Philip's party, but Robert, my boyfriend, hates spending time around that particular crowd, so we decided instead to sample one of the latest delights on offer down at the local multiplex cinema. As it turned out, we both enjoyed the film in question, but we definitely did not appreciate the two guys sitting in front of us, who were very tall and very noisy.

2. Consider the following words. Try to identify which of them respectively exemplify compounding, derivation and inflection.

grapes	*proven*	*bookshelf*	*sisters'*
seaside	*frighten*	*tightrope*	*adores*
brightly	*oldish*	*sweaty*	*media*
lice	*Tim's*	*oxen*	*instep*
lousy	*doorbell*	*tended*	*unfit*

3. In 3.3 we saw some examples of English noun plural forms which departed from the normal (+ -(e)s) pattern. Try to think of five further examples of such irregular noun plurals in English and try also to think of five examples of English past tense forms which do not conform to the normal (+ -ed) pattern. Also, reflect on the inflectional morphology of any language you know other than English and try to identify some examples of inflectional irregularity in this other language too.

4. Group the following words into those which show a 'neutral' impact on the base form on the part of the relevant bound morpheme and those which show a 'non-neutral' impact.

active	*houses*	*motion*	*bulbous*
action	*poetic*	*movement*	*harshly*

had	normal	hooves	Chomskyan
has	swollen	roofs	Hallidayan
proceeded	paying	gracious	titular

5. The following words are often thought of as posing problems for morphologists. Can you say why this might be? Can you think of some further words that might pose similar kinds of problems?

bilberry	contain	fission	equine
cranberry	maintain	fissile	equestrian
unkempt	retain	locate	invade
dishevelled	select	locomotion	evade
disparage	elect	frantic	pensive

4

Lexical partnerships

4.1 Collocation: the togetherness factor

We saw in Chapter 1 and again in Chapter 2 that a great deal of what was traditionally seen as coming under the heading of grammar is now considered to be essentially lexical in nature. The basic point we noted was that once a particular lexical choice has been made in a given sentence, this choice has a major impact on the determination of what else may or may not occur in the sentence in question. In addition to this strongly determinant aspect of lexical choice there is also an effect in respect of word selection which is rather more probabilistic in nature. This latter effect has to do with the fact that – for a variety of reasons – particular words are frequently to be found in the company of certain other words. In such cases the selection of one or more of the words concerned in a given context is quite likely – or even very likely – to be accompanied by the selection of another word or other words from its habitual entourage. For instance, if a radio or television presenter uses the word *breaking*, we are anything but surprised if the word *news* follows. Similarly with:

at this moment in	*time*
law and	*order*
the Middle East peace	*process*

As has already been indicated in earlier chapters, this phenomenon of words 'keeping company' together is referred to as collocation. *Collocation* comes from two Latin words, the word *cum* ('with') and the word *locus* ('place'). Words which form collocations are repeatedly 'placed with' each other; that is to say, they often co-occur within a short distance of each other in speech and in written texts. In this chapter we shall briefly explore the notion of collocational range, look at fixed expressions and compounds, examine the role of collocational information in traditional dictionaries, review some of the recent corpus-based research into collocations, consider the question of the extent to which language use is based on prefabricated multi-word chunks, and discuss some of the implications of the collocation phenomenon for our understanding of the notion of lexical unit.

4.2　Collocational range

Even the most casual reflection on the way in which we put words together in the languages we know will lead us to an awareness of the fact that some words enter into a great number and variety of lexical partnerships, whereas other words are, as it were, a great deal more 'choosy' about the combinations they become involved with. At the many-partnered end of the scale is, for example, the English word *nice*. The list of items with which this word frequently co-occurs seems to be almost endless; the following is a tiny sample of the vast array of *nice* collocations: *nice body, nice day, nice food, nice house, nice idea, nice job, nice manners, nice move, nice neighbourhood, nice person, nice time, nice weather*. At the other end of the scale is the word *addled*, which in its literal sense of 'rotten' collocates only with *egg(s)*, and which in its metaphorical sense of 'muddled' collocates only with words such as *brain(s)* and *mind*. The term used to refer to these different patterns of combinability is *collocational range*; thus, *nice* would be said to have a very wide collocational range, whereas *addled* would be said to have a very restricted collocational range.

One obvious issue that arises in the context of looking at collocational range – indeed in the context of collocational research generally – is how far away from each other two words can be in a piece of speech or writing and still be regarded as 'keeping company'. For example, taking the word *garden* as our starting point or *node*, which other words in the following sentences are to be considered as occurring close enough to *garden* to qualify as candidates for having a collocational relationship with that word.

> *They invited me to a garden party.*

> *County Wicklow is sometimes called the Garden of Ireland.*

> *The children were playing in the garden.*

> *None of these houses has a decent garden.*

> *The garden was totally devoid of flowers.*

> *These gardens are famous for their exotic trees.*

> *I planted those tulip bulbs I bought in Amsterdam in the garden this year.*

Party in the first sentence obviously counts, since there are no intervening words between it and *garden*, but just how many intervening words between the node and a potential lexical partner are we prepared to accept? If one is the answer, then *Ireland* in the second sentence comes into the frame, if up to five, then so do *playing* (sentence 3), *houses* (sentence 4), *flowers* (sentence 5) and *trees* (sentence 6). What about *tulip* and *bulbs* in the final sentence? Can we accept six or seven intervening words and still talk about 'keeping company'? Different researchers will set the limits differently in this connection, but it is clear that there is no straightforward solution to this problem, and that whatever decision is taken will be open to debate.

4.3   Fixed expressions and compounds

A particular grouping of words may recur so frequently in a language that it comes to be seen as a *fixed expression*. Some examples of fixed expressions in English are:

once in a blue moon

seeing is believing

the more the merrier

the other side of the coin

to throw in the towel

Obviously, some fixed expressions are more fixed than others. In some of the above instances, for example, almost no change to either the order of the words or the actual words used is possible without the general meaning or the acceptability of the expression being affected. Thus, in *seeing is believing*, it might just be possible to insert an adverb before *is* (e.g. *seeing really is believing*), but otherwise the expression has to be used as it is. Similarly with *the more the merrier*; here the only admissible change is the placing of an intensifying word (usually a taboo word or a euphemism for a taboo word) before *merrier* (e.g. *the more the bleedin' merrier*). In other cases changes in the syntax and in the actual components of the expression can be made without the force of expression being undermined. Thus, *the other side of the coin* can be manipulated in various ways while still maintaining its essential identity:

Moving on to the cost of the project, here we see the <u>negative side of the coin</u>.

Of the French economy it has been remarked that <u>this is a coin that has two very different sides</u>.

As for the present political situation, well, <u>which side of the coin</u> shall I begin with?

Fixed expressions vary also in relation to the extent to which their overall meanings can be arrived at by simply adding together the meanings of the words out of which they are composed. For example, *seeing is believing* is interpretable simply on the basis of a knowledge of the normal meanings of the individual words involved in this expression. However, in the case of *to throw in the towel*, it would not be possible to interpret this as 'to give up', 'to surrender' unless one actually knew that this meaning attached to the whole expression – or unless one knew enough about boxing (where a towel thrown into the ring has traditionally been a way of conceding defeat) to be able to decode the metaphor. Expressions such as these which are 'semantically opaque' in this kind of way are generally referred to as *idioms*.

Lexical items which very frequently co-occur with each other often fuse together into compound words (see above, Chapter 3). Examples of this are *blackboard* (*black + board*), *keyhole* (*key + hole*) and *paintbrush* (*paint + brush*). In such instances the relationship between the meaning of the compound word and the meanings of its individual constituent words is not always a simple one. Thus, for example, *blackboard* does not denote any old board which is black, but a very specific kind of black board, usually found in classrooms, on which it is possible to write (and make excruciating noises!) with chalk.

The rule of thumb commonly appealed to for distinguishing between compound words and fixed expressions is based on an orthographic criterion. If two words are joined together in written form we tend to label them as a compound word; if not, we tend to treat them as participating in a fixed expression. However, this is a highly arbitrary distinction. Within a particular language a given expression may be transcribed in various ways. For example:

air bag	*air-bag*	*airbag*
coffee shop	*coffee-shop*	*coffeeshop*
gold mine	*gold-mine*	*goldmine*

It is also worth saying that, as we saw in Chapter 1, some languages are written down using systems which do not mark word boundaries, and some languages are not written down at all; clearly, in these cases the orthographic approach to distinguishing between fixed expressions and compounds would be totally irrelevant.

A phonological approach to this conundrum does not get us very far either. As, again, we saw in Chapter 1, whereas, for example, in most English words we can identify one syllable carrying the main stress, in many multi-word expressions that on the orthographic criterion, and according to native speakers' own intuitions, would not be classed as compound words, only one main stress occurs over the whole group. Thus:

<u>bar</u>ber shop group

<u>feel</u> good factor

<u>skin</u> care ointment

We might also note that phonological usage in this regard varies within language communities. The expression *New Year* (as in *Happy New Year!*), for instance, is given just one main stress by some speakers of English (<u>New</u> Year), while other speakers of English place a stress on both words (<u>New</u> <u>Year</u>).

Nor does there seem to be a simple way of distinguishing between compound words and fixed expressions in semantic terms. We have seen some examples of compounds whose meanings are not straightforwardly computable from the meanings of the words which compose them. However, as we have also noted, it is equally easy to find examples of collocations with similarly peculiar semantics: *heavy smoker* is not typically understood as 'overweight nicotine-user'; *criminal lawyer* is in most contexts taken to mean something other than 'law-breaking attorney'; and *artificial florist* will not usually be interpreted as 'flower-seller of unnatural origin'! On the other hand, fixed expressions as well as compounds often mean exactly what they look as if they might mean. Thus, *heavy vehicle* uncomplicatedly denotes a vehicle which is heavy; *criminal behaviour* denotes behaviour which is criminal; and *artificial additive* denotes an additive beyond Mother Nature's range. Similarly, *coalminer* denotes someone who mines coal, *sunlight* denotes the sun's light, and *workplace* denotes the place where one works.

4.4   Collocations and the dictionary

Whether it is possible to differentiate rigorously between compound words and collocations, and whether the meaning generated by the co-occurrence of two or more particular lexical items is a straightforward sum of the individual meanings of the items concerned, it is clear that the combinations into which a given word may enter and the meanings that attach to the various combinations in question are important elements in that word's profile. This is recognized at a practical level by dictionary-makers, as is demonstrated by the fact that (leaving aside the very tiniest pocket dictionaries) dictionary entries have traditionally not only treated the individual words concerned but have also referred to items with which they frequently co-occur. The following entry from the 1940 edition of the *Harrap's Shorter French and English Dictionary* is fairly representative.

> fatigue [fatig], *s.f.* **1.** (*a*) Fatigue, tiredness, weariness. **Tomber de fatigue,** to be dropping with weariness. **Brisé de fatigue,** dog-tired; dead-beat. (*b*) **Souliers de fatigue,** strong walking shoes. **Habits de fatigue,** working clothes. **Cheval de fatigue,** cart-horse. *Mec. E:* **Pièces de fatigue,** parts subject to strains. **2.** Wear and tear (of machines, clothes etc.).

As was mentioned in Chapter 2, the suggestion was made many years ago by the British linguist J. R. Firth that investigating the lexicon was essentially a matter of exhaustively investigating collocations, and, in fact, he specifically referred to lexicography (i.e. dictionary-making) in this context. The idea that dictionary-making needs to be founded on collocational research is a point of view which continues to have its champions today. Indeed, it is an idea which has been gaining ground over the last 10–15 years. Moreover, since Firth's time information technology has developed to the point where it is now possible – through the use of computerized corpora (see above, 2.2) – to undertake the kind of exhaustive investigation of collocations that Firth called for, and such corpora are indeed drawn on in the preparation of dictionaries, as well as being exploited in many other ways.

4.5   Corpora and collocations

The present view of many linguists is that the investigation of collocations is inextricably bound up with the exploitation of computerized corpora, for the simple reason that only through the use of such corpora – with their vast amounts of authentic data and their concordancing software – is it possible to come to any reliable conclusions about which words 'keep company' with which. Collocations were certainly studied before the advent of electronic corpora; the work of J.R. Firth in the 1950s has already been mentioned in this connection, and before him, in the 1930s, another British linguist, H.E. Palmer, was already deep into collocational research; however, there is no doubt that the creation of such corpora has enabled this area of research really to come into its own.

The potentialities of electronic corpora in this regard have been dramatically demonstrated by the *COBUILD* project. *COBUILD* (Collins Birmingham University International Language Database) involves a partnership between the Collins (now HarperCollins) publishing house and the School of English of the University of Birmingham. It has assembled a vast and still growing corpus of naturally occurring English data, now known as the *Bank of English*. Recent reports indicate that the corpus currently runs to more than 320 million words of spoken and written English text. There were, admittedly, corpora in existence before *COBUILD*, and other corpora were developed alongside and after *COBUILD*; however, the *COBUILD* project went further than its predecessors in showing how useful a corpus could be not only to researchers focused on language description but also in very practical domains such as the production of dictionaries and language-teaching materials, and, in so doing, it blazed a trail for the many corpus-based projects that followed and imitated it. It should perhaps also be noted in the present context that the director and leading light of the *COBUILD* project, John Sinclair, was deeply involved in collocational research long before the project was ever thought of, and that he always saw one of the principal attractions of the project as being its capacity to shed light on collocational issues.

Materials and language descriptions arising out of the *COBUILD* project base their definitions and illustrations on the combinatorial patterns discernible in the corpus. The following is a typical *COBUILD* dictionary entry. The meaning it assigns reflects an exhaustive analysis of the environments in which the word in question has been found to occur in the corpus — some of which are cited in the entry.

> **veritable** /vɛritəbəl/ is used to emphasize a description of something and used to suggest that, although the description might seem exaggerated, it is really accurate. EG *The water descended like a veritable Niagara . . . I'm sure the audience has a veritable host of questions . . . . . . a veritable passion for the cinema.*

We can see the same kind of approach in the *Collins COBUILD English Grammar*, as the following excerpt demonstrates.

Many nouns can be used after 'make'.

. . . There is usually a related verb which can be used followed by a reported clause.

She <u>made a remark</u> about the weather.

Allen <u>remarked</u> that at times he thought he was in America.

Now and then she <u>makes a comment</u> on something.

Henry Cecil <u>commented</u> that the ground was too firm.

. . .

Here is a list of nouns which are used after 'make' and have a related reporting verb:

arrangement	confession	protest	suggestion
claim	decision	remark	
comment	promise	signal	

Other nouns used with 'make' express speech actions other than reports or describe change, results, effort, and so on.

I'll <u>make some enquiries</u> for you.

They agreed <u>to make a few minor changes</u>.

McEnroe was desperate <u>to make one last big effort</u> to win Wimbledon again.

Here is a list of other nouns which are used after 'make':

appeal	contribution	noise	sound
attempt	effort	point	speech
change	enquiry	progress	start
charge	impression	recovery	success

Theoretical/descriptive linguists drawing on the *COBUILD Bank of English* use it as a basis for making statements about how words are combined that go beyond syntactic generalizations. For example, faced with a sentence such as *The bushes and trees were blowing in the wind, but the rain had stopped*, a syntactician would wish to analyse it in terms of finite clauses, noun phrases and verb phrases; the collocationally oriented corpus linguist, on the other hand, would be inclined to look at the whole range of instances in the databank in which combinations like *blow–wind, rain–stop* occurred in order to be able to comment on the lexical frame 'SOMETHING blowing in the wind' (which, as it turns out, is a great deal more likely to occur than the lexical frame 'the wind blowing SOMETHING') or to be able to note that *rain* followed by *stop* is much more typical that *rain* followed by *end*.

Some further electronic English-language corpora which are frequently referred to in the lexicological literature, and which to a greater or lesser extent have been used in collocational research, are mentioned below. We shall be revisiting some of them, as well as the *COBUILD* corpus, in Chapter 10 when we return to the topic of dictionary-making.

- the *Brown Corpus* (*Brown University Standard Corpus of Present-Day American English),* started in 1961, comprising one million words of written American English;
- the *LOB Corpus* (*London, Oslo, Bergen Corpus*), compiled between 1970 and 1978, involving the collaboration of the University of Lancaster, the University of Oslo and the Norwegian Computing Centre for the Humanities at Bergen, comprising one million words of written British English;
- the *London–Lund Corpus*, available since 1987, based mostly on the University of Lund's *Survey of Spoken English (*1975), which in turn was mostly based on the (non-computerized) *Survey of English Usage* compiled at University College London (1959), comprising approximately half a million words of spoken English;
- the *Longman–Lancaster Corpus*, dating from 1996, comprising 30 million words of spoken and written English from British and American sources;
- the *BNC* (*British National Corpus*), compiled between 1991 and 1995, involving collaboration between Oxford University Press, Longman

Chambers Harrap, the University of Lancaster, the British Library and Oxford University Computing Service, comprising 90 million words of written British English and 10 million words of spoken British English;
- the *CIC* (*Cambridge International Corpus* – formerly known as the *Cambridge Language Survey*), available since 1996, an initiative of Cambridge University Press, comprising 95 million words of written English (the spoken language annexe of *CIC*, compiled in collaboration with the University of Nottingham and comprising five million words, is known as the *CANCODE* – *Cambridge and Nottingham Corpus of Discourse in English*).

4.6   Creativity and prefabrication in language use

Linguists have put a good deal of emphasis in the last three or four decades on what Noam Chomsky calls the 'creative' dimension of language use – on the fact that knowledge of a language enables one to 'understand an indefinite number of expressions that are new to one's experience . . . and . . . to produce such expressions'. While it is undoubtedly true that we can and do use language innovatively and open-endedly in precisely the way Chomsky suggests, it certainly is not the case that our use of language is exclusively 'creative' in this sense. Large numbers of the sequences of words that we deploy and encounter in everyday speech and writing are clearly combinations that we have available to us as more or less prefabricated chunks – such combinations ranging from fixed idiomatic expressions like *cats and dogs* (= 'hard' as in *It's raining cats and dogs*) to 'semi-fixed' combinations such as *to know one's onions/stuff* and *to know/be up to all the tricks*. An analysis of authentic data in preparation for the *Oxford Dictionary of current idiomatic English*, for example, yielded literally thousands of such stable multi-word units. Similarly, it has been estimated that the *Oxford Dictionary of phrasal verbs* and the *Oxford Dictionary of English idioms* between them contain some 15,000 multi-word expressions. There is also psycholinguistic evidence to suggest that fixed expressions and formulas have an important economizing role in speech production; that is to say that they enable us to produce speech which is very much more fluent than it would be if we had to start from scratch and build up piece by piece every expression and every structure we use.

This notion has been taken a stage further by Sinclair, on the basis of his experience with the *COBUILD* data, and developed into the so-called 'idiom principle'. (The term *idiom* is used here with a much broader application than in 4.3, where mention was made of its more usual usage as a label for fixed expressions with meanings that cannot be deduced from the meanings of their component parts). The idiom principle states that, when we are putting together phrases in a language we know, although it may look as if we operating on the basis of open choices at every stage (the only constraints being that what we produce has to be broadly grammatical and make sense), what we are doing most of the time is drawing on our knowledge of pre-constructed or semi-preconstructed phrases that constitute single choices, varying lexical content within the chosen patterns to a fairly limited extent. Why we do this, rather than going through the process of constructing new phrases out of individual words every time, may, says Sinclair, have to do with our capitalization on the fact that similar situations recur in life and tend to be referred to in similar ways; it may have to do with the fact that we in any case prefer to economize on effort whenever possible; and/or it may have to do with the fact that the demands made on us by the extreme rapidity of speech production are such that we have to exploit every opportunity to make savings on processing time.

Some examples of the kind of thing Sinclair has in mind are:

- the phrase *set eyes on*, which usually has a pronoun subject and which is usually associated with either *never* or an expression such as *the moment, the first time* – as in *I've never set eyes on him; The first time he set eyes on her he knew he would always love her* etc.;
- the phrasal verb *set about*, which (in the sense of 'begin') tends to be associated with a following (usually transitive) verb in the *-ing* form – as in *We set about packing our bags; Bill finally set about earning some real money* etc.;
- the verb *happen*, which tends to occur in a particular kind of semantic environment – one where unpleasant occurrences, such as accidents, are being referred to – as in *No one knew how the catastrophe has happened; Such appalling events can never be allowed to happen again* etc.

4.7   Collocations, the lexicon and lexical units

What are the implications of collocational patterning for our conception of the lexicon and in particular for our understanding of what constitutes a lexical unit? If the lexicon represents that part of our knowledge of language that revolves around words, then, clearly, collocations have to be seen as included in the lexicon. It is obvious from all that has been said that we need to know about collocational patterns in order to function smoothly in lexical terms in either our mother tongue or any other language we may know. Anyone listening to news reports in English about recent military conflicts, for example, who did not know the terrible meanings that emerge when *ethnic* 'keeps company' with *cleansing, collateral* with *damage* or *friendly* with *fire* would be deeply mystified by what they heard. Similarly, and on a lighter note, anyone trying to express great excitement and pleasure in English who used a combination such as *I'm on top of the moon* (rather than *I'm on top of the world* or *I'm over the moon*) would certainly run the risk of incomprehension.

With regard to defining the lexical unit, one approach is to take the word as the typical lexical unit and to say that a group of words can be considered as a lexical unit only if its meaning is associated with the group as a whole rather than a sum of the individual meanings of the constituent words. According to this view *black* is a lexical unit; so is *blackbird* (as opposed to *black bird*), since *blackbird* denotes a particular species of bird (*turdus merula*) rather than just a bird of a particular colour; and so is *in black and white* (as in *He wants it in black and white*), since the meaning of this whole expression ('written', 'in writing') cannot be arrived at simply by combining the normal meanings of the individual items out of which it is formed.

There are at least two possible objections to this approach. On the one hand, the issue of semantic transparency or opacity in relation to multi-word expressions (i.e. whether or not the meaning of a expression can or cannot be seen as a straightforward composite of its component words) is somewhat problematic. It is not the case that multi-word expressions are either self-evidently transparent or self-evidently opaque. There are degrees of opacity. Thus, *blackbird* is less opaque than *ladybird* (which in many varieties of English is the word used for the insect that in American English is called *ladybug*); and *ladybird* (given that ladybirds do at least fly like birds!) is less opaque than *strictly for the birds* (= 'trivial', 'uninteresting'). Even many apparently transparent examples like *fish and chips* turn out on closer inspection to have opaque aspects; thus, in order to qualify to be described as *fish and chips* a culinary product has to involve one of a particular range of types of fish (sardine, trout or tuna will not do) and has to have been cooked and presented in a particular way.

Another problem is that using a purely semantic criterion is a rather narrow way of looking at the matter. It leaves out of account the question of whether in the use of a particular expression – whatever its degree of semantic opacity – the individual words are selected and are perceived to function singly or together. For example, the following expressions are all relatively transparent, but there is little doubt that they are selected and understood as wholes rather than being processed in a word by word manner.

midnight

good-natured

diesel engine

bread and butter

say it with flowers

As we have seen, it has been suggested that most of our use of language relies on the exploitation of collections of words that to a greater or lesser extent function together as entire packages. Whether or not this is true, it does seem clear that groups of words which are transparent in their meaning may nevertheless operate as units.

To sum up, even a conservative approach to the question of what counts as a lexical unit based on a criterion of semantic unitariness has to concede that there are lexical units which consist of more than one word. An approach which makes reference to the broader issue of the selection and perception of multi-word expressions as wholes (whatever their degree of semantic transparency/opacity) yields the conclusion that many multi-word expressions which are semantically transparent are none the less to be seen as lexical units.

4.8   Summary

This chapter looked at the commonly observed fact that certain words habitually 'keep company' with certain other words. It showed that a particular word may have a wider or more restricted collocational range, that is, enter into frequent partnership with a greater or lesser quantity and variety of other words; it explored the relationship between compound words and fixed expressions, concluding that there was no hard and fast way of distinguishing between these two categories of collocation; it touched on collocational description in traditional lexicography; it discussed the way in which collocational research has been enhanced by the advent of electronic corpora; it reported on evidence from corpus-based research that language users incorporate very large numbers of pre-constructed and semi-preconstructed multi-word expressions into their speech, and noted a suggestion that most language use relies on sequences of words that are to a greater or lesser extent prefabricated; and, finally, it examined the implications of the results of collocational research for our understanding of the nature of lexical units.

Sources and suggestions for further reading

See 4.2. The treatment of the notion of collocational range, which originates in A. McIntosh, 'Patterns and ranges' in A. McIntosh and M. A. K. Halliday, *Patterns of language: papers in general, descriptive and applied linguistics* (London: Longman, 1966), owes much to Chapter 3 of R. Carter's book *Vocabulary: applied linguistic perspectives* (second edition, London: Routledge, 1998). Carter's chapter was in fact also a valuable source for much of the rest of the discussion of collocations.

See 4.3. The *heavy smoker*, *criminal lawyer* and *artificial florist* examples are borrowed from F. Palmer's *Grammar* (Harmondsworth: Penguin, 1971, 45, 54).

See 4.4. The illustrative dictionary entry in 4.4 are taken from the 1965 reprint of J. E. Mansion (ed.), *Harrap's Shorter French and English Dictionary* (London: George G. Harrap & Company, 1940, 259). A concise account of Firth's collocational approach to lexicographical issues – in his own words – is to be found on pages 26–7 of his article 'A synopsis of linguistic theory' in *Studies in linguistic analysis* (Special Volume of the Philological Society, Oxford: Blackwell, 1957).

See 4.5. On the question of the connection between electronic corpus-based studies and collocation research, a typical pronouncement is that of Moon: 'collocation studies are now inevitably associated with corpus studies, since it is difficult and arguably pointless to study such things except through using large amounts of real data' (R. Moon, 'Vocabulary connections: multi-word items in English', in N. Schmitt and M. McCarthy (eds), *Vocabulary: description, acquisition and pedagogy*, Cambridge: Cambridge University Press, 1997, 41). H. E. Palmer's work, and in particular his *Second interim report on English collocations* (Tokyo: Institute for Research in English Teaching, 1933) is cited by G. Kennedy in his *Introduction to corpus linguistics* (London: Longman, 1998, 108).

See 4.5. The two main sources for the description of the *COBUILD* project in 4.5 are: J. Sinclair (ed.), *Looking up: an account of the COBUILD project in lexical computing and the development of the Collins COBUILD English Language Dictionary* (London: Collins, 1987) and J. Sinclair, *Corpus, concordance, collocation* (Oxford: Oxford University Press, 1991). The figure of 320 million words is quoted by R. Carter (*Vocabulary*, London: Routledge, 1998, 167). The *COBUILD* dictionary entry is cited and discussed by R. Krishnamurthy in his article 'The process of compilation' (in J. Sinclair (ed.), *Looking up*, London: Collins, 1987). The extract from the *Collins COBUILD English grammar* (London: Collins, 1990, 150–1) is taken from the section entitled 'Verbs with little meaning: delexical verbs'. The brief discussion of the sentence *The bushes and trees were blowing in the wind, but the rain had stopped* is based on R. Moon's comments on p. 41 of her article 'Vocabulary connections: multi-word items in English' (in N. Schmitt and M. McCarthy (eds), *Vocabulary: description, acquisition and pedagogy*, Cambridge: Cambridge University Press, 1997).

See 4.6. The Chomsky quote is to be found on p. 100 of N. Chomsky, *Language and mind* (enlarged edition, New York: Harcourt Brace Jovanovich, 1972). The report on the research leading to the *Oxford Dictionary of current idiomatic English* (eds A. Cowie, R. Mackin and I. A. McCaig, two volumes, Oxford: Oxford University Press, 1975/1983) is that of A. Cowie in his article 'Stable and creative aspects of vocabulary use' (in R. Carter and M. McCarthy (eds), *Vocabulary and language teaching*, London: Longman, 1988). The *Oxford Dictionary of phrasal verbs* and the *Oxford Dictionary of English idioms* are both published in Oxford by Oxford University Press (1993); the quantitative figure put on their content (15,000 multi-word expressions) is cited by R. Moon ('Vocabulary connections: multi-word items in English', in N. Schmitt and M. McCarthy (eds), *Vocabulary: description, acquisition and pedagogy*, Cambridge: Cambridge University Press, 1997, 48). Psycholinguistic evidence regarding the facilitating role of prefabricated patterns in speech production is referred to by, among others, A. Peters in *The units of language acquisition* (Cambridge: Cambridge University Press, 1983). The discussion of John Sinclair's idiom principle is based on the section entitled 'The idiom principle' in his book *Corpus, concordance collocation* (Oxford: Oxford University Press, 1991, 110–15); the examples used in this context are taken from pp. 111–12 of this book.

See 4.7. The importance of the contribution of collocational knowledge to linguistic competence, referred to in 4.7, is discussed by, among others, M. Benson ('Collocations and idioms', in R. Ilson (ed.), *Dictionaries, lexicography and language learning*, Oxford: Pergamon/The British Council), G. Kjellmer ('A mint of phrases', in K. Aijmer and B. Altenberg (eds), *English corpus linguistics: studies in honour of Jan Svartvik*, London: Longman, 1991), and T. Van Der Wouden (*Negative contexts: collocation, polarity and multiple negation*, London: Routledge, 1997). The semantically based approach to the definition of lexical units summarized in this section is essentially that proposed by D. A. Cruse in his book *Lexical semantics* (Cambridge: Cambridge University Press, 1986, Chapter 2). The *blackbird*, *ladybird* and *fish and chips* examples are all borrowed from Cruse, this source.

Good introductions to the collocational aspect of the lexicon are to be found in Chapter 3 of R. Carter's *Vocabulary: applied linguistic perspectives* (second edition, London: Routledge, 1998), in Chapter 9 of E. Hatch and C. Brown's *Vocabulary, semantics and language education* (Cambridge: Cambridge University Press, 1995), in R. Moon's above-mentioned article in N. Schmitt and M. McCarthy's edited volume *Vocabulary: description, acquisition and pedagogy* (Cambridge: Cambridge University Press, 1997), and in the first section of T. Van Der Wouden's *Negative contexts: collocation, polarity and multiple negation* (Amsterdam: John Benjamin, 1997).

Numerous books on the use of corpora in collocational research (and linguistic research generally) are now available. Some of the relevant titles are:

- K. Aijmer and B. Altenberg (eds), *English corpus linguistics: studies in honour of Jan Svartvik* (London: Longman, 1991);
- G. Kennedy, *Introduction to corpus linguistics* (London: Longman, 1998);
- T. McEnery and A. Wilson, *Corpus linguistics* (Edinburgh: Edinburgh University Press, 1996);
- J. Sinclair (ed.), *Looking up: an account of the COBUILD project in lexical computing and the development of the Collins COBUILD English Language Dictionary* (London: Collins, 1987);
- J. Sinclair, *Corpus, concordance, collocation* (Oxford: Oxford University Press, 1991);
- J. Thomas and M. Short (eds), *Using corpora for language research: studies in the honour of Geoffrey Leech* (London: Longman, 1996).

Focusing questions/topics for discussion

1. At the beginning of the chapter some clichés commonly used in journalism were mentioned (*breaking news, law and order* etc.). Try to think of five more such clichés in English and also try to think of one or two in any other language you know.

2. In 4.2 we looked at the notion of collocational range, comparing the very wide collocational ranges of *nice* with the very restricted collocational range of *addled*. Consider the following words and try to categorize them likewise according to their collocational range – that is to say, into items with very wide collocational ranges and items with much more restricted ranges. In each case give examples of collocations in which they occur.

big	*bright*	*centrifugal*	*improper*
loud	*premeditated*	*rancid*	*right*
sad	*short*	*trenchant*	*unwarranted*

3. In our discussion of fixed expressions and compound words in 4.3 we noted that some compounds and fixed expressions are semantically transparent (i.e. have meanings which are essentially combinations of the meanings of their component parts) and that others are semantically opaque (i.e. have meanings which are not simply sums of the meanings of their component parts). Consider the following compounds and fixed expressions and try to decide which are semantically transparent and which are semantically opaque. In the case of those which are semantically opaque demonstrate their opacity by providing definitions of their meanings.

air circulation system	*eye strain*	*to pop off*
airhead	*to see eye to eye*	*to pop the question*
blue skies	*foxglove*	*to look on the sunny side*
blue language	*to go fox-hunting*	*sun-dried*
a weekend in the country	*good grief!*	*to sing out of tune*
country music	*grievous bodily harm*	*he who pays the piper calls the tune*

4. In 4.4 we saw some examples of the way in which information about collocational patterns have been incorporated into traditional dictionary entries. Imagine you are writing dictionary entries for the following words and decide what kind of collocational information and examples you would include in these cases.

day   all   fire   high   middle   rat   spirit   tell   twist   way

5. It seems that some kinds of writing are full of well-worn expressions and phrases, while others are characterized by a relative absence of frequent collocations. Horoscopes tend to fall into the former category and poetry into the latter. Have a look at some horoscopes and some poems and try to decide why the writers of these texts took the approach they did in relation to the use of collocations.

5

Lexis and meaning

5.1 Words making the difference

It is quite obvious to any user of any language that there is an intimate connection between the lexicon and meaning. A brief glance at the following two brief passages – which are identical but for one word – will persuade anyone who needs convincing just how much difference to the meaning of an entire stretch of language a single word can make.

The interrogating officer moved closer to the prisoner.

'Let's see how you like this', he said.

He then hit the prisoner with a truly vicious <u>question</u>.

The interrogating officer moved closer to the prisoner.

'Let's see how you like this', he said.

He then hit the prisoner with a truly vicious <u>truncheon</u>.

Of course, the use of different sequences of words does not always yield vastly different overall meanings. Indeed, the English expression *in other words* normally introduces a phrase or a sentence which is differently formulated from but similar in meaning to what went before it, for example:

I worship the ground you stand on, dearest Patricia. I bless the day that you were born, and I rejoice in every breath you take. In other words, sweet Patty, I love you.

Usually, in such cases, as in the above example, some kind of summary of the preceding material is involved.

There is also the fact that individual words may resemble each other semantically to the point where they are *synonymous*, i.e. can replace each other in some contexts without any noticeable change in meaning being involved, for example:

They stumbled into the sitting room and collapsed on to the <u>couch</u>.

They stumbled into the sitting room and collapsed on to the <u>sofa</u>.

The questions on this paper were too <u>hard</u> for us to answer.

The questions on this paper were too <u>difficult</u> for us to answer.

Josie and I are the best of <u>pals</u> now.

Josie and I are the best of <u>friends</u> now.

However, it is generally true to say that the meaning of what we say or write is carried to a very large extent by the words that we choose, and that changing words more often than not changes meanings, for example:

Sue lives up <u>North</u>, well in the <u>Midlands</u> really, not too far from Leicester.

It says here in the paper that he lived off '<u>immortal</u> earnings'. I suppose they mean '<u>immoral</u>'.

I used to <u>jog</u> around the park, but now I just <u>walk</u>!

In what follows we shall explore some of the ways in which linguists have tried to come to grips with the relationship between words and meaning. We shall start by looking at the notion that lexical meaning is essentially about expressions being applied to objects, places, people, attributes, states, actions, processes etc. in the 'real world'. We shall then consider that dimension of meaning which has to do with relations between words. Our next port of call will be the suggestion that the meaning of any given word can be analysed into a set of sense components. Finally, we shall examine some 'cognitive' approaches to word meaning – that is, approaches which are based on the idea that the ways in which linguistic meanings are constructed and organized come out of our experience of the world and our perception and processing of that experience.

5.2 Meaning seen as reference or denotation

It is self-evident that language conveys meaning partly by as it were pointing to various kinds of phenomena in the 'real world'. In fact, physically pointing to something can often perform the same function as naming it. For example, if I am in the queue for lunch in the university canteen, and, on reaching the servery, I am asked for my order, I may say 'The egg curry please', or I may point to the steaming concoction in question, or I may do both. When a linguistic expression 'points' in this way in a particular context to a specific entity, attribute, state, process etc., linguists talk about an act of *reference*, the phenomenon thus identified being labelled as the *referent*.

There is another way in which linguistic expressions can be applied to 'real world' phenomena. Instead of picking out a specific phenomenon in a particular context, an expression may identify a whole class of phenomena.

For instance, in the following sentence the expression *the wolf* does not refer to one particular wolf but to an entire category of mammals.

The wolf is a much misunderstood animal.

Similarly with *baked beans* and *Sunday night* in the sentences below.

Even though they taste nice, baked beans are actually quite good
for you.

Sunday night is as quiet as the grave around these parts.

Many linguists call this kind of meaning *denotation,* labelling the class of entities to which an expression is applied as its *denotatum* (plural: *denotata*). (However, it should be noted that the terms *refer, reference* and *referent* are often used in a broad sense to cover both reference as defined earlier and denotation.)

Traditionally, language has been seen as communicating meanings via concepts constructed out of our experience of the relevant denotata. On this view, each linguistic form is associated with a concept, and each concept is the mental representation of a phenomenon in the 'real world'. This notion is sometimes represented diagrammatically as shown in Figure 5.1.

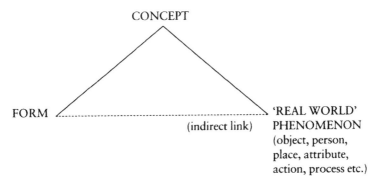

Figure 5.1 Linguistic forms associated with 'real world' phenomena.

One difficulty with this kind of representation is that, in implying that each particular form is uniquely associated with a single particular concept, it fails to provide any account of cases where more than one expression is associated with a single meaning or of cases where a single expression is associated with a more than one meaning (see below) and there is also the problem that this whole approach leads to an 'atomistic' view of semantics which treats each form and its meaning as isolated and self-contained.

There are other reasons too for taking a wary approach to the notion that meaning is only about expressions being applied to 'real world' phenomena, whether referentially or denotationally. For one thing, there are words whose meaning simply cannot be accounted for in this way – words like *if*, *and*, *should*, *nevertheless*. All of these items have meaning, but certainly not by virtue of identifying observable phenomena or classes of phenomena in the 'real world'. There are also expressions that relate to phenomena which do not exist – *mermaid*, *tooth-fairy*, *unicorn* etc. Can we say that such expressions have no meaning just because they have no corresponding denotata in the 'real world'? Certainly not.

Also worth noting is that two (or more) expressions may be applied to exactly the same phenomenon and yet have different meanings. The classic example of this is the designation of the planet Venus as both the *Morning Star* and the *Evening Star* (because – owing to its brightness – Venus is still visible at dawn and already visible at dusk). The expressions *Morning Star* and *Evening Star* clearly have different meanings, and yet they are applied to precisely the same object. Some further illustrations of expressions with different meanings being applied to the same phenomenon follow.

the Lionheart	*half-empty*	*to tell lies*
King Richard I of England	*half-full*	*to be economical with the truth*

5.3   Structuralist perspectives on meaning

Much of the discussion in previous chapters has been concerned with structure of various kinds – sentence-structure, the internal structure of words, sound-structure etc. This is very much the hallmark of the whole approach to language taken by modern linguistics, which is usually taken to date from the work of the Swiss linguist Ferdinand de Saussure, the generally recognized 'founding father' of what became known as *structuralism*. According to the structuralist conception, in the words of the British linguist John Lyons, 'every language is cut to a unique pattern', and the units of a given language 'can be identified only in terms of their relationships with other units in the same language'. What this view implies in respect of lexical meaning is that it has to be seen in the light of relations between expressions in the same language system.

This is not to say that structuralism denies the relationship between linguistic forms and phenomena in the 'real world'. It does, however, insist that this relationship is only part of the story. Saussure draws an analogy in this connection with monetary systems. Just as the value of a given coin (e.g. five francs) is based, he says, both on the kinds of goods it will buy and on its relationship with other coins in the same system (e.g. one franc), so, says Saussure, the 'value' of a linguistic unit derives both from the concepts for which it may be 'exchanged' and from its set of relationships with other words in the language.

The first manifestation of structuralist semantics was *lexical field theory*. This is an approach based on the idea that it is possible to identify within the vocabulary of a language particular sets of expressions (*lexical fields*) covering particular areas of meaning (*semantic fields*) where the lexical organization is such that the relevant lexical units precisely mark out each other's territory, so to speak. One of the early exponents of lexical field theory, Jost Trier, wrote in terms of 'a net of words' cast over meaning 'in order to capture and organize it and have it in demarcated concepts'. A much-cited example of a semantic field is that of colour. Colour is an undifferentiated continuum in nature; it is organized into red, orange, yellow, green etc. by the words which are used to identify particular areas of the spectrum. Moreover, different languages divide up colour differently. For example, Russian recognizes two colours in the blue range where English recognizes only one; the words Russian *goluboj* and *sinij* – which are customarily translated as 'light blue' and 'dark blue' respectively – are in fact understood as identifying quite distinct colours, not different varieties of the same colour.

The fact that lexical field theory talked so much about concepts was, however, off-putting for some structuralist linguists, especially North American structuralists who took their inspiration from the work of the American linguist Leonard Bloomfield. Bloomfield was determined to see linguistics recognized as a fully-fledged science and so he and his followers were interested only in those areas of language which were amenable to rigorous objective analysis. Meaning, defined in terms of unobservable concepts, did not come into that category as far as the Bloomfieldians were concerned, and they saw the scientifically accurate definition of meaning in terms of the 'real world' phenomena to which words were applied as being possible for only a minority of expressions. Bloomfield claimed, for example, that defining the names of minerals was relatively straightforward thanks to the resources made available by chemistry and mineralogy; the problems arose in the cases of words like *love* or *hate*, 'which concern situations that have not been accurately classified', these latter being 'in the great majority'.

This is a very limited and naïve view of meaning. On the other hand, the dependence of lexical field theory on the notion of conceptually defined semantic fields is undoubtedly a weakness. There are certainly some areas of meaning – like colour, the human body etc. – which have a clearly identifiable objective reality which can be detached from other areas of meaning, but what about a semantic field such as the 'intellectual domain of meaning', on which Jost Trier did his pioneering work? For Trier the 'intellectual domain' covers a whole range of types of knowledge – scholarly, social, mystical, technical, aesthetic – but his definition of the domain is essentially arbitrary; for some researchers the 'intellectual domain of meaning' might be much more narrowly defined, and for others it might be more broadly defined.

It was the above-mentioned British linguist, John Lyons, who found a widely acceptable way forward for a structuralist approach to lexical meaning. He acknowledges that aspect of meaning which derives from some expressions' relationship with the world beyond language – their application in terms of reference and denotation as defined earlier. However, in common with Saussure and the lexical field theorists, Lyons also recognizes that the meaning of an individual expression crucially depends on the network of relations with other expressions into which it enters. This latter aspect of meaning Lyons labels *sense*, and his approach to the analysis of sense is such that it does not require the prior identification of a conceptual area or semantic field; the lexical field or subsystem in this perspective is defined in terms of the observable relations between lexical expressions within partic-ular contexts.

This last point about context needs emphasizing because of the fact that a given expression may have more than one meaning. For example, the word *mouth* may refer to a facial feature in some contexts (e.g. *He has rather a small mouth*) and to a geographical feature in other (e.g. *The mouth of this river is difficult to navigate*). Where the meanings attached to a given form are clearly connected in this kind of way, linguists are happy to regard them as meanings of the same word and to talk about *multiple meaning* or *poly-semy*. There are, however, other cases where a particular form is associated with more than one meaning and the meanings in question are totally unre-lated (e.g. *bank* denoting a financial institution and *bank* denoting the edge of a river, canal etc.). In this sort of instance, linguists consider that two dis-tinct words are involved which simply happen to coincide formally, the term used to signify this situation being *homonymy*. Homonyms may be com-pletely identical – as in *bank–bank*; they may be identical only at the phono-logical level – as in *meet–meat* (in which case they are called *homophones*); or they may be identical only at the orthographic level – as in *row* /rəʊ/ = 'propel a boat using oars' and *row* /raʊ/ = 'quarrel' – (in which case they are called *homographs*). Unfortunately, it is not necessarily always crystal-clear in specific instances whether polysemy or homonymy is involved.

With regard to the kinds of relations Lyons has in mind, he distinguishes between those which are *paradigmatic* (or *substitutional*) in nature and those which are *syntagmatic* (or *combinatorial*). Paradigmatic relations are defined as those which hold 'between intersubstitutable members of the same grammatical category', and syntagmatic relations are defined as those which hold 'typically, though not necessarily, between expressions of dif-ferent grammatical categories (e.g. between nouns and adjectives, between verbs and adverbs etc.), which can be put together in grammatically well-formed combinations (or constructions)'. Syntagmatic sense-relations are clearly one aspect of the colligational and collocational dimensions of the lexicon, which have already been discussed (in chapters 2 and 3, respec-tively). For example, the fact that the adjective *rancid* combines with only a limited range of nouns (*butter*, *lard*, *oil* etc.) can be seen as a set of semantic relationships, since the meanings of the nouns in question are clearly the determining factor. As far as paradigmatic relations are concerned, Lyons focuses on *synonymy*, *hyponymy* and *incompatibility*, which he defines and demonstrates in terms of logical relations between sentences, or *meaning postulates*. The two important logical notions that Lyons uses in his approach are those of *entailment* and *negation*. One sentence *entails* another sentence in a given context if the one necessarily implies the other (e.g. *I am a man* entails *I am a human being* where the two *Is* refer to the same individual. One sentence *negates* another in a given context if the one necessarily denies the truth of the other (e.g. *I am a man* negates *I am a centipede* where the two *Is* refer to the same individual).

Synonymy

The relation of synonymy has already been briefly mentioned in 5.1. It is defined by Lyons in terms of minimally different sentences entailing each other. Where two or more sentences entail each other and differ by only one expression, the distinguishing expressions are taken to be synonymous. For example, the following sentences all entail each other.

Ethelred the Unready <u>died</u> in 1016.

Ethelred the Unready <u>expired</u> in 1016.

Ethelred the Unready <u>passed away</u> in 1016.

Ethelred the Unready <u>popped off</u> in 1016.

Ethelred the Unready <u>kicked the bucket</u> in 1016.

Ethelred the Unready <u>snuffed it</u> in 1016.

They differ by only the expressions underlined, and so, according to the terms of the above definition, all of these expressions are synonymous. The above examples illustrate two further points which are relevant to the rest of the discussion of lexical relations. The first is that such relations can hold between individual words (e.g. *die*, *expire*), between individual words and multi-word expressions (e.g. *die*, *snuff it*) and between multi-word expressions (*pass away*, *kick the bucket*). The second point is that it is not a condition for the establishment of a particular semantic relation that it should hold in all contexts. For example, there are instances where the expression *kick the bucket* is interpreted literally, as in: *The window-cleaner tripped and kicked the bucket which was standing at the bottom of his ladder, spilling water all over the pavement.* Obviously, this last sentence does not entail *The window-cleaner tripped and expired which was standing at the bottom of his ladder, spilling water all over the pavement*; accordingly, in this context *kick the bucket* is not synonymous with *expire, die, pass away* etc. Issues of contextual appropriacy also arise: the contexts in which we might use *snuff it* in the above sense would tend not to be the same as those in which we would use *expire*. For these reasons, statements about semantic relations between lexical expressions always have to take context into consideration.

Two further examples of sets of synonyms are set out and illustrated below.

Aid, assistance, help

The crisis cannot be solved without the <u>aid</u> of the international community.

The crisis cannot be solved without the <u>assistance</u> of the international community.

The crisis cannot be solved without the <u>help</u> of the international community.

Fast, quickly, speedily, swiftly

He was travelling so <u>fast</u> that everything around him became a blur.

He was travelling so <u>quickly</u> that everything around him became a blur.

He was travelling so <u>speedily</u> that everything around him became a blur.

He was travelling so <u>swiftly</u> that everything around him became a blur.

Hyponymy

Hyponymy, the relation between more specific (*hyponymous*) terms (e.g. *spaniel*) and less specific (*superordinate*) terms (e.g. *dog*) is defined in terms of one-way rather than two-way entailment. Thus *I own a <u>spaniel</u>* entails *I own a <u>dog</u>*, but *I own a <u>dog</u>* does not entail *I own a <u>spaniel</u>*. Hyponymous relations can be represented as inverted tree diagrams in which the lower intersections or nodes represent terms which are hyponymous to the ones above them, and these latter in turn are hyponymous to the ones above them. Thus in the (incomplete) Figure 5.2 below *cocker spaniel* is hyponymous to *spaniel*, which is in turn hyponymous to *dog*, which is in turn hyponymous to *mammal*, which is in turn hyponymous to *animal*.

Another characteristic of hyponymy is that it is what semanticists call *transitive*, in the sense that the relation can be seen as 'in transit' all the way along the line, so that if X is hyponymous to Y and Y is hyponymous to Z then X is hyponymous to Z. Thus, *cocker spaniel* is hyponymous not only to *spaniel* but also to *dog*, *mammal* and *animal*.

Further examples of expressions in hyponymous–superordinate relationships are given below.

Claret, wine, drink

You'll find some <u>claret</u> on the table.

You'll find some <u>wine</u> on the table.

You'll find some <u>drink</u> on the table.

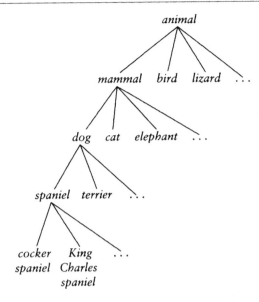

Figure 5.2 Hyponymous relations.

Claret is hyponymous to *wine*; wine is hyponymous to drink; and claret is also hyponymous to drink.

Hatchback, car, vehicle

The firm bought him a new <u>hatchback</u>.

The firm bought him a new <u>car</u>.

The firm bought him a new <u>vehicle</u>.

Hatchback is hyponymous to *car*; *car* is hyponymous to *vehicle*; and *hatchback* is also hyponymous to *vehicle*.

Incompatibility

With regard to incompatibility, this can be defined in general terms, and also more specifically for particular types of incompatibility, namely, *complementarity*, *polar antonymy* and *converseness*. Incompatibility in general is simply defined in terms of negative entailment: *Johnny's shirt is <u>pink</u>* entails *Johnny's shirt is not <u>green</u>*; *Johnny's shirt is <u>green</u>* entails *Johnny's shirt is not <u>pink</u>*; and so *pink* and *green* can be taken to be incompatible. Similarly with:

Metal, wood

The chair is entirely made of <u>metal</u>.

The chair is entirely made of <u>wood</u>.

Plain, striped

The tie I was wearing was <u>plain</u>.

The tie I was wearing was <u>striped</u>.

Complementarity

Turning now to particular subcategories of incompatibility, let us begin with the relation of complementarity (also known as *simple antonymy* or *binary antonymy*), which is a sort of 'one or the other' relation. In the case of complementarity not only does the assertion of one lexical item in a complementary pair (such as *alive* and *dead*) imply the denial of the other but the denial of the one implies the assertion of the other. Thus *Nessie is <u>alive</u>* entails *Nessie is not <u>dead</u>*, and *Nessie is not <u>dead</u>* entails *Nessie is <u>alive</u>*. Some further examples follow.

Pass, fail

Janet <u>passed</u> the exam.　　　*Janet <u>failed</u> the exam.*

Janet did not <u>pass</u> the exam.　　*Janet did not <u>fail</u> the exam.*

Janet <u>passed</u> the exam entails *Janet did not <u>fail</u> the exam*; *Janet <u>failed</u> the exam* entails *Janet did not <u>pass</u> the exam*; *Janet did not <u>pass</u> the exam* entails *Janet <u>failed</u> the exam*; *Janet did not <u>fail</u> the exam entails Janet <u>passed</u> the exam*.

True, false

What he says is <u>true</u>.　　　*What he says is <u>false</u>.*

What he says is not <u>true</u>.　　*What he says is not <u>false</u>.*

What he says is <u>true</u> entails *What he says is not <u>false</u>*; *What he says is <u>false</u>* entails *What he says is not <u>true</u>*; *What he says is not true* entails *What he says is <u>false</u>*; *What he says is not <u>false</u>* entails *What he says is <u>true</u>*.

Polar antonymy

Polar antonymy (also known as *gradable antonymy*) differs from complementarity by virtue of the fact that the items in question are not in a 'one or the other' relationship but imply the possibility of gradations between them. The assertion of one of a pair of polar antonyms (e.g. *rich* and *poor*) implies the denial of the other, but the denial of the one does not necessarily imply the assertion of the other. *Liz is <u>rich</u>* entails *Liz is not <u>poor</u>*, and *Liz is <u>poor</u>* entails *Liz is not <u>rich</u>*. However, *Liz is not <u>poor</u>* does not entail *Liz is <u>rich</u>*, and *Liz is* *not rich* does not entail *Liz is poor*, since it is fairly easy to think of expressions identifying states somewhere between being rich and being poor (e.g. *comfortably off*); *rich* and *poor* are therefore said to be polar antonyms with respect to each other. Where polar antonyms are used there is always some kind of implicit or explicit standard or norm involved against which judgments are made and in the light of which qualities are attributed. For instance, the same person, let us say a teacher by the name of Rothschild, may be described as rich when compared with other members of his/her profession but poor when compared with other members of the Rothschild family. Whenever we use the terms *rich, poor, comfortably off* etc. we always have some kind of yardstick in mind on the basis of which we make the evaluations signalled by the words used. Similarly with the following examples.

Big, small

Tom's house is <u>big</u>.	*Tom's house is <u>small</u>.*
Tom's house is not <u>big</u>.	*Tom's house is not <u>small</u>.*

Tom's house is <u>big</u> entails *Tom's house is not <u>small</u>*, but *Tom's house is not <u>small</u>* does not entail *Tom's house is <u>big</u>*. *Tom's house is <u>small</u>* entails *Tom's house is not <u>big</u>*, but *Tom's house is not <u>big</u>* does not entail *Tom's house is <u>small</u>*. Intermediate terms between <u>big</u> and <u>small</u> exist, e.g. *middle-sized.*

Hot, cold

The water is <u>hot</u>.	*The water is <u>cold</u>.*
The water is not <u>hot</u>.	*The water is not <u>cold</u>.*

The water is <u>hot</u> entails *The water is not <u>cold</u>*, but *The water is not <u>cold</u>* does not entail *The water is <u>hot</u>*. *The water is <u>cold</u>* entails *The water is not <u>hot</u>*, but *The water is not <u>hot</u>* does not entail *The water is <u>cold</u>*. Intermediate terms between *hot* and *cold* exist, e.g. *tepid.*

Converseness

Finally under the heading of incompatibility, we come to converseness (otherwise known as *relational oppositeness*). This is the relation that holds between expressions in sentences (differing only in respect of the converse expressions in question) which imply the denial of each other but which, after particular kinds of syntactic permutation have been effected, actually entail each other: *Fred <u>lent</u> the flat to Michael* entails the denial of *Fred <u>borrowed</u> the flat from Michael* (and vice versa), but *Fred <u>lent</u> the flat to Michael* entails and is entailed by *Michael <u>borrowed</u> the flat from Fred*, and so *lend* and *borrow* are taken to be converses of each other. Converseness is further exemplified below.

Buy, sell

Rick bought the car from Sarah.   *Rick sold the car to Sarah.*

Sarah bought the car from Rick.   *Sarah sold the car to Rick.*

Rick bought the car from Sarah entails the denial of *Rick sold the car to Sarah* (and vice versa). *Sarah bought the car from Rick* entails the denial of *Sarah sold the car to Rick* (and vice versa). *Rick bought the car from Sarah* entails *Sarah sold the car to Rick* (and vice versa). *Rick sold the car to Sarah* entails *Sarah bought the car from Rick* (and vice versa).

Husband, wife

Hilary is Vivian's husband.   *Hilary is Vivian's wife.*

Vivian is Hilary's husband.   *Vivian is Hilary's wife.*

Hilary is Vivian's husband entails the denial of *Hilary is Vivian's wife* (and vice versa). *Vivian is Hilary's husband* entails the denial of *Vivian is Hilary's wife* (and vice versa). *Hilary is Vivian's husband* entails *Vivian is Hilary's wife* (and vice versa). *Hilary is Vivian's wife* entails *Vivian is Hilary's husband* (and vice versa).

Meronymy

A lexical relation not focused on particularly by Lyons but discussed at length by other lexical semanticists is that of *meronymy*. This relation covers part–whole connections. *X* is a *meronym* of *Y* if it can form the subject of the sentence *An X is a part of a Y. Y* in such a case is labelled a *holonym* of *X*. For example, *finger* is a meronym of *hand*, and *hand* is a holonym of *finger* on the basis of the way in which the two words feature in the sentence: *A finger is a part of a hand.*

As in the case of hyponymy, it is possible to represent meronym–holonym relations in inverted tree diagrams, where meronymy is represented as the relationship between a lower node and a higher node. Thus, in the diagram on page 75 (Figure 5.3), *finger* is a meronym of *hand*, which in turn is a meronym of *arm*, which in turn is a meronym of *body*.

However, meronymy is not consistently transitive in the way that hyponymy is. For example, despite the fact that *finger* is a meronym of *hand* and *hand* is a meronym of *arm*, we might have some hesitation about the sentence *A finger is a part of an arm.*

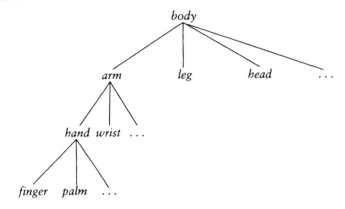

Figure 5.3 Meronymy.

Two further examples of meronym–holonym pairs follow.

Petal, flower

A *petal* is a part of a *flower*.

Petal is a meronym of *flower*. *Flower* is a holonym of *petal*.

Roof, house

A *roof* is a part of a *house*.

Roof is a meronym of *house*. *House* is a holonym of *roof*.

5.4   Componential analysis

Some linguists have tried to take structuralist semantics a stage further by trying to analyse lexical meaning into *components*, otherwise labelled *semantic markers* or *semantic features*, which might underlie sense-relations. For example, in a componential analysis the relations between *human being, man, woman, boy, girl* and *lad* might be accounted for in terms of plus or minus values attaching to the components HUMAN, MALE and ADULT. Thus:

human being	*man*	*woman*	*boy*	*girl*	*lad*
+ HUMAN	+ HUMAN	+ HUMAN	+ HUMAN	+ HUMAN	+ HUMAN
	+ MALE	– MALE	+ MALE	– MALE	+ MALE
	+ ADULT	+ ADULT	– ADULT	– ADULT	– ADULT

In this perspective the synonymy between *boy* and *lad* would, for example, be seen as explicable in terms of the fact that their features and their feature-values totally match (+ HUMAN, + MALE, – ADULT); the hyponymy between *man* and *human* being would be seen as explicable in terms of the fact that *man* shares a feature and feature value (+ HUMAN) with *human being* and, despite being endowed with other features besides, exhibits no feature-values which are at odds with the componential profile of *human being*; and the incompatibility between *man* and *woman* would be seen as explicable in terms of the fact that the two words differ in terms of the respective values attached to the feature MALE.

This approach to lexical meaning obviously has strong similarities to the traditional dictionary definition. For example, a typical dictionary definition of *girl* would be 'female child' (i.e. – MALE, – ADULT, in the above terms). Componential analysis has long been used in anthropological linguistics – in, for example, studies of kinship terms, and it has also been associated with broadly Chomskyan perspectives, but it has also been favoured by semanticists without any specific research task preoccupations or theoretical predispositions.

Despite its apparently wide appeal, componential analysis has been subject to a fair amount of criticism. Perhaps most controversial has been the claim made by some linguists that the semantic components on which componential analysis is based are universal – in other words that they underlie the expression of meaning in all languages and cultures. This claim is undermined by the fact that even concepts which in common sense terms look as if they might be independent of particular cultures turn out on closer inspection not to be. For example, the feature MALE, which, in view of its association with a clear biological category, looks as if it might well be a candidate for universality, appears distinctly less universal when one considers the fact that – at least as far as human maleness is concerned – the concept of maleness is also a product of socio-cultural traditions and perceptions which diverge widely from society to society. For example, males are involved to vastly differing degrees in nurturing and rearing children from culture to culture; the extent to which and manner in which they 'beautify' themselves is also highly culture-dependent, as is their role in courtship and in the sexual arena generally.

Componential analysts insist that the labels are language-neutral and indeed that they could be replaced by arbitrary symbols (+ ♣, – ♣, + Ƴ etc.). However, in practice, real words from natural languages are used (*human, male, adult* etc.) which inevitably carry the particular cultural baggage of the language communities with which they are associated. Moreover, because in the binary system of values (+ or –) often adopted by componentialists just one term is chosen to carry either value, componential analysis constantly runs the risk of seeming to be sexist, ageist and indeed many other 'ists'. How many women, for instance, are content to see the meaning of the word *woman* being characterized as including the feature – MALE?

A further frequent charge levelled at componential analysis is that it treats meaning in too 'cut and dried' a manner, and that it cannot therefore deal with contextual and metaphorical effects. For example, we know that there are circumstances where the words *boy* and *lad* are frequently used for adult males, in other words as synonyms of *man*. Thus, in the context of social interaction in the dressing-room in the aftermath of a rugby match between two teams of males of mature years the following sentences are entirely equivalent:

Are we going for a pint, men?

Are we going for a pint, boys?

Are we going for a pint, lads?

How does an analysis of *boy* and *lad* as [+ HUMAN, + MALE, – ADULT] sit with this? Similarly, the word *girlfriend* is applied by males and females alike to female companions of any age from nine to ninety, which casts more than a modicum of doubt on the analysis of girl as simply [+ HUMAN, – MALE, – ADULT].

These and other points have not gone without response from those who advocate a componentialist approach, although at least some componentialists are prepared to admit that componential analysis is not the whole story. On the other hand, non-componentialists like Lyons are perfectly happy to recognize that, because it is based on structural notions of sense, componential analysis is, 'at least in principle, fully compatible with [other approaches to structural semantics]'.

5.5   Cognitive approaches to meaning

One version of the componential approach which appears to meet some of the above criticisms is that which starts from the notion of *prototypical* sense (otherwise labelled *stereotypical*, *focal* or *nuclear*). The notion of prototype arises from the work of psycholinguists and cognitive linguists – in other words from research which is interested in how language relates to the mind. According to advocates of prototype theory, on the basis of our experience of the world we construct in our minds 'ideal exemplars' of particular categories of 'real world' phenomena with ideal sets of characteristics. These 'ideal exemplars' are the prototypes postulated by prototype theorists, who suggest that when we come across further candidates for inclusion in the same category, we judge them against the prototypes we have established. However, the matching process is envisaged as flexible. There does not have to be a complete match. Thus, for example, our prototype of a bird would undoubtedly include features such as 'HAS WINGS', 'FLIES', but this would not prevent us from recognizing a penguin as a bird, even though penguins have flippers rather than wings and swim rather than fly.

Similarly, our prototype of *chair* would probably include the feature 'HAS FOUR LEGS', but that would not lead us to reject as chairs the kinds of seats that have appeared in offices and around tables in modern times – items with single tubular steel stems attached to wide, heavy bases. On the other hand, in some instances it is unclear where a particular item fits in terms of prototypical categories. For example, there are drinking vessels on the market these days which are large and have no saucers – and to that extent resemble the mug prototype, but which on the other hand have an elegantly curved cup-like shape – and to that extent resemble the cup prototype. In other words, prototypes have 'fuzzy' boundaries.

The prototypical view of lexical meaning obviously takes us away from what Lyons calls a 'checklist theory of definition' which allows for absolutely no indeterminacy of meaning. Clearly, prototype theory can cope far better than classic 'checklist' componential analysis with the fact that – in particular contexts – terms like *boy* and *girl* may be applied to adults and that terms like *beast, rat, shark, snake* may be applied to human beings. On the other hand, prototype theory is not without its drawbacks either. It appears to relate more to a traditional denotational view of meaning than to recent structuralist perspectives. In consequence, the prototypical approach may be not be able to cope equally well with all types of words; words which do not identify concrete 'real world' phenomena with observable characteristics – *alas, albeit, become* etc. – would seem to pose some problems in this connection. In any case, prototype theory has very little to say about *sense*, that important dimension of meaning – explored in 5.3 and also (in its collocational aspects) in Chapter 4 – which derives from relations holding between lexical expressions.

Another approach to meaning which can be characterized as cognitive in nature is that proposed by linguists working within the 'conceptual semantics' framework. Conceptual semantics, whose best-known proponent is Ray Jackendoff, essentially says that semantic structure exactly coincides with conceptual structure and that, therefore, any semantic analysis is also an analysis of mental representations. Jackendoff claims that we human beings come into the world equipped with (a) some very basic concepts ('primitives' – such as spatial concepts, concepts of time, even some social concepts like possession and dominance) which are applicable to the interpretation and categorization of a whole variety of experiences, and (b) some principles of concept-combination. Lexical meanings, on this view, are constructed on the basis of interaction among: our inborn conceptual primitives, our inborn concept-combining principles, our experience of the world and our experience of language.

There are, therefore, according to conceptual semantics, limits on the kinds of lexical meanings that we can generate – limits having to do with 'conceptual well-formedness' in terms of what kinds of combinations of concepts our innate primitives and principles will permit. A further aspect of the conceptual semantics perspective is that, because the process of meaning formation is combinatorial, lexical meanings so formed can necessarily be analysed into the concepts out of which they were composed. However, the kind of conceptual structure envisaged by Jackendoff goes far beyond the listing of features with plus or minus signs attached; for example, he suggests that lexical entries for physical object words include three-dimensional model representations – basically the prototypical images posited by proto-type theorists but with more structure.

Conceptual semantics has been criticized on the ground that there is not sufficient hard evidence to support the view that linguistic meaning exactly parallels conceptual structure. It is also claimed that linguistic meanings do not actually reflect the fuzziness of concept structure. For instance, the above-discussed semantic relation of complementarity (as in *true:false*) operates as if truth and falsehood ruled each other out (as we saw in 5.3, *X is true* entails and is entailed by *X is not false*; and *X is false* entails and is entailed by *X is not true*. The fact is, though, that 'in real life', as it were, we can quite easily conceive of Xs that partake of both truth and falsehood. Jackendoff's remark that 'People have things to talk about only by virtue of having represented them' is difficult to argue with, but it is as yet unclear precisely how close the relationship is between mental representation and linguistic meaning.

Finally in the context of cognitive approaches to lexical meaning, it is worth noting that a further development in the prototype concept in seman-tics is the idea that not only individual entities but also entire events may have prototypical features. This is a notion born of script theory, according to which we interpret experience via *scripts* – general prototypes of or tem-plates for particular types of activity. For example, the prototypical scenario for going on a train journey will include going to the railway station, buying a ticket, standing on the station platform, boarding the train, finding a seat and presenting one's ticket to the ticket inspector when he passes through the train. According to script theory, event templates such as this allow us to fill in any information gaps from what we know about the typical way in which things happen. Related to and overlapping with the notion of script is the notion of *frame*; frames are conceived of as mental frameworks or plans relating to specific domains of knowledge which assist us in dealing with rel-evant situations. A railway station frame, for instance, would include a ticket office, a waiting room, a cafeteria, an arrivals and departures infor-mation board, a station master etc. Also connected with script theory and the frame concept are *schema–theoretic* models of comprehension which are based on the idea that comprehension always taps into one's knowledge of the world as well as one's linguistic knowledge.

The relevance of scripts, frames and schemata for lexical semantics has at least two aspects. On the one hand, scripts and frames provide a plausible underpinning for at least some aspects of syntagmatic lexical relations. That is to say, the fact that the same lexical expressions repeatedly recur in each other's company is partly explicable in terms of the fact that the same kinds

of scenarios involving the same kinds of entities recur in the life of a particular culture and in the lives (including the mental lives) of those who partic-
ipate in that culture. On the other hand, scripts, frames and schemata also
relate to paradigmatic aspects of meaning, and, in particular to the contextual dimension of such relations. For example, the noun *stump* in some contexts denotes the remnant of a cut or fallen tree and in other contexts
denotes one of the three uprights of the wicket defended by the batsman in
the game of cricket. Now, it so happens that in the contexts where *stump* has
the first of the above meanings the relevant prototypical frame ('in the
forest') centrally involves trees and does not involve at all the accoutrements
of cricket, while in contexts where *stump* has its 'wicket' sense the relevant
prototypical frame ('a game of cricket') involves a large open pitch where
trees have no place (except perhaps as peripheral background).

5.6   Summary

This chapter has been devoted to exploring some of the different ways in
which lexical meaning has been approached by linguists. The exploration in
question has covered the traditional, referential/denotational account of
word-meaning, has talked about Saussure's perspective and the lexical field
theory to which it gave rise, has defined and exemplified lexico-semantic
relations as they have been understood in recent decades by Lyons and
others, and has sketched out the componential analysis approach to expli-
cating such relations. Mention has also been made of a number of 'cognitive'
perspectives on lexical meaning. It is clear from discussion in the chapter
that lexical meaning is no different from other aspects of language in being
in part a function of the network of interrelations between linguistic units. It
is also clear that such relations hold not only between words, but also
between words and multi-word lexical expressions and within pairs and
groups of multi-word expressions. This underlines the fact – already clear
from the discussion in earlier chapters – that the lexicon is not just an inven-
tory of individual words but also covers a large variety of combinations of
words. Finally, it is noteworthy that a consideration of context is necessary
to the very definition of lexical sense-relations and that contextual influence
on meaning is a major issue in lexical semantics – which leads to the conclusion that orientation to context is fundamental to the way in which the
lexicon operates.

Sources and suggestions for further reading

See 5.2. The diagram in 5.2 is based on the model proposed by C. Ogden
and I. Richards in their book *The meaning of meaning* (fourth edition,
London: Routledge and Kegan Paul, 1936, 11). The objection that the

Ogden and Richards model is 'atomistic' is voiced by, among others, S. Ullmann in his *Semantics: an introduction to the science of meaning* (Oxford: Blackwell, 1962, 63). The problems surrounding a view of meaning which is purely based on reference or denotation have been discussed by philosophers for more than a century. The name usually mentioned in this connection is that of Gottlob Frege, and in particular his article 'Über Sinn und Bedeutung' (*Zeitschift für Philosophie und philosophische Kritik* 100, 1892, 25–50). Frege's work is available in English translation in P. Geach and M. Black's *Translations from the philosophical writings of Gottlob Frege* (Oxford: Blackwell, 1952). The *Morning Star/Evening Star* example is Frege's. The discussion of referential/denotational meaning in 4.2 was informed mostly by the work of J. Lyons – especially his *Structural semantics* (Oxford: Blackwell, 1963, Chapter 4) and his *Introduction to theoretical linguistics* (Cambridge: Cambridge University Press, 1968, Chapter 9). Other sources drawn on were R. Carter, *Vocabulary* (second edition, London: Routledge, 1998, Chapter 1) and Stephen Ullmann, *Semantics* (Oxford: Blackwell, 1962, Chapter 3).

See 5.3. The Lyons quotations at the beginning of 5.3 are taken from his article 'Structuralism and linguistics' (in D. Robey (ed.), *Structuralism: an introduction*, Oxford: Clarendon Press, 1973, 6). Ferdinand de Saussure's *Cours de linguistique générale* (first published 1916) is available in a modern critical edition prepared by Tullio de Mauro (Paris: Payot, 1973). It is also available in English translation: *Course in general linguistics*, translated by W. Baskin with an introduction by J. Culler (Glasgow: Fontana/Collins, 1974). The monetary analogy is to be found in Chapter IV of the Second Part of the *Cours*. The words cited (and translated) from J. Trier are from his book *Der deutsche Wortschatz im Sinnbezirk des Verstandes*. (Heidelberg: Carl Winter, 1931, 2). The colour example is borrowed from J. Lyons's *Introduction to theoretical linguistics* (Cambridge: Cambridge University Press, 1968, 56–7). Leonard Bloomfield's comments on meaning are taken from his book *Language* (New York: Holt, Rinehart and Winston, 1933, 139). The discussion of synonymy, hyponymy and the various types of incompatibility is based very largely on the ideas of Lyons as set out in his books: *Structural semantics: an analysis of part of the vocabulary of Plato* (Oxford: Blackwell, 1963), *Introduction to theoretical linguistics* (Cambridge: Cambridge University Press, 1968), *Semantics* (two volumes, Cambridge: Cambridge University Press, 1977), *Language, meaning and context* (London: Fontana, 1981), *Linguistic semantics: an introduction* (Cambridge: Cambridge University Press, 1995). The principal source for the treatment of meronymy is Chapter 7 of Cruse's *Lexical semantics* (Cambridge: Cambridge University Press, 1986).

See 5.4. An example of componential analysis being put at the service of anthropological linguistics is F. Wallace and J. Atkins's (1960) article 'The meaning of kinship terms' (*American Anthropologist* 62, 58–80).

Examples of componential analysis partaking of a Chomskyan perspective are J. Katz and J. Fodor's (1963) much cited article 'The structure of a semantic theory' (*Language* 39, 170–210) and R. Jackendoff's *Semantic structures* (Cambridge, MA: MIT Press, 1990). An example of a componentialist without a particular methodological or theoretical axe to grind is G. Leech (see, for example his book *Semantics: the study of meaning*, second edition, Harmondsworth: Penguin, 1981). The critique of componential analysis in 5.4 draws on comments by D. Bolinger (1965) ('The atomization of meaning', *Language* 41, 555–73); J. Lyons (*Introduction to theoretical linguistics*, Cambridge: Cambridge University Press, 1968, 470 ff.; *Linguistic semantics: an introduction*, Cambridge: Cambridge University Press, 1995, 114 ff.) and J. Saeed (*Semantics*, Oxford: Blackwell, 1997, 259 ff.). The Lyons quote which ends 5.4 is taken from p. 117 of his *Linguistic semantics: an introduction* (Cambridge: Cambridge University Press, 1995).

See 5.5. The sources for the discussion of prototype theory in 5.5 include: L. Coleman and P. Kay (1981), 'Prototype semantics: the English word "lie"' (*Language* 57, 26–44); W. Labov, 'The boundaries of words and their meanings' (in J. Fishman (ed.), *New ways of analyzing variation in English*, Washington, DC: Georgetown University Press, 1973). G. Lakoff, *Women, fire and dangerous things: what categories reveal about the mind* (Chicago: University of Chicago Press, 1987); S. Pulman, *Word, meaning and belief* (London: Croom Helm, 1983); E. Rosch, 'Principles of categorization' (in E. Rosch and B. Lloyd (eds), *Cognition and categorization*, Hillsdale, NJ: Lawrence Erlbaum, 1978). The definition of prototype as 'ideal exemplar' is borrowed from J. Aitchison's book *Words in the mind: an introduction to the mental lexicon* (second edition, Oxford: Blackwell, 1994, 55). Lyons's description of componential analysis as a 'checklist theory of definition' is to be found on p. 99 of his book *Linguistic semantics: an introduction* (Cambridge: Cambridge University Press, 1995). The criticisms of prototype theory sketched here draw on the discussion by A. Lehrer in his article 'Prototype theory and its implications for lexical analysis' (in S. L.Tsohatzidis (ed.), *Meanings and prototypes: studies in linguistics categorization*, London: Routledge, 1990). The account of conceptual semantics is largely based on the first four chapters of R. Jackendoff's book *Languages of the mind* (Cambridge, MA: MIT Press, 1992) and on W. Fawley's discussion of the topic in his *Linguistic semantics* (Hillsdale, NJ: Lawrence Erlbaum, 1992, Chapter 2). The discussion of scripts, frames and schemas draws on: R. Anderson, R. Reynolds, D. Schallert and E. Goetz (1977), 'Frameworks for comprehending discourse' (*American Educational Research Journal* 14, 367–81); M. Minsky, 'A framework for representing knowledge' (in P. Winston (ed.), *The psychology of computer vision*, New York: McGraw-Hill, 1975); R. Schank and R. Abelson, *Scripts, plans, goals and understanding* (Hillsdale, NJ: Lawrence Erlbaum, 1977); R. Schank and A. Kass, 'Knowledge representation in people and machines' (in U. Eco,

M. Santambrogio and P. Violi (eds), *Meaning and mental representations*, Bloomington, IN: Indiana University Press, 1988).

Accessible introductions to lexical semantics are provided by: Chapter 1 of R. Carter's *Vocabulary: applied linguistic perspectives* (second edition, London: Routledge, 1998), chapters 1–4 of J. Lyons's *Language, meaning and context* (London: Fontana, 1981) and chapters 2–4 of the same author's *Linguistic semantics: an introduction* (Cambridge: Cambridge University Press, 1995), chapters 1–7 of G. Leech's *Semantics: the study of meaning* (second edition, Harmondsworth: Penguin, 1981), and chapters 1–7 of E. Hatch and C. Brown's *Vocabulary, semantics and language education* (Cambridge: Cambridge University Press, 1995). With regard specifically to 'cognitive' approaches to lexical semantics the interested reader may also care to consult J. Aitchison, *Words in the mind: an introduction to the mental lexicon* (second edition, Oxford: Blackwell, 1994, especially chapters 4–8), and F. Ungerer and H. J. Schmid, *An introduction to cognitive linguistics* (London: Longman, 1996).

Focusing questions/topics for discussion

1. In the introductory section of the chapter it was claimed that changing even a single word can make a radical difference to the meaning of a sentence or indeed a longer stretch of speech or writing. Try to think of five pairs of sentences differing by a single word where the effect of the word-changes in question is to transform the meanings of the sentences in a fundamental way.

2. We noted in 5.2 that two or more expressions with different senses can identify the same object, person, place, attribute, action etc. in the real world, one example being the way in which the expressions *Morning Star* and *Evening Star* both refer to the planet Venus. Try to think of five further examples of words or phrases with different senses being applied to the same 'real world' phenomenon.

3. Section 5.3 defined and illustrated a number of sense-relations. Re-read this section and then – avoiding the examples already given in the section – try to supply the following: two pairs of synonyms, two pairs of expressions linked to each other by the relation of hyponymy-superordinateness, two pairs of complementaries, two pairs of polar antonyms, two pairs of converses, and two pairs of expressions linked to each other by the relation of meronymy–holonymy. In each case illustrate the relations in question, taking the illustrative sentences in the section as your model.

4. In 4.4 we saw some examples of the way in which componential analysts treat lexical meaning. Using these examples as your guide, suggest

a possible componential analysis of the meanings of the following sets of words:

bitch: dog: puppy

duck: drake: duckling

ewe: ram: lamb

goose: gander: gosling

mare: stallion: foal

Indicate any problems you perceive in relation to the analysis you arrive at.

5. In 5.5 we saw some examples of items which were less close to the 'ideal exemplar' of their category than certain other items (e.g. *penguin* in relation to *bird*). For each of the following categories specify one member of the category in question which is close to the 'ideal exemplar' and one member which is less close. Give reasons for your proposals.

country	(*France, Germany, Spain* etc.)
fruit	(*apple, pear, orange* etc.)
garment	(*blouse, jacket, sweater* etc.)
mammal	(*bear, cow, panda* etc.)
tree	(*ash, elm, oak* etc.)

|6|

Lexis, phonology and orthography

6.1   Lexis and 'levels of articulation'

In our discussion so far we have been concentrating mostly on what the French linguist Martinet calls the *primary level of articulation*, the level of language at which meaningful units (morphemes, words etc.) combine into larger meaningful units (phrases, sentences etc.). It is clear that what happens at this level is very largely determined by lexical choice. It would be fairly natural to speculate that things might be rather different at the *secondary level of articulation* – the level at which meaning*less* units (in speech, minimal phonemes; in alphabetic writing, individual letters) combine to form meaning*ful* units (inflections, affixes, words etc.).

However, as we shall see, there is enough evidence of interaction between lexis and phonology on the one hand and lexis and orthography on the other to rule out any idea that sound-systems and writing systems are partitioned off from the lexical domain. One self-evident sense in which lexis and the secondary level of articulation interact relates to the fact that the choice of any given lexical unit determines the particular combination of phonological or orthographical units that is deployed. A less obvious – and for that reason more interesting – dimension to the issue is the question of whether the phonological or orthographic realization of specific words draws on semantic and grammatical information about the word concerned which the lexicon has to supply and whether individual lexical items or categories of items have specific sounds or symbols associated with them.

6.2   Phonemes, stresses and tones

Let us begin with that aspect of the interaction between the lexicon and phonology which is labelled above as 'self-evident'. Given that knowledge of a lexical expression typically includes knowledge of how that expression is pronounced, we have to assume that an entry in the lexicon contains information about the sounds out of which the item in question is composed – just as entries in dictionaries may contain 'phonetic' transcriptions. The sound components of a lexical unit include: (i) the relevant sequence of individual sound segments, (ii) (in languages such as English) the pattern of stress-distribution in the unit in question, and (iii) (in languages such as Chinese and Thai) the specific pitch or tone characteristic of the expression concerned when used in a particular sense.

With regard to individual sound segments, we saw in Chapter 1 that some differences between sounds were critical in differentiating between words and that some were not. We noted that distinctions that are critical in this way are labelled *phonemic*, and that the sound units which are, as it were, kept apart by such distinctions are called *phonemes*. Phonemes can thus be looked upon as collections of *distinctive features*. Examples of such features are:

- *plosiveness*: whether or not air is completely blocked before being released in the production of a sound – as in /p/ – or not – as in /f/;
- *labiality*: whether the lips are involved in the production of a sound – as in /p/ – or not – as in /k/;
- *nasality*: whether air passes through the nose in the production of a sound – as in /n/ – or not – as in /d/;
- *voice*: whether the vocal cords are in vibration in the production of a sound – as in /z/ – or not – as in /s/;
- *frontness/backness/centrality*: whether the tongue is positioned towards the front of the mouth in the production of a vowel – as in /ɪ/ (the vowel sound in *lid*), towards the back – as in /uː/ (the vowel sound in *boot*), or centrally – as in /ʌ/ (the vowel sound in *but*);
- *highness/lowness/midness* (whether the tongue is high in the mouth in the production of a vowel – as in /ɪ/, low in the mouth – as in /ɑː/ (the vowel sound in the standard British English pronunciation of *bath*), or in a mid position – as in /ɛ/ (the vowel sound in *bet*).

Correspondingly, the phonological dimension of each lexical entry can be conceived of as an array or *matrix* of distinctive features as well as a sequence of phonemes. Thus, a simplified version of the matrix for *pin* might be represented as follows:

	/p/	/ɪ/	/n/
Plosive	+		−
Labial	+		−
Nasal	−		+
Voiced	−		+
Front/back/central		Front	
High/low/mid		High	

Turning now to the question of stress patterns, in many languages, including English, the ways in which stresses are distributed are important in differentiating between words. For example there are a number of pairs of nouns and verbs in English where grammatical category is signalled partly by stress distribution. Thus:

Student numbers are continuing to decrease [VERB].

There has been a continuing decrease [NOUN] *in student numbers.*

He's going to record [VERB] *a new single.*

He's going to make a new record [NOUN].

In Europe we no longer implant [VERB] *growth-promoting substances in cattle.*

The growth-promoting implant [NOUN] *is no longer used in Europe.*

In some instances, stress distribution is a factor in distinguishing between distinct meanings of similar sequences of sounds. For example, the word *process*, when used as a verb, means something like 'to treat', 'to work on' – as in:

The new information had to be processed very rapidly by the research team.

When the stress in *process* is shifted to the second syllable, however, the verb means 'to walk in procession' – as in:

The bishop, the priests, the acolytes and the choir processed solemnly up the aisle.

Not dissimilar is the case of the adjective *contrary*. When stressed on its first syllable, this form means 'opposed', 'opposite' – as in:

This idea is contrary to good sense.

When stressed on its second syllable, on the other hand, it means 'self-willed', 'perverse', 'cantankerous' – as in the nursery rhyme:

Mary, Mary, quite contrary,
How does your garden grow?
With silver bells and cockle shells
And pretty maids all in a row.

With regard to tone, in a number of languages of Asia – such as Chinese, Thai and Burmese, as well as in many African and Native American languages, the pitch at which a particular sequence of sounds is uttered and/or the direction of the pitch (rising or falling) will determine what is understood by the sound-sequence in question. For instance in Thai, the sequence /kao/ means 'he' or 'she' if spoken with a high or rising tone, 'rice' if spoken with a falling tone, 'white' if spoken with a low tone, and 'news' if spoken with a mid-tone. Similarly with the sequence /naa/, which means 'young maternal uncle or aunt' if spoken with a high tone, 'thick' if spoken with a rising tone, 'face' if spoken with a falling tone, 'nickname' if spoken with a low tone, and 'rice paddy' if spoken with a mid-tone.

6.3 Lexical phonology as a reflection of lexical grammar and lexical meaning

We have already seen that there is a connection between the way in which a particular form is pronounced and its grammatical category. In other words, there is in some cases a relationship between the grammatical category assigned to a given entry in the lexicon and the manner in which it is stressed. On the other hand, this kind of variation in stress placement, according to whether a noun or a verb is involved, is not systematic. In other cases the main stress remains in the same place irrespective of grammatical category, for example: *delay* [VERB]; *delay* [NOUN]; *off*er [VERB]; *off*er [NOUN]; *repeat* [VERB]; *repeat* [NOUN]. What this means is that the lexicon has to specify which nouns and verbs follow the *record*: *record* pattern and which do not, and that the pronunciation of a particular word will need to be based on this information as well as information about grammatical category.

As for the question of the relationship between lexical phonology and meaning, one obvious set of circumstances in which this relationship can be seen to exist is any situation where onomatopoeia is involved. In such instances part of the meaning conveyed by the word is the sound made by the entity or activity to which the word is applied – *buzz, crackle, cuckoo, plop, tinkle* etc. In other words, in cases such as these the particular phonological shapes involved are determined in large measure by the meanings they are intended to convey. It is worth emphasizing, perhaps, that the phrase 'in large measure' is very deliberately chosen here. There is no question of the forms of onomatopoeic words being *completely* determined by the sounds they imitate; the conventions of the particular language in which an onomatopoeic form occurs also play a role. This is even true of words that are used to represent animal noises. For instance, in English, the sound made by a crowing cock is represented as *cock-a-doodle-doo*. Not so in other languages, as the following examples indicate.

German	*kikeriki*
Japanese	*kokekokou*
Persian	*gogoligogo*
Spanish	*quíquiriquí*
Thai	*ek-i-ek-ek*

Nevertheless, the relationship between the phonological forms of onomatopoeic words and their meanings is clear and indisputable.

Somewhat more subtle demonstrations of a relationship between meaning and specific sounds are instances where particular combinations of sounds are avoided because they are associated with taboo words. For example, in Luganda, the /nj/ combination (which corresponds roughly to the combination of sounds in the middle of the English word *onion* – /ˈʌnjən/) occurs in taboo items like /kunja/ 'defecate' and /kinjo/ 'anus'. Because of its association with such words, it tends to be replaced in other items by /ŋ/ (which corresponds to the *ng* sound in English *sing*). Thus /kanja:la/ ('immature banana') and /munjo:ngo/ ('miserable') tend to be pronounced as /kaŋa:la/ and /muŋo:ngo/ respectively.

To return briefly to the question of interaction among grammar, the lexicon and phonology, it is interesting to note that there is a whole theoretical approach to phonology – known as *Lexical Phonology* – which is based on a recognition of this interaction. In this conception of phonology, phonological processes are seen as operating together with word-formation rules in a cyclic fashion in such a way as to specify the lexical items in a language. Affixes are seen as being divided into different subsets (called *levels* or *strata*), to which different word-formation rules apply, these word-formation rules correlating with different phonological rules.

6.4 Association between particular sounds and particular (categories of) lexical items

Let us now consider the notion that particular sounds in a language may be closely, even exclusively, associated with particular words or categories of words. A revealing case to examine in this connection is that of the /ŋ/ sound in Modern Standard French (the sound corresponding to *ng* in English *sing*). This sound, which features in the pronunciation of words like *vin* and *pain* in many non-standard varieties of French spoken in Southern France, is an innovation in the more prestigious varieties of the language – the French of educated speakers in Paris, Brussels, Geneva etc. It was brought into these latter varieties via loanwords from English – especially words ending in the morpheme *-ing*. When such words first came into Standard French their *-ing* ending was pronounced by most people using phonemes from the Standard French repertoire. Thus *-ing* was pronounced as the nasal vowel /ẽ/ (which normally corresponds to the spelling *in* in Standard French), as /in/ (which normally corresponds to the spelling *ine* in Standard French) or as /iɲ/ (which normally corresponds to the spelling *igne* in Standard French). In more recent times, however, *-ing* words like *parking, casting, lifting* etc. have increasingly been pronounced using an /ŋ/ sound.

The interesting point about /ŋ/ in the present context is that, although the distinction between this sound and other sounds is phonemic (differentiating, for example, *shopping* ('shopping') from *chopine* ('bottle [of wine]'), it occurs in a very limited set of words. Moreover, the words in question are rather difficult to place under a common heading. It certainly is not the case that /ŋ/ is systematically associated with the spelling *ing*. In many words *ing* simply indicates the presence of a nasal vowel (*coing* = /kwẽ/ – 'quince'; *poing* = /pwẽ/ – 'fist' etc.). Nor can one even say that the /ŋ/ phoneme is systematically associated with English loanwords ending in -*ing*; for instance, the -*ing* in the loan-word *shampooing* is pronounced not as /ŋ/ but rather as the same nasal vowel as in *coing*, i.e. /ẽ/. In any case, many of the -*ing* words in French pronounced with final /ŋ/ are not so much loans as new coinages, for example *footing* meaning 'jogging', *lifting* in the sense of 'face lift'. To sum up, there is a phoneme in Modern Standard French which is exclusively associated with a small and rather ill-defined assortment of lexical items and whose occurrence is, therefore, entirely dependent on the selection of one of these words.

In the above case the particular sound discussed can be seen as the result of language contact. However, lexically determined aspects of phonology are not necessarily connected to the borrowing of sounds. The process known as *lexical diffusion* may or may not involve cross-linguistic influence, but what it always does involve is an association between specific sets of lexical items and the sounds that are likely to occur. Lexical diffusion is a phenomenon that has been observed by linguists tracking phonological changes over time in particular languages and dialects. It refers to the fact that such changes develop gradually – affecting different portions of the vocabulary as they progress.

It used to be thought that changes in sound-systems operated simultaneously across the board according to laws that admitted no exceptions, the same sound in the same environment always developing in precisely the same way. It now appears that this view of sound change was fundamentally mistaken. The current indications are that when a sound change gets under way it spreads on a word-by-word basis through the lexicon, so that whether or not the new sound is likely to occur is dependent not on the general phonetic/phonological environment but on specific lexical selection. A good illustration of such lexical diffusion comes from data on Belfast English collected in the 1970s. From these data it emerges that there is a sound shift in process in Belfast English from [ʉ] (which is fairly close to the French *u* sound or the German *ü* sound) to [ʌ] (which is the *u* sound in Standard British English pronunciations of words like *but* and *cut*). However, the [ʌ] innovation is affecting different lexical items to varying degrees. Thus, the word *pull*, for instance, was pronounced [pʌl] in the data in question in about three-quarters of its occurrences, whereas the word *look* attracted the pronunciation [lʌk] in only about a quarter of its occurrences. In other words, whether or not [ʌ] occurs is closely related to the selection and deployment of specific lexical items.

6.5 Lexis and orthography

Much the same kind of situation applies in relation to the lexis/orthography interface as has been described in respect of lexis and phonology. That is to say, it is obvious that lexical selection determines the particular sequence of letters (in an alphabetic system), the character (in a logographic system) etc., that is deployed; it is also true to say that orthographic representations draw on lexicosemantic and lexicogrammatical information; and it is in addition the case that certain aspects of a writing system may be particularly, or even exclusively, associated with a specific set of lexical items.

Writing systems vary enormously around the world, and have varied enormously through history. This book is written using an alphabetic system, where there is a clear relationship between written signs and the sounds of the words represented by those signs. For example, in the following written versions of English words, each letter represents a different phoneme occurring in the words in question:

den   /dɛn/

men   /mɛn/

ten   /tɛn/

English, in common with all western European (and numerous other) languages, uses Roman script, which, as its name implies, was developed by the Romans, and was the form in which Latin was written. The Roman alphabet was based on the Greek alphabet, which exhibits the same basic principle of clear correspondence between written signs and individual sounds – as the following examples from Modern Greek demonstrate:

να   /na/   'that', 'in order to'

σα   /sa/   'when', 'as soon as' (= σαν)

τα   /ta/   definite article (neuter nominative/accusative plural)

Also based on the Greek alphabet, and on the same principle of correspondence between letters and phonemes, is the Cyrillic alphabet, in which many Slavic languages, such as Russian, Bulgarian and Serbian, are written.

As is well-known, there is a fair amount of variation in alphabetic systems in relation to the precise degree of consistency of correspondence between letters and sounds. In a language like Spanish or Finnish, the level of consistency is very high indeed. That is to say, in these systems it is more often than not the case that for any given sequence of phonemes there is only one possible spelling and that for any given sequence of letters there is only one possible pronunciation. Compare this with the situation in English, Modern Greek or French, where the relationship between sounds and letters is a good deal more fluid. In English, for example, the vowel sound /iː/ can be written as *e* (as in *be*), *ee* (as in *bee*), *ea* (as in *bean*), *ie* (as in *brief*), *ei* (as in *receive*), *ey* (as in *key*), *i* (as in *ravine*), even *ae* (as in *encyclopaedia*).

An earlier version of the alphabetic approach was the system used to transcribe Semitic languages, starting with Phoenician. Semitic languages, represented in the modern world by Arabic and Modern Hebrew, have the characteristic of showing morphological contrasts (for verb tense etc.) through the alternation of vowels within the word rather than by the addition of endings. We have this to some extent in English too, for example *run–ran, sing–sang, write–wrote*; however, in the Semitic languages this type of grammatical patterning operates throughout. What this means is that the basic form of any given word is its 'consonantal shell' – the counterpart of English *s-ng* in the *sing–sang* case – and that the vowels are, as it were, supplied by the grammatical context. Probably for this reason, the Phoenician alphabet represented consonants only, the vowel sounds being left for readers to work out for themselves. Hebrew and Arabic were also originally written in the same way, with only consonants being represented, and, indeed, writing Hebrew and Arabic in this way remains an option even today. However, in the case of both languages, the writing systems have with the passage of time developed ways of indicating vowel sounds.

The original Phoenician alphabet was the source of the Greek alphabet; what the Greeks did was to 're-cycle' consonantal signs that they did not require as vowel signs. Thus, for example, the Phoenician sign for a glottal stop (which involves holding air by totally closing the vocal cords and then releasing it) was ⟨. Since this particular consonant was not a phoneme of Ancient Greek, it could be borrowed to represent the vowel /a/, and so it was that, with some minor adjustments, it became the Greek letter *alpha* – A α – and subsequently found its way – in much the same form and with much the same value – into both the Roman alphabet and the Cyrillic alphabet.

An alternative to the alphabetic approach to representing the sounds of words in written form is to take the syllable rather than the individual phoneme as the basis of the system. Systems which take this approach – known as *syllabaries* – include the Japanese *kana* script, the script used by the Cherokees, and the script invented by the Minoan Greeks – called *Linear B* by archaeologists – long before the development of the Greek alphabet. As far as Japanese is concerned, the *kana* script is used in two forms, *hiragana* and *katakana*, to represent, respectively, on the one hand, particles, verb-inflections etc. and, on the other, words borrowed from Western languages such as English. However, this is only part of the story; non-Western content words (nouns, verbs etc.) are represented in Japanese using a totally different system – a system based on Chinese characters (*kanji*), which takes meanings rather than sounds as its starting point.

The most extreme version of this last-mentioned kind of system is that in which the objects, animals etc. referred to in writing are represented pictorially.

This takes us right back to the origins of writing in human history. Thus, the earliest-known form of writing was associated with the Sumerian culture of Mesopotamia, the area between the rivers Tigris and Euphrates stretching from the Persian Gulf towards modern-day Baghdad. The Sumerians wrote on clay tablets, and the first written signs they used were in effect simplified drawings. For example, the sign for 'cow' was a simplified representation of a bovine head, the sign for 'bird' was a simplified representation of the neck and body of a bird, and the sign for 'woman' was a simplified representation of a vulva (Figure 6.1):

'ox'   'bird'   'woman'

Figure 6.1 The earliest-known form of writing associated with the Sumerian culture of Mesopotamia.

As Sumerian writing developed, such pictorial representations, or *pictograms*, became progressively stylized – literally, because the changes can largely be ascribed to the particularities of the stylus used to make them. The scribes of the time wrote on wet clay using a reed which had had one of its ends cut into a triangular shape. Accordingly, the impressions made in the soft clay tended to be wedge-shaped or cuneiform (< Latin *cuneus* = 'wedge'), and these triangular shapes were increasingly used to form the signs based on the earlier drawings. So it was that the sign for 'cow' was first turned on its side and eventually took on a form which was very far indeed from the original representational pictogram (Figure 6.2):

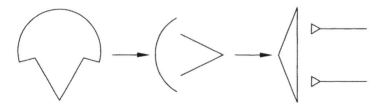

Figure 6.2 Stylization of pictograms.

Through the combination of pictograms it became possible to express concepts other than those covered by the original basic repertoire of simplified drawings. Thus by combining the pictogram for 'woman' with that representing 'mountains' it became possible to express in writing the notion of 'woman from beyond the mountains' = 'foreign woman' = 'female slave' (Figure 6.3):

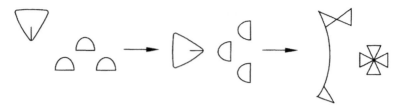

Figure 6.3 Expression of concepts through combination of pictograms.

Since in such cases the signs no longer simply or directly reflect the visual appearance of the entity represented, but can be thought of rather as representing ideas, they are often referred to as *ideograms*. To the extent that this kind of sign represents an idea encapsulated in a single word, it can also be seen as a *logogram* (< Greek λόγος – lógos – 'word').

Other pictographic systems underwent similar evolutions. For instance, in the Chinese writing system the notion of 'sheep' was initially represented in writing by a simplified drawing of ram's horns. Later developments of this character rendered it increasingly less representational (Figure 6.4):

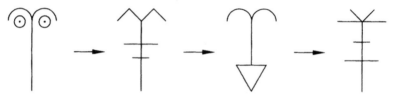

Figure 6.4 Evolution of the Chinese character for 'sheep'.

On the other hand, some Chinese characters retain some of the representational nature of their original forms, as the historical development of the character for 'tree' illustrates (Figure 6.5):

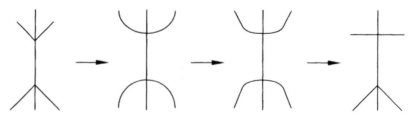

Figure 6.5 Retention of the representational nature of the original form: Chinese character for 'tree'.

As well as undergoing changes in form, some pictographic systems also underwent developments in terms of what the signs stood for. Thus, the Sumerian cuneiform system sometimes used signs for a particular meaning to represent the syllable corresponding to the word in question, and indeed sometimes used the sign for a particular meaning to represent a word sounding the same as the word associated with the original meaning. For example, the pictogram for 'arrow' – for which the Sumerian word was *ti* – was also used to represent 'life' – for which the word was also *ti*.

To return to the case of Sumerian, it is clear from the above that the way in which the Sumerian writing system came to be used contained the seeds of a sound-based system. These seeds germinated when the Sumerian system was used to transcribe other languages in the region. For instance, the Akkadians (ancestors of the Arabs and Hebrews) used Sumerian signs to represent both the syllables for which they stood in Sumerian and the meanings associated with the original Sumerian words. Thus, in the Akkadian system the Sumerian sign for 'sky'/'heaven' – in Sumerian *an* – was used both to represent the syllable /an/ and the Akkadian word for 'sky'/'heaven' – *shamu*. (The use of pictures or symbols representing words with particular sound shapes to stand for words with similar sound shapes – sometimes labelled the *rebus principle* – is familiar to us in the modern world from wordgames, riddles, jokes and advertising.) In further developments, the Sumerian writing system actually became the basis for an alphabet. Thus, cuneiform script was used to transcribe a Semitic language spoken in ancient Syria – almost certainly proto-Phoenician – and in this case signs which in Akkadian had represented syllables were used to represent single consonants. For example, the sign which in Akkadian had stood for the syllable /pa/ was used to represent /p/.

The Egyptian writing system underwent a similar kind of development. In this case the *hieroglyphs* (< Greek 'ιερός – *hierós* – 'holy', γλύφειν – *glúphein* – 'to engrave') familiar to us from pictures of Egyptian tombs were originally pictograms. In hieroglyphic writing – and in the simpler writing systems based on it which were used for writing on papyrus – a sign representing an entity associated with a particular word often also came to be used to represent a word with a similar sound-shape – as in the Sumerian system. For example the sign for 'scarab', for which the Ancient Egyptian word was *khéper* (the initial *kh* being pronounced as /x/ – the *ch* sound in the Scottish-English word *loch*, German *Dach* etc), was in addition used to represent 'become', the word for which was also *khéper*. Moreover, particular signs were also deployed to represent the sounds of the 'consonantal shell' of the words with the meanings of which they were originally associated. Thus the hieroglyph for 'scarab' also more generally represented the 'consonantal shell' /xpr/. Where only one consonant was involved in a word for which the corresponding sign was used in this way, the signs in question effectively functioned in this particular role as 'letters' standing for individual consonants. For example, the hieroglyph for 'seat' – □ – was also used to represent the sound /p/.

Whether a writing system is sound-based or meaning-based – or indeed a mixture of the two – the written signs which constitute the system obviously need to be distinct from each other. Thus in the Roman alphabet, for instance, the letter *t* is distinguished from the letter *l* by the horizontal stroke through its upper part, and *d* is distinguished from *l* by the *c* shape attached to its bottom-left side. Similarly, the Egyptian hieroglyph □ ('seat', /p/) is distinguished from ⬭ ('mouth', /r/) by shape, and from ● ('grill', /x/) by shape and by the absence/presence of shading. Because written signs are contrastive units in written language in much the same way as phonemes are in speech, they are sometimes referred to as *graphemes* (< Greek γραφή – *graphē* – 'writing'). Moreover, just as phonemes have allophones, so graphemes can be thought of as having *allographs*; that is to say, each written sign may be realized in a variety of ways. Thus, for example, **A**, **a** and *a* are all variant forms of the same letter.

We have seen that in alphabetic systems the correspondences between graphemes and phonemes can sometimes be quite variable, even within the same language. Examples have already been given from English, Modern Greek and French. A further – indeed *the* classic example – from English of variation in grapheme-phoneme correspondence is the case of the combination of the letters *o, u, g* and *h*. This may correspond to /ʌf/ (as in *rough*), /ɒf/ (as in *cough*), /əʊ/ (as in *though*), /ɔː/ (as in *thought*) or /ɒx/ (as in Irish-English *lough*). Likewise, grapheme-meaning correspondences can vary. For example the Sumerian sign ▶▶Ⴤ corresponds not only to 'sky'/'heaven' (*an*), but also to 'god' (*dingir*). We have also seen that signs may stand both for sounds and for meanings. With regard to alphabetic systems, it has sometimes been claimed that variation in grapheme–phoneme correspondences can be of assistance in distinguishing between homophones. It is noted that, thanks to a certain looseness of fit between graphemes and phonemes in French, for example, it is possible to distinguish orthographically between identically pronounced pairs such as the adjectives *sûr* ('sure') and *sur* ('sour'), the plural nouns *maux* ('evils') and *mots* ('words') and the verbs *pécher* ('to sin') and *pêcher* ('to fish'). Unfortunately for this particular line of argument, French, in common with English, goes only a rather limited distance along this road. For instance, it does not distinguish between the identically pronounced pairs *sur* ('sour') and *sur* ('on') or *pêcher* ('to fish') and *pêcher* ('peach-tree'). Moreover, there are cases in French of homographs, i.e. identically spelt items – which are in fact differently pronounced. Thus *fils* meaning 'threads' is pronounced /fil/, while *fils* meaning 'son' or 'sons' is pronounced /fis/.

As well as signs standing for phonemes and syllables and signs standing for meanings, writing systems may also contain signs indicating how words are stressed. For example, in Modern Greek, every word containing more than one syllable has a diacritic symbol (´) over the syllable bearing the main word stress. Thus:

φορά	/foˈra/	'time'
σπίτι	/ˈspiti/	'house'
τράπεζα	/ˈtrapeza/	'bank'

It is, then, perfectly possible for written forms of languages to incorporate information about word stress in what appears on the page. As it happens, the written conventions of different languages vary in the extent to which they make use of this possibility. The written form of English, for instance, provides absolutely no information about stress distribution. Similarly with the transcription of tone. The writing systems of some tone languages – such as the Thai system – indicate the tone associated with a particular lexical item, whereas others do not.

6.6 Orthography as a reflection of lexical grammar and lexical meaning

Just as the pronunciation of particular words may draw on information about their grammatical characteristics and about their meaning, so too may the way in which they are written. With regard to grammar, one very clear demonstration of the influence of a word's grammatical profile on its spelling is the way in which all nouns are written with initial capital letters in German. Thus, in the following sentence, apart from the first word (*wir* = 'we') – capitalized simply because it begins the sentence – all capitalized items are nouns:

Wir finden das <u>Essen</u> und das <u>Bier</u> besonders gut in dieser <u>Kneipe</u>.

('We find the food and the beer especially good in this pub.')

It is worth noting that capitalization is not triggered simply by the form of the word. Thus, for example, the form *e–s–s–e–n*, which here means 'food', can also be used as a verb, meaning 'to eat' (as in *Sollen wir essen?* – 'Shall we eat?'). In the latter circumstances, the word is not capitalized.

In English (and in many other languages) capitalization in the spelling of nouns is restricted to the subcategory of proper nouns, that is to nouns which identify very specific persons, places, ideas etc. in any particular context. For example, *Beethoven*, *Paris* and *Islam* are all proper nouns. However, once again, capitalization is not triggered simply by the form of the word. For instance, the word *Ulster* may be used as a proper noun to refer to the nine northernmost counties of Ireland or, more loosely, to refer to Northern Ireland, which extends over six of the counties in question. However *ulster* may also be used as a common noun to refer to an entire class of entities, i.e. long loose overcoats of coarse cloth. Thus:

The ancient province of <u>Ulster</u> is the setting for many of Ireland's best-known legends.

The stranger was wearing a dark <u>ulster</u>, which flapped in the wind as he walked.

As far as the relationship between the lexicon and meaning is concerned, this has already been dealt with in the discussion of different types of writing system in the last section. We saw there that some writing systems (for example the Sumerian and the Ancient Egyptian systems) actually began as attempts to represent the entities referred to in pictorial form. However, from the way in which these systems subsequently developed – with, for example, particular signs sometimes being used to represent words with sound-shapes similar to those of the words associated with the original meanings represented – it is clear that the meanings on which such pictographic systems were based were essentially word-meanings. It is for this reason that such systems are often described as *logographic*.

An example of a modern logographic system is that used in association with Chinese. As we saw earlier, the Chinese system also began life as a straightforwardly pictographic system, but the characters gradually lost contact with their original pictorial role. It should be noted that the situation in Chinese is actually a little more complicated than one in which an individual word is always represented by an individual character. For instance, the character 木 used alone stands for *mu* ('tree'); doubled (木 木) it stands for *lin* ('wood', 'small forest'); and tripled (木木木) for *sen* ('large forest', 'numerous', 'dark'). Also, as in Sumerian and Ancient Egyptian, certain characters may be combined with others in order to indicate phonetic characteristics of the word represented. These and other considerations have led some linguists to question whether the Chinese system is truly logographic – some scholars continuing to assert that it is essentially pictographic, others that it is a system which primarily represents syllables or morphemes rather than word-meanings. However, whichever line one wants to take on the terminology which most succinctly captures the most salient characteristics of the Chinese system, it is clear that at least part of what determines the forms of the characters deployed is the word-meanings to which they relate. Thus, for example, the sequence /nan/ can mean 'difficult', 'south' or 'male', and each of these meanings is differently represented in the shape of the character used for /nan/.

In alphabetic writing systems, too, there is often a relationship between what a word means and how it is spelt. In the previous section we looked at some examples of French homophones whose spelling varied in accordance with their meaning. Some further examples – from English – of identically pronounced items with different spellings depending on their different meanings are:

beat:beet

grate:great

sole:soul

As we also saw, this kind of differentiation of homophones by spelling is not universal. For instance, the following pairs of English words are identical in both pronunciation and spelling, even though their meanings are completely unrelated:

cope (applied to priest's vestment):	*cope* (= *manage*)
pen (applied to enclosure for, e.g. sheep):	*pen* (applied to writing implement)

However, there are enough orthographically differentiated homophones around in languages such as English and French to demonstrate that in at least some alphabetic systems word meaning can play an important role in the determination of orthographic form.

6.7   Association between particular written signs and particular (categories of) lexical items

As is the case of the relationship between sounds and lexis, one can often point to particular written signs which are linked with particular lexical items or categories of lexical items. An obvious demonstration of this phenomenon is provided by logographic systems, such as those discussed earlier, where specific written characters are associated with specific words – or sets of words. However, there are also instances of particular signs being associated with particular words or types of words in syllabaries and alphabetic systems.

With regard to syllabaries, a rather dramatic example of specific signs being associated with specific sets or types of words comes from Japanese. It was mentioned earlier – in 6.5 – that the Japanese *kana* syllabary script, has two forms. On the one hand, there is the 'normal' form – *hiragana* – used for Japanese particles, verb-inflections etc., but, on the other hand, there is a version of *kana* – *katakana* – which is specifically and exclusively used to represent words borrowed from Western languages such as English. That is to say, in the Japanese system a particular category of words – loanwords from Western languages – has an entire script all of its own dedicated to it.

As far as alphabetic systems are concerned, a case of a particular letter being associated with a particular type of word is that of the letter *c* in German when it is used outside the clusters *ck* and *ch* and outside proper names such as *Celle* and *Claus*. When it is used alone in common nouns, verbs, adjectives and adverbs, *c* is exclusively associated with foreign borrowings. Some examples of borrowed expressions in which *c* is used are: *Comeback, Comics, Cornflakes*. As foreign words become increasingly integrated into German, both their written form and their pronunciation are Germanized, *c* being written as *k* or *z* depending on whether it is to be pronounced as /k/ or as /ts/. Thus what was originally written as *Copie* is now written as *Kopie*, and what was originally written as *Penicillin* is now written as *Penizillin*. Other examples are: *Spectrum* → *Spektrum, Centrum* → *Zentrum, Accusativ* → *Akkusativ*. Where *c* is retained or reverted to in the spelling of such words, this is often a deliberate act on the part of advertisers who thus seek to give a product or an event foreign chic or exotic connotations. One notes, for example, that cigarette advertisements sometimes contain the spelling *Cigaretten* rather than *Zigaretten*, and circus posters frequently prefer *Circus* to *Zirkus*. Clearly, such an advertising ploy would not be possible were it not the case that *c* is associated with a particular type of lexical item – namely foreign words.

A further point worth noting is the way in which grapheme–phoneme correspondences are, at least in some languages, highly dependent on the particular lexical item in which particular letter-combinations occur. For example, mention was made earlier of the combination *ough* in English. Now, it so happens that there is just one word in English in which this sequence of letters is pronounced as /ɒx/, namely *lough*. *Lough* is a word used for 'lake', with particular reference to lakes in Ireland. (It is derived from the Gaelic word *loch*, which exists in both Irish Gaelic and Scots Gaelic.)

6.8 Summary

This chapter has concerned itself with evidence of interaction between the lexicon and phonological and orthographic systems. With regard to phonology, it pointed to the rather obvious fact that the choice of a lexical item determines the particular sound-shape, the particular combination of phonological units – phonemes, allophone, stressed and unstressed syllables, and (in languages like Thai) tones – that is deployed. It also looked at evidence in favour of the notions that phonological realizations of lexical items are informed by grammatical and semantic considerations and that individual lexical items or groups of items may have particular sounds associated with them. In relation to orthography, the chapter noted that lexical choice determines orthographic shape no less than it determines phonological shape. The chapter also set out evidence showing that, again as in the case of phonology, on the one hand, orthographic realizations draw on grammatical and semantic information, and, on the other, certain features of a writing system, and/or particular grapheme–phoneme correspondences, are often associated with a specific set or category of lexical items.

Sources and suggestions for further reading

See 6.1. The notion of double articulation referred to is discussed in A. Martinet's articles 'La double articulation linguistique' (*Travaux du Cercle Linguistique de Copenhague* 5, 1949, 30–7) and 'Arbitraire linguistique et double articulation' (*Cahiers Ferdinand de Saussure* 15, 1957, 105–16).

See 6.2. The discussion in 6.2, 6.3 and 6.4 owes some of its inspiration to F. Katamba's treatment of the topics in question in his book *An introduction to phonology* (London: Longman, 1989). The first of the Thai examples in 6.2 was provided by Jennifer Pariseau; the second was taken from V. Fromkin and R.Rodman, *An introduction to language* (sixth edition, New York: Harcourt Brace, 1998, 241).

See 6.3. The examples in 6.3 of the different ways in which the cockcrow is designated in different languages are borrowed from V. Cook's *Inside language* (London: Arnold, 1997, 53). The examples from Luganda are to be found on p. 256 of F. Katamba's *An introduction to phonology*. Lexical Phonology is the brainchild of P. Kiparsky – see, e.g. his articles 'Lexical phonology and morphology' (in I. S. Yang (ed.), *Linguistics in the morning calm*, Seoul: Hanshin, 1982) and 'Some consequences of lexical phonology' (*Phonology Yearbook* 2, 83–138). Other treatments of the topic include K. P. Monahan's book *The theory of lexical phonology* (Dordrecht: D. Reidel Publishing, 1986) and M. Kenstowicz's chapter 'Lexical Phonology' in his volume *Phonology in generative grammar* (Oxford: Blackwell).

See 6.4. The discussion of the /ŋ/ phoneme in French broadly follows what I had to say on the matter in my little volume *French: some historical background* (Dublin: Authentik, 1992, 49f.). The notion of lexical diffusion derives from the work of W. Wang – e.g. W. Wang, 'Competing changes as a cause of residue' (*Language* 45, 1969, 9–25); M. Chen and W. Wang, 'Sound change: actuation and implementation' (*Language* 51, 1975, 255–81); it is discussed by, among others, J. Aitchison, in her book *Language change: progress or decay?* (London: Fontana, 1981, 95), R. Hudson, in his book *Sociolinguistics* (Cambridge: Cambridge University Press, 1980, 168ff.) and S. Romaine, in her book *Socio-historical linguistics: its status and methodology* (Cambridge: Cambridge University Press, 1982, 254ff.). The Belfast data are discussed in articles by R. Maclaran ('The variable (ʌ): a relic form with social correlates, *Belfast Working Papers in Language and Linguistics* 1, 1976, 45–68) and J. Milroy ('Lexical alternation and diffusion in vernacular speech', *Belfast Working Papers in Language and Linguistics* 3, 1978, 101–14).

See 6.5. Section 6.5 draws liberally on the following three sources: chapters 2–6 of L.-J. Calvet's *Histoire de l'écriture* (Paris: Plon, 1996); Chapter 6 of V. Cook's *Inside language* (London: Arnold, 1997); and chapters 1–3 of Georges Jean's *Writing: the story of alphabets and scripts* (London: Thames & Hudson, 1992). The Sumerian, Chinese and Ancient Egyptian examples cited in the section are all borrowed from these authors. The English, French, Modern Greek and Spanish examples are my own.

See 6.6. The brief mention of the controversy about the nature of the Chinese writing system was inspired by articles contributed by W. C. Brice, M. A. French and E. Pulgram to the collection of papers edited by W. Haas under the title *Writing without letters* (Manchester: Manchester University Press, 1976) and by J. DeFrancis's article 'How efficient is the Chinese writing system?' (*Visible Language* 30, 1996, 6–44).

See 6.7. The examples of German words spelt with *c* are taken from D. Berger, G. Drosdowski and O. Käge's *Richtiges und gutes Deutsch* (Mannheim: Dudenverlag, 1985, 160). The examples of words exchanging their *c* for a *k* or a *z* are taken from G. Drosdowski, W. Müller, W. Scholze-Stubenrecht and M. Wermke's *Rechtschreibung der deutschen Sprache* (Mannheim: Dudenverlag, 1991, 29).

Good introductions to phonology – all of which refer in varying degrees to lexical matters – are:

V. Cook, *Inside language* (London: Arnold, 1997, Chapter 4);

H. Giegerich, *English phonology: an introduction* (Cambridge: Cambridge University Press, 1992);

F. Katamba, *An introduction to phonology* (London: Longman, 1989).

More theoretical treatments of phonology are to be found in:

P. Carr, *Phonology* (London: Macmillan, 1993);

J. Goldsmith, *The handbook of phonological theory* (Oxford: Blackwell, 1995);

M. Kenstowicz, *Phonology in generative grammar* (Oxford: Blackwell, 1994);

A. Spencer, *Phonology: theory and description* (Oxford: Blackwell, 1996).

Accessible introductory publications on writing systems and orthography include:

L.-J. Calvet, *Histoire de l'écriture* (Paris: Plon, 1996);

V. Cook, *Inside language* (London: Arnold, 1997, Chapter 6);

F. Coulmas, *The Blackwell encyclopedia of writing systems* (Oxford: Blackwell, 1996);

Georges Jean, *Writing: the story of alphabets and scripts* (London: Thames & Hudson, 1992);

J. L. Swerdlow, 'The power of writing' (*National Geographic* 1962, 1999, 110–32).

The reader looking for more in-depth discussion of orthographic and related issues may wish to consult one or more of the following:

E. Carney, *A survey of English spelling* (London: Routledge, 1994);

P. T. Daniels and W. Bright (eds), *The world's writing systems* (Oxford: Blackwell, 1996);

G. Sampson, *Writing systems: a linguistic introduction* (London: Hutchinson, 1985);

M. Stubbs, *Language and literacy* (London: Routledge & Kegan Paul, 1980).

Focusing questions/topics for discussion

1. In 6.2 and 6.3 we saw some examples of different stress distributions in relation to similar sound-sequences being associated with different

grammatical categories – e.g. *reject* [VERB] vs. *reject* [NOUN]. Try to find further pairs of English words which are differentiated in this way.

2. In 6.4 we looked at the association between particular sounds and particular (categories of) lexical items. Consider the nasalized vowel sound /ã/ as it occurs, for example, in the final syllable of many English-speakers' pronunciation of the word *restaurant*. In what other English words does this sound occur? What kinds of words are these?

3. In 6.5 the notion of *allograph* was briefly discussed. It was noted that a particular grapheme – the first letter of the Roman alphabet – has the allographs **A**, **a** and *a*. Taking any writing system(s) with which you are familiar, try to find some further examples of 'families' of allographs.

4. In 6.5 and 6.6 it was shown that orthography is sometimes used to differentiate between homophones (e.g. *meat:meet*). Illustrate this phenomenon further from any language(s) you know.

5. In 6.7 we observed that some written signs are associated with particular words or categories of words. Try to think of some further instances of this in any language(s) with which you are familiar. Note that sometimes the specific association has to do with *where* the particular sign occurs as well as with the nature of the sign itself. For example, the letter *x* rarely occurs at the beginning of words in English, and almost all the words which feature *x* in this position are of Greek origin.

7

Lexis and language variation

7.1 Variety is the spice of language

So far we have been looking at the lexical aspects of language largely as if the same range of forms and functions of any given language were deployed in all circumstances of language use. A moment's reflection, however, will bring us to the conclusion that this is a simplification and that, in fact, languages are characterized by high degrees of variation. Regional accents immediately spring to mind in this connection, as do the different words that people from different regions use for the same object.

Similar kinds of variation occur across the social and ethnic spectrum, as well as between the genders. With regard to gender, for instance, there are languages in which males and females pronounce the same words differently; thus, in Gros Ventre, a Native American language of the north-eastern United States, words which male speakers pronounce with a /dj/ sound (the sound in the middle of *Indian*) are pronounced by women with a /kj/ sound (the sound in the middle of *Slovakian*) – so that the word for 'bread' in this language is either *djatsa* or *kjatsa*, depending on whether the speaker is male or female. In other languages certain pronouns and particles are gender-specific; thus, in Japanese, female speakers indicate their gender by using the particles *ne* or *wa* at the end of sentences they produce.

Also, it is clear that we vary our use of language from situation to situation – so that, for example, the way we talk or write to a prospective employer is likely to differ significantly from the way in which we talk or write to close personal friends. For example, over a cup of coffee with a friend we might explain that we are too busy to go somewhere or do something using a form of words such as: *Can't. I'm up to my eyes.* In a formal interaction with an employer or a prospective employer we might be more likely to express the same thought rather differently: *I am unfortunately unable to make myself available at that particular time because of pressure of work.*

The study of language variation falls within the ambit of that branch of linguistics known as *sociolinguistics*. In this chapter we shall begin with some discussion around a few of the basic concepts and terms developed by sociolinguists in connection with their study of language variation. We shall then home in on the extremely important lexical dimension of language variation in its different manifestations. Finally, we shall take a brief look at the question of the relationship between lexical variation and cultural variation and the impact, if any, of lexical variation on perceptions and thought patterns.

7.2 Language variation: sociolinguistic perspectives

With all this variation in evidence, a legitimate question to ask is: when are the differences so great as to indicate that we are dealing with distinct languages rather than two or more versions of the same language? Compare, for example, the expressions in the first two columns below:

auf dem Fahrrad	*op de Fiets*	'on the bicycle'
es zieht	*et drekkt*	'there's a draught'
wir trinken Schnaps	*we drenken Söpis*	'we're drinking schnaps'

Can these two sets of expressions possibly be from the same language? In fact the expressions from the first column are from Standard High German (*Hochdeutsch*), whereas the expressions in the second column are from what is generally regarded as a 'dialect' of German spoken in a part of Germany which lies very close to the Dutch border. The 'dialect' in question is in fact a variety of *Plattdeutsch* or Low German.

Now consider three more sets of expressions:

et bord til to	*et bord til to*	*ett bord för två*	'a table for two'
hva koster det	*hvad koster det?*	*vad kostar det?*	'what does it cost?'
jeg er tørst	*jeg er tørstig*	*jag är törstig*	'I'm thirsty'

Are these perhaps also from different dialects of the same language? In fact, the first column contains expressions from Norwegian, the second column contains expressions from Danish, and the third column contains expressions from Swedish. In other words, in this case we are talking about sets of expressions from what are regarded as three separate languages.

What is interesting is that, whereas a Norwegian, Dane and a Swede, can, each using his/her own language, to a very large extent converse with each other intelligibly, a speaker of Standard German with no knowledge of *Plattdeutsch* would have great difficulty understanding the German 'dialect' from which the earlier examples are taken, including the examples themselves. Actually, a speaker of Dutch would fare better in this regard. This demonstrates clearly that whether we call something a *dialect* or a *language* is really more a matter of politics than of linguistics. If the part of Germany where the above-exemplified type of *Plattdeutsch* is spoken had happened to be situated in the Netherlands, the linguistic variety in question would have been designated as a 'dialect' of Dutch. As it turns out, much the same variety is spoken on the Dutch side of the border, where it is indeed regarded as a 'dialect' of Dutch.

The way in which sociolinguists deal with this problem terminologically is to apply the neutral term *variety* to any set of linguistic items and patterns which coheres into a means for communication – not only in the context of geographic variation but also in the context of social, ethnic, gender-related or context-related variation. For example, one ethnic variety which has been much studied by sociolinguists is *Black English*, otherwise known as *Black Vernacular English* or *Afro-American Vernacular English*. This variety – used, as its various labels indicate, by many Black people in the United States – diverges very noticeably from varieties used by Whites. It has a fairly well-defined set of characteristics, one of which is a tendency for word-final plosive consonants to be voiceless; thus, the Black English consonants corresponding to Standard English /g/ in *big*, /b/ in *cub* and /d/ in *kid* may occur as /k/, /p/ and /t/.

A feature such as a word-final plosive whose differing realization can, as in the case of Black English, contribute towards the identification of a particular variety is labelled a *variable* in sociolinguistics. Another example of a variable is that of /h/ in British English. Most British English-speakers would consider the dropping of *h*'s at the beginnings of words to be a 'working-class' phenomenon. As it turns out, *h*-dropping is not the exclusive preserve of any particular social stratum in Great Britain, although the degree to which it occurs is correlated with class, as is evident from the following figures from a study conducted in the 1970s showing the percentages of word-initial /h/s dropped by samples from different social groupings in Bradford and Norwich:

	BRADFORD	NORWICH
Middle middle-class	12%	6%
Lower middle-class	28%	14%
Upper working-class	67%	40%
Middle working-class	89%	60%
Lower working-class	93%	60%

What this set of figures illustrates is that linguistic varieties are not necessarily characterized by the absolute presence or the absolute absence of a specific realization of a variable – in this case the suppliance or the dropping of the word-initial *h* sound. Thus, while it seems to be the case that, in both Bradford and Norwich, middle-class speakers pronounce word-initial *h* more often than they fail to pronounce it, there are nevertheless occasions when they drop it. Varieties, in other words, are often characterized by tendencies or probabilities in terms of the presence or absence of particular variants of variables rather than by categorical attributes. Another dimension of the way in which variables relate to varieties which is illustrated by the above figures is the fact that different varieties are not necessarily discrete, self-contained systems neatly divided off from each other, but may form a continuum and blur into each other.

A continuum of variation is precisely what one usually finds in social context-related variation, which is sometimes referred to as *style-shifting*. In all languages people adjust their language style according to the situation in which communication is taking place and according to the relationship that exists between the participants in the interaction. For example, consider the expression *going to* in English, as in: *I'm going to leave tomorrow*. This expression can undergo a range of reductions – indicated below – and its most reduced forms are more frequently used in informal styles of speech and less frequently used in formal styles:

/gəʊɪŋ tuː /	('*going to*')
/gəʊɪŋ tə/	('*going tuh*')
/gəʊɪn tə/	('*goin' tuh*')
/gən tə/	('*guhn tuh*')
/gənə/	('*guhnuh*' – the form usually written as '*gonna*')

That is not to say that 'one or the other' situations are unknown in language variation. Where two or more varieties have attained the status of standard regional, national or international languages and their patterns have been fixed and prescribed for by grammar books, dictionaries, and language academies, the differences between them are more categorical. For example, in Standard Swedish the form *två* will always be used for 'two', whereas in Standard Danish the form used will be *to*. Similarly with the pairs of forms below representing Castilian (Standard Spanish) and Catalan respectively:

CASTILIAN	CATALAN	
ciudad	*ciutat*	'city'
descuento	*descompte*	'discount'
dirección	*direcció*	'direction'
mas	*més*	'more'
podemos	*podem*	'we can'
tambien	*també*	'also'
tiempo	*temps*	'time'

Two important points remain to be made before we move on to examine the lexical dimension of language variation in more detail. The first is that the various factors in language variation do not operate in isolation from each other but on the contrary constantly interact. For example, there is an interplay between geographical variation and social variation, with non-standard regional accents and expressions being more frequently found in working-class language use than in the language use of the middle classes. There is also interaction, to take another example, between geographical variation and social context-related variation; thus, an individual with a knowledge of both a national standard variety (such as Standard German) and a non-standard regional variety (such as a variety of *Plattdeutsch*) will tend to use the non-standard variety in situations of intimacy and informality – in the home and with friends and acquaintances from his/her locality – and will use the standard variety in more formal circumstances – with strangers and in the world of officialdom.

The second point is that the particular variety or varieties that we use are not deterministically imposed on us but rather reflect the models we ourselves adopt and the attachments and affiliations we enter into; I was born and raised in a working-class home in Dorset, but – because at some stage in my childhood I began to identify with the norms, including the linguistic norms, of my Standard English-speaking educators – I no longer (alas!) speak with a Dorset accent. Sometimes a particular affiliation can take speakers in a less rather than a more standard direction. For instance, a much-cited study conducted in Martha's Vineyard (an island off the coast of Massachusetts) some years ago revealed that the use of a particular non-standard vowel sound was increasing among the islanders – apparently reflecting a heightened sense of local solidarity and a negative reaction to the values and behaviour of the large numbers of mainlanders who holidayed on the island in the summer.

7.3   Lexical aspects of geographical variation

A very frequently cited illustration of lexical variation related to geography is the case of lexical divergence between American and British English, for example:

AMERICAN ENGLISH	BRITISH ENGLISH
apartment	*flat*
billfold	*wallet*
diaper	*nappy*
gas(oline)	*petrol*
trunk (of a car)	*boot*

Also well-known are pronunciation and spelling differences between British English and American English such as:

AMERICAN ENGLISH	BRITISH ENGLISH

PRONUNCIATION DIFFERENCES

*har**ass*** /haˈras/	*h**a**rass* /ˈhærəs/
*l**a**boratory* /ˈlabrətɒrɪ/	*lab**o**ratory* /ləˈbɒrətrɪ/
*l**ei**sure* /ˈliːʒər/	*l**ei**sure* /ˈlɛʒə/
*m**a**gazine* /ˈmagəzin/	*maga**zine*** /mægəˈziːn/
*m**i**ssile* /ˈmɪsəl	*m**i**ssile* /ˈmɪsaɪl/

SPELLING DIFFERENCES

center	*centre*
defense	*defence*
favorite	*favourite*
plow	*plough*
traveler	*traveller*

In a number of cases where British and American English have what look like identical words, there are differences in morphological behaviour. For example, the verb *to dive*, which in British English has *dived* as its preterite (simple past) form, in at least some varieties of American English has *dove* as its preterite. Other cases where – at least to judge by the usage of many current American popular writers – British and American preterites diverge include: *to fit* – British *fitted*, American *fit*; *to sneak* – British *sneaked*, American *snuk*; *to strive* – British *strove*, American *strived*. There is also the case of the past participle of the verb *to get*, which in British English is *got* and in American English *gotten*.

Probably more problematic in communicative terms are instances of 'false friends' – words which seem to be identical but which have different meanings. The case of *bum* is probably too well known to cause misunderstandings; in American English it means 'tramp', whereas in colloquial British English it denotes 'buttocks' (= colloquial American English *buns*). The metaphorical use of the expression *pissed*, on the other hand, might just be a source of difficulty. In colloquial British English *I'm really pissed* means 'I'm really drunk'; in American English, however, it means 'I'm really annoyed', which British English speakers express by adding *off*: *I'm really pissed off*. A British English speaker buying a small item – such as a book or a card – in downtown Indianapolis may also be taken aback (as I was!) to be asked 'Do you want a sack for that?'; the word *sack*, which in American English can be applied to bags of any description, is in British English applied only to very large bags – such as those used for coal or fertilizer.

Much the same kind of situation as one finds in relation to lexical differences between the English of Great Britain and the English of North America applies to the Castilian Spanish of Spain and the Spanish of Latin America. Thus, for example, in America the Spanish for 'bean' is *frijol*, whereas the Castilian word is *alubia* or *judia*; in America the Spanish for 'bus' is *bus*, whereas the Castilian version is *autobús*; in America the words used when answering the telephone are *aló*, *hola* or *bueno*, whereas in Castilian the expressions used are *digame* or *diga*. There are a number of 'false friends' in this connection too. For instance, the word *carro*, which in Castilian means 'cart' or 'wagon', also means 'car' in America (= Castilian *coche*); the word *estampilla*, which in Castilian means 'rubber stamp', is also used in Latin America for 'postage stamp' (= Castilian *sello*); and the word *coger*, which in Castilian has the innocent enough meaning 'to take hold of', in Latin America is a slang word for 'to have sex with' (= Castilian *joder*).

Not that the interposition of a large ocean is a necessary prerequisite for lexical divergences. Such divergences are also found from country to country within Europe. For example, the number system in French operates differently in Francophone parts of Belgium and Switzerland from the way it operates in France. In France the words used for 'seventy', 'eighty' and 'ninety' are, respectively, *soixante-dix* (literally 'sixty-ten'), *quatre-vingts* (literally 'four-twenties') and *quatre-vingt-dix* (literally 'four-twenty-ten'). In Belgium and Switzerland, on the other hand, the words used for 'seventy' and 'ninety' are, respectively, *septante* and *nonante*; also, in Switzerland the word *huitante* is frequently used for 'eighty'. There are also differences between the English of Ireland (sometimes called Hiberno-English) and British English. For instance, most British English speakers would have difficulties with the Irish English expressions: *boreen* ('narrow track'), *garsoon* ('boy'), *gurrier* ('ruffian'), *locked* (in the sense of 'drunk'), and *yoke* (in the sense of 'thing').

Even national frontiers are of only limited value as guides to lexical divergence. That is to say, particular lexical forms or usages do not necessarily stop at frontiers – as we saw in the earlier discussion of the *Plattdeutsch* examples – and lexical differences are to be observed within as well as between varieties spoken in any given country. Thus, for example, although the statement in the last paragraph about the use of *soixante-dix* for 'seventy' in France – as opposed to *septante* in Belgium and Switzerland – is generally true, in fact, *septante* is also used by some speakers in eastern France. A further case of lexical variation within a country is that of the German words for 'Saturday'; in northern Germany the word used is typically *Sonnabend*, whereas in southern Germany the word *Samstag* tends to be used.

7.4   Lexical aspects of social variation

Whereas relating the way in which people speak and write to the country or region they come from is relatively uncontroversial, making the same kinds of connections between language varieties and social background is a some-what more sensitive matter, since the description of particular variants of lin-guistic variables as being associated with a particular social class is liable to be interpreted as feeding into snobbery, élitism and/or anti-democratic polit-ical philosophies. Indeed, one early attempt to analyse lexical usage in social terms was immediately put at the service of elitist attitudes. This was the work of the English linguist, A.S.C. Ross, which set out – in a rather impres-sionistic manner – to isolate markers of upper-class ('U') and non-upper-class ('non-U') language use in respect of pronunciation, grammar and most especially vocabulary. Ross's dictates were seized upon and added to by lin-guistic snobs all over the English-speaking world and led to the establish-ment of a veritable glossary of 'U' and 'non-U' terms. For example, in the U/non-U scheme of things, the words on the left below are supposedly 'U', and the words on the right their 'non-U' equivalents:

'U'	'NON-U'
bicycle/bike	*cycle*
looking glass	*mirror*
lavatory	*toilet*
lunch(eon)	*dinner*
(table-)napkin	*serviette*
scent	*perfume*
pudding	*sweet*
wireless	*radio*

One rather amusing point in this connection is that the so-called 'upper-class' variants in many cases precisely coincide with the variants used in working-class circles. For example, in my own working-class home in the 1950s we listened to the *wireless* rather than the *radio*, looked forward to *pudding* not *sweet*, rode *bikes* not *cycles*, and occasionally presented my mother with bottles of *scent* not *perfume*. Ogden Nash's suitably sceptical comment on the whole U/non-U discussion was that the Wicked Queen in the Snow-White story, by uttering the words 'Mirror mirror on the wall', 'exposed herself as not only wicked but definitely non-U'.

Other early attempts to examine the relationship between language – including lexis – and social class were rather more scientific. As far back as the late 1930s the American linguist Charles Fries compared a number of aspects of the language used in letters on similar topics sent to the same des-tination (an administrative department of the armed forces) by lower working-class and professional correspondents. Among the lexical differ-ences that emerged from Fries's work were the following:

the professional subjects in the study tended to intensify the force of adjectives using forms ending in -*ly* (as in <u>*awfully*</u> *difficult*), whereas the more common intensifiers used by the working-class subjects were items like *awful, mighty, pretty, real, right.*

the professional subjects used a single form *you*, whether the reference was singular or plural, whereas the working-class subjects often used forms such as *youse, you all, you people* to indicate plurality;

the working-class subjects often used double prepositions such as *off from*, whereas the professional subjects tended not to use such forms.

Another early study, this time dating from the 1950s, found that, on being interviewed about a tornado in Arkansas, working-class speakers, unlike middle-class speakers, used *we, they* and persons' names without further explanation for the benefit of the interviewer, and that they used expressions like *and stuff like that* instead of going into detail.

A more recent account of language and class is that of the British sociologist Basil Bernstein. Bernstein talks about two 'codes' to which, he claims, lower working-class and middle-class speakers have differential access. The two 'codes' in question are, on the one hand, *restricted code* (originally labelled *public language*) and, on the other, *elaborated code* (originally labelled *formal language*). Restricted code, according to Bernstein, is the code of intimacy, the code we all use when with people and in circumstances where we can communicate a great deal without saying very much because there is so much shared information and there are so many shared expectations in the situations in question. Elaborated code, for its part, says Bernstein, is the code we use when we need to be explicit in our speech and writing because the person(s) to whom we are addressing ourselves is/are not familiar with the people, places, ideas etc. we are referring to, which means that we need to contextualize everything we are producing in order to be understood. Bernstein contends that, whereas all users of a language have access to restricted code, lower working class speakers have little experience of elaborated code and so are likely to be disadvantaged in situations, such as school, where the use of elaborated code is required.

The linguistic characteristics of restricted and elaborated code, as described by Bernstein, include the following:

RESTRICTED	ELABORATED
short, often unfinished or fragmentary sentences	well-ordered complete sentences with syntactic norms observed
simple and repetitive use of conjunctions (e.g. *because, so*) and very limited use of subordinate clauses	use of a wide range of conjunctions and subordinate clauses
rigid and limited use of adjectives and adverbs	appropriate use of a wide range of adjectives and adverbs

With regard to the lexicon, what all of the above amounts to is a claim that lower working-class language users produce fewer conjunctions, adjectives and adverbs than middle-class language users, and in fact, a number of studies appear to show that this is indeed the case. On the other hand, Bernstein's claims and his interpretation of the relevant evidence have been called into question by some linguists on the basis that the quantitative findings he cites do not necessarily indicate two qualitatively different orientations, and that, in any case, a narrower vocabulary in some grammatical categories may perhaps be compensated for by a wider vocabulary in other categories hitherto uninvestigated.

A final point on the question of lexis and social class concerns 'bad' language or 'vulgar' language. It seems to be quite widely assumed that such language is mostly to be found on the lips of people at the lower end of the social scale. Indeed, the very word *vulgar* comes from a Latin word, *vulgus*, which means 'the common people', and there has been a longstanding tendency to associate the use of choice language with stigmatized social categories. However, oaths, curses profanities and obscenities have also been a royal and an aristocratic prerogative. Queen Elizabeth I, for instance, was famous for her foul mouth, and the traditionally choice language of the nobility is reflected in the expression *to swear like a lord*.

In the modern age, at least in the West, there seems to have been an increase in the use and acceptability of words which would once have been regarded as offensive (see Chapter 8) and this phenomenon has apparently affected the entire social range. Serious research into the social distribution of 'swear-words' remains to be done, but it is likely that the extent of the use of such items will depend on factors rather more complex than simply adherence to a particular social class. For example, among the working-class population of Great Britain there are sizeable numbers of practising Christians, Hindus, Muslims and Sikhs for whom the use of explicitly sexual words or irreverent references to sacred matters would be unthinkable.

7.5   Lexical aspects of ethnic variation

We turn now to the issue of the relationship between language variation and ethnicity. Ethnicity is that aspect of culture which signifies 'belongingness' to a community in terms other than socio-economic terms; it is been recently defined as 'the identificational dimension of culture'. Racial factors may or may not be present among the criteria by which an ethnic group defines itself and/or is defined by other groups. For example, the small Vietnamese community in Dublin has characteristics of both a cultural and a racial kind which distinguish it from the majority of the population, whereas most Scots residing in the same city would not be identifiable in racial terms but would nevertheless see themselves as culturally distinct from the Irish people among whom they live.

Obviously, one component of a culture which very often plays an important role in identifying an ethnic group is language. For many members of particular communities there is an absolutely vital connection between their language and their ethnicity; thus, for instance, one of the slogans frequently heard in the context of the revival of the Irish language is '*Gan teanga, gan tir*' – 'Without a language, without a country' – and among Jews it has been claimed that Hebrew 'emerges from the same fiery furnace from which the soul of the people emerges'.

In some countries and regions there is a high degree of separation of ethnic groupings defined largely in linguistic terms. For example, in Belgium the longstanding linguistico-cultural conflict between the Dutch-speaking Flemings and the French-speaking Walloons has resolved itself into a division of the country – with the exception of the bilingual territory of Brussels – into two large unilingual regions, Dutch-speaking Flanders to the north, and French-speaking Wallonia to the south. There is in addition an officially recognized small German-speaking area in eastern Belgium (Eupen, St Vith). In other situations, members of different ethnic groupings are living and working side by side, communicating with each other via the standard language of the country and largely reserving their use of ethnic varieties distinct from that standard language for use with family and friends of the same ethnic background. This would be true, for example, of the community of Turkish immigrants in the Netherlands. In still other situations the varieties spoken by particular ethnic groups may have strong resemblances to and connections with the varieties of other ethnic groups, including the standard variety of the country or region in question. Examples of this kind of scenario would include the cases of speakers of American English, Australian English, Hiberno-English, West Indian English etc. living in Great Britain.

Further to this last point, a particularly interesting study of patterns of language use among West Indians in Great Britain was conducted in the 1980s by the British linguist Viv Edwards. According to her account, the variety – or *patois* – used (especially in informal and intimate contexts) by the Jamaican community is very closely related to Standard English but has a large number of specific features, including lexical features, which set it apart from the latter. Some of the lexical differences between Jamaican Patois and Standard English reported by Edwards are detailed below.

JAMAICAN PATOIS	STANDARD ENGLISH
PLURAL MARKING OF NOUNS	
mostly zero marking, e.g.	mostly -*s*
He give me two book.	*He gave me two books.*
-*dem*, where the context does not suffice to indicate plurality, e.g.	
Clovis gone up a Elaine fi you record-dem.	*Clovis went up Elaine's for your records.*

JAMAICAN PATOIS	STANDARD ENGLISH
PERSONAL PRONOUNS	
me	*I, me, my*
yu	*you, your*
im	*he, him, his, she, her*
i	*it, its*
we	*we, us, our*
unu	*you, your*
dem	*they, them, their*

INFINITIVES OF VERBS

fi + base form of verb, e.g.	*to* + base form of verb
Dem want me fi go up dere go tell dem.	*They want me to go up there and tell them*

EXPRESSION OF LOCATION

deh + expression of place, e.g.	*to be* + expression of place
When me deh at school, di whole a dem hate me	*When I was at school, they all hated me.*

Finally in this connection, it may be worth mentioning that some ethnic groups mark their identity by *conversational code-switching* – switching to and fro – apparently quite arbitrarily – *between* the languages at their disposal. For example, some groups within the Hispanic (or *Latino*) communities in the United States – whether from parts of the country which once belonged to Mexico or immigrants from Cuba, El Salvador, Guatemala, Mexico or Puerto Rico – signal their ethnicity in all its biculturality by inserting English expressions into their discourse when speaking Spanish and insert Spanish expressions into their discourse when speaking English. In some instances there actually seems to be a convention to the effect that roughly equal amounts of both languages should be used in any given conversation. One oft-cited study of code-switching among Puerto Ricans in New York demonstrates this kind of balanced approach in its very title – quoted from one of the members of the community in question: 'Sometimes I'll start a sentence in English *y termino en español*' (Sometimes I'll start a sentence in English and finish it in Spanish.').

7.6 Lexical aspects of gender-related variation

Gender-related variation, as we saw from the Gros Ventre and Japanese examples mentioned at the beginning of the chapter, may in some cases be very clear and noticeable by all. In other cases the differences between male and female speech are more subtle and users of a given language may or may not be conscious of them. With regard to English and many other European languages, for instance, the differences are often said to reside in the tendency of female language use to be closer to the 'prestige variety' than male language use. Thus, for example, as far as accent is concerned, it has been observed that female British English speakers are more likely than their male counterparts to produce pronunciations which resemble those of radio and television announcers. An explanation commonly offered for this kind of difference is that women have traditionally been expected to be more 'correct' and conforming in their behaviour than men and that this expectation and its consequences carry over into the linguistic sphere.

With regard to lexis, a test case for 'good behaviour' among women as far as language is concerned is that of 'swear-words'. It is certainly true to say that there is – or at least until recently was – a certain reluctance on the part of many men to utter such words in the presence of women. The expression *not in mixed company*, which really means 'not in front of the women', was frequently used as an interdiction in respect of jokes and anecdotes which contained sexually explicit references and/or 'four-letter words'. One presumes from this kind of approach on the part of some men that women have traditionally *heard* less 'bad language' than men, but what about their *production* of such language?

Queen Elizabeth I was mentioned in the last section as a user of choice language. One interesting comment about her in the present context depicts her as having 'sworn like a man'. This implies that in Renaissance England – at least in well-to-do circles – swearing was associated more with men than with women, but it also implies, of course, that individual women (including the Supreme Governor of the Church of England) refused to be bound by this particular convention. In seventeenth century England the association between maleness and swearing was still, apparently, very much in place if the following quotation is anything to go by.

> The Grace of Swearing has not obtain'd to be a Mode yet among the Women; God damn ye, does not sit well upon a Female Tongue; it seems to be a Masculine Vice, which the Women are not arrived to yet . . .
> Defoe, *An essay on projects*, 1697

To bring the discussion a little closer to our own times, in an influential study published in 1975 under the title of *Language and women's place*, the American linguist, Robin Lakoff claims that 'If a little girl "talks rough" like a boy, she will be ostracized, scolded or made fun of' (p. 5). Lakoff provides the following example (p. 10):

(a)   Oh dear, you've put the peanut butter in the refrigerator again.

(b)   Shit, you've put the peanut butter in the refrigerator again.

It is safe to predict that people would classify the first sentence as 'women's language' the second as 'men's language'.

Actually, 25 years on, the above prediction would not be at all safe. In Great Britain and Ireland at any rate many women now say *shit* no less readily than they drink pints. Whether this means that women have entirely caught up with men in the 'four-letter word' stakes is not clear, but there is little doubt that – to say the very least of the matter – the gap is closing.

Lakoff also claims that some other words are more frequently used by women than by men. Thus, for example, she maintains that certain colour words such as *aquamarine, chartreuse, lavender* and *magenta* are more likely to be produced by women than by men, and that much the same applies to adjectives such as *adorable, divine* and *precious*. Among the many aspects of British upper middle-class behaviour parodied in the television series *Absolutely Fabulous!* is the vocabulary used by women of that background – *darling, gorgeous, sweetie* etc. Vivian Cook found in an informal survey conducted in association with his book *Inside language* that 90% of his 48 respondents identified *Absolutely gorgeous* and *It's nice, isn't it?* as coming from female speakers.

Just how far lexical divergences genuinely differentiate between speakers of different genders in a language like English is, as can be seen from the above discussion, a matter of some debate – whatever may be the situation in languages like Gros Ventre and Japanese. It is worth saying, however, that in the major European languages, including English, and presumably in all languages there are certain words which, when used literally and self-referentially, will very clearly designate the speaker or writer as male or female. The particular items will vary from language to language but their denotation will typically have to do with biological attributes and/or with roles or positions assigned to one gender or the other in a given society. Here are some examples from English:

MALE-IDENTIFYING	FEMALE-IDENTIFYING
I'm extremely <u>virile</u>.	*I'm extremely <u>pregnant</u>.*
I'm a <u>monk</u>.	*I'm a <u>nun</u>.*
I'm a <u>widower</u>.	*I'm a <u>widow</u>.*

Moreover, in languages with grammatical gender the particular morphological shape of certain words will have much the same effect, as the following examples from French demonstrate:

MALE-IDENTIFYING	FEMALE-IDENTIFYING
Je suis <u>étudiant</u>.	*Je suis <u>étudiante</u>.*
'I'm a student'	'I'm a student'
Je suis <u>heureux</u>.	*Je suis <u>heureuse</u>.*
'I'm happy'	'I'm happy'
Cela m'a <u>surpris</u>.	*Cela m'a <u>surprise</u>.*
'That surprised me'	'That surprised me'

7.7   Lexical aspects of context-related variation

As has already been indicated, and as a moment's reflection on our own use of language will confirm, language varies not only in accordance with speakers'/writers' geographical, social, ethnic and gender profiles but also in accordance with the context in which the speaking or writing takes place. The examples given earlier were of people using a very different speech style with their friends from that used with employers or prospective employers, and of people who speak *Plattdeutsch* at home and with friends switching to Standard German when in the presence of strangers or bureaucrats.

This second example illustrates a phenomenon which the American linguist Charles Ferguson called *diglossia* - in an article bearing that name published in 1959. In the cases described by Ferguson diglossia refers to situations where two related but very different varieties are in use within a given community, one of which – labelled High (H) – is used for formal, high-status functions, and the other – labelled Low (L) – is used in more intimate, informal circumstances. The cases in question are Classical Arabic and Egyptian Arabic in Egypt, Standard German and Swiss German in Switzerland, French and Haitian Creole in Haiti, and *Katharevousa* and Demotic Greek in Greece. A word or two of explanation about each of these cases follows.

- Classical Arabic is the language of the Koran; in its modern form it is nowadays more usually called Modern Standard Arabic (MSA). MSA is used as a means of communication throughout the Arab world, but each Arabic-speaking country and region has its own local variety of Demotic Arabic, these different varieties being unintelligible to speakers of other local varieties.
- The case of Standard German (*Hochdeutsch*) and Swiss German (*Schweizerdeutsch, Schwyzertüüsch*) in Switzerland is comparable to the case of *Hochdeutsch* and *Plattdeutsch* in northern Germany. That is to say, Swiss German is very different from Standard German – to the point of being largely unintelligible to Standard German speakers who have not learnt Swiss German.
- The official language of Haiti is French, the language of the colonists who populated it with African slaves and ruled it until 1804. However, the native variety of most of its population is Haitian Creole. A *creole* develops when a simplified system of communication between two groups speaking mutually unintelligible languages (*pidgin*), is adopted as a mother tongue (by, for example, children born of sexual relationships between members of the two groups). Haitian Creole, like most creoles, took most of its vocabulary from the language of the economically dominant group, i.e. French in this instance, but has some grammatical elements derived from the languages – in this case African languages – of the economically subordinate group.

- *Katharevousa* is a supposedly 'pure' (= Greek καθ αρός – *katharós*) form of Modern Greek which is much closer to Ancient Greek than is Demotic Greek (= δημτική – *dhimotikí*). *Katharevousa* was invented in the nineteenth century by certain scholars concerned to re-connect Greeks with their ancient culture and to rid Modern Greek of elements borrowed from Turkish. It was for a considerable period after Greek independence from Turkey the official language of the country and the language of education. Modern Demotic Greek, on the other hand, is the vernacular language which naturally evolved from Ancient Greek, borrowing fairly extensively from Turkish and other languages. It was adopted as the language of administration and education in Greece in 1976 (so that the linguistic situation in Greece is now very different from that described by Ferguson in the 1950s).

Ferguson's representation of the functional distribution of H and L varieties in these instances is given below.

	H	L
Sermon in church or mosque	x	
Instructions to servants, waiters, workmen, clerks		x
Personal letter	x	
Speech in parliament, political speech	x	
University lecture	x	
Conversation with family, friends, colleagues		x
News broadcast	x	
Radio 'soap opera'		x
Newspaper editorial, news story, caption on picture	x	
Caption on political cartoon		x
Poetry	x	
Folk literature		x

With regard to the lexical differences between the H and L varieties he discusses, Ferguson gives the following examples (among others) of *lexical doublets*.

	H	L	
Arabic in Egypt			
	'al'āna	*dilwa'ti*	'now'
	'anfun	*manaxīr*	'nose'
	mā	*'ēh*	'what'

	H	L	
German in Switzerland			
	jemand	*öpper*	'someone'
	klein	*chly*	'small'
	nachdem	*no*	'after'
French and Creole in Haiti			
	âne	*bourik*	'donkey'
	beaucoup	*âpil*	'much', 'a lot'
	donner	*bay*	'give'
Greek			
	éteke	*eyénise*	'gave birth'
	ídhor	*neró*	'water'
	íkos	*spíti*	'house'

What Ferguson describes under the heading of diglossia can be seen as a special case of *code-switching*. We have already (at the end of 7.5) looked at *conversational code-switching*, where the practice of alternating between two distinct varieties seems to be just an unspoken convention of a particular group. However, there is another type of code-switching – *situational code-switching* – where the switch between varieties is triggered by the situation in which communication is proceeding. The switch from Swiss German to Standard German as a speaker moves from a conversation with family to giving a lecture or filling in a form in a tax office is precisely such a case. In classic diglossic cases, as we have seen, the two varieties are widely perceived as High and Low versions of the 'same language'. In other instances of situational code-switching this need not apply. To take a very obvious example, if I take a train from London to Paris, I shall begin my journey (buy my ticket etc.) in one language – English – and end it (ask directions to my hotel etc.) in another – French.

A third type of code-switching which needs to mentioned – for the sake of completeness – is that known as *metaphorical code-switching*. This term is applied where the switch between varieties is triggered by a change of topic. When the topic changes the effect on language use is *as if* the situation were changed; hence 'metaphorical'. A much-quoted example of metaphorical code-switching refers to the linguistic goings on in a community administration office in Norway, where the clerks used standard or local dialect phrases with each other according to whether or not they were talking about official matters, and where members of the public interacted with the clerks in the standard variety or local dialect depending on whether they were transacting business or engaging in small talk at the beginning or end of the transaction.

Most of us who have acquired and made use of more than one language during the course of our lives will have been involved in code-switching of some kind or other at some point. *All* of us will have been involved in what is usually called *style-shifting* – that is to say, in making relatively subtle changes in the language we use in response to differences in context – adjusting what we say or write to make it appropriate to more formal or less formal situations, for instance. With regard to the lexical aspects of style-shifting, some expressions are relatively neutral in respect of the kinds of contexts in which they are likely to occur, some are identifiable as unlikely to be used in formal circumstances, whilst others are unlikely to be associated with informal communication. The following examples illustrate this for British English.

FORMAL	NEUTRAL	INFORMAL
diminutive	*small*	*teeny-weeny*
garments	*clothes*	*threads*
offspring	*child*	*sprog*
voluminous	*large*	*whopping*
weep	*cry*	*blub*

The association of given words with particular kinds of contexts has a major influence on what impact they will have in other contexts. Thus, for example, between close friends or colleagues at the end of a hard day an expression like *I'm shagged* (in the sense of 'I'm really tired') will cause not a ripple. Offered as a contribution to polite small talk with a visiting dignitary at a glittering civic reception, on the other hand, its effect will be somewhat different. There is another sense too in which context determines how words are received. One of the most interesting books on language of the twentieth century was a small volume called *How to do things with words* published by a philosopher by the name of John Langshaw Austin. Austin was particularly interested in what he called *performative* utterances, the saying of which both perform specific acts and explicitly refer to the acts in question, for example:

ENTERING INTO MARRIAGE

With this ring I thee <u>wed</u> . . .

PUTTING ONESELF UNDER OATH

I <u>swear</u> by Almighty God that the evidence which I shall give will be the truth, the whole truth and nothing but the truth.

NAMING A SHIP

I <u>name</u> this ship Titanic II . . .

Austin also noted that in order for acts such as those referred to above to take effect, certain *felicity conditions* had to be fulfilled. In order for *With this ring I thee wed* to 'work', for instance, the marriage has to have been consented to by both the parties to it and by the religious and/or civic authorities validating it, vows have to have been taken, a ring has to be put on the finger of the addressee, and the entire ceremony has to take place in front of witnesses, including at least one witness (priest, mayor, registrar, captain of ship etc.) empowered by Church and/or State to be the official overseer of proceedings. The same words uttered by a deeply smitten ten-year-old romeo to his giggling girlfriend behind the school bicycle-sheds (even if accompanied by the offering of a ring) will simply not do the job – at least not the job of admitting the happy couple to the holy estate of matrimony!

Actually, as Austin himself noted, and as other writers on the topic have since emphasized, we perform an act of some kind not only when we make a highly conventionalized utterance in a formal public ceremony such as a wedding, but every single time we use language. There may be some kind of ritual involved – as in the above cases; we may explicitly name the act we are performing – as in the above cases and also in cases like *I hereby* <u>*approve*</u> *this claim* (APPROVAL), *I* <u>*congratulate*</u> *you on your success* (CONGRATULA-TION), *I* <u>*promise*</u> *I'll be there* (PROMISE); or the act may be signalled by an interaction between the words we use and the context in which we use them; for example, *Could you please pass the salt?* and *Is there any salt?* will both be interpreted as requests (for the salt cellar to be passed) if uttered at table by a diner too far from the salt to reach it him/herself. The acts in question usually go under the label of *speech acts* in the relevant literature, but they would more appropriately be called *language acts*, since they are the substance and the results of any kind of linguistic communication – whether in speech, writing or sign.

To return to the question of the role of context, the act performed by any set of words will vary according to the situation in which they are produced. For example, *Is there any salt?* uttered by an irritated teenager to his/her poor harassed parents in the presence of an open cupboard from which salt is very obviously missing performs the act of complaining rather than (or as well as) requesting; in other contexts, such as the collective inspection of the partially stocked kitchen of a flat being borrowed for the weekend by a group of friends, the same utterance will constitute a simple enquiry. Similarly, the word *cheers* uttered to the accompaniment of the raising of a glass constitutes a toast; uttered in the context of the departure of the utterer it constitutes a leave-taking; uttered in response to a kindness it constitutes an act of thanking.

7.8 Lexical variation, culture and thought

Finally in this chapter we shall very briefly explore lexical variation in a somewhat different sense. If we look at the language varieties used in different countries and communities around the world we shall quickly come recognize that, while in many instances they have different words for the same concepts, for example American English *gasoline*, British English *petrol*, French *essence*, German *Benzin* etc., there are many other instances in which they lexicalize reality differently. That is to say, the range of concepts covered by vocabulary and the ways in which the concepts in question are bundled together in words will tend to diverge from variety to variety. We saw this in our discussion of structuralist perspectives on meaning in Chapter 5, when we noted that different languages deal differently with the colour spectrum. Similarly, different languages deal differently with how they package concepts of kinship. Even two languages as relatively close as English and Swedish differ in this regard; thus, whereas English has just one word, *grandmother*, to signify female grandparents on both the mother's and the father's side, and one word, *grandfather*, to signify male grandparents on both the mother's and the father's side, Swedish has separate words for 'mother's mother' (*mormor*) and 'father's mother' (*farmor*), and, similarly, separate words for 'mother's father' (*morfar*) and 'father's father' (*farfar*). Another example – this time from two varieties of English – concerns the dividing up of the day. In British English each day has a *morning* period, an *afternoon* period, an *evening* period and a *night* period; in some varieties of Hiberno-English, on the other hand, *afternoon* is missing, and *evening* covers the entire period from noon until the onset of the *night* period. Two questions arise from such divergences: (i) do they reflect meaningful cultural distinctions relative to the groups using the varieties in question (*culture* and *cultural* in this context being applied to whole pattern of life in a society rather than just to its 'high cultural' activities such as poetry and music), and (ii) do they result in differences in the ways in which different groups perceive the world.

With regard to the first of the above questions, it is widely assumed that the greater the lexical differentiation in a linguistic variety in respect of any given semantic field, the greater the cultural significance of that field for the community using the variety in question. The old cliché in this connection about Eskimos having dozens of words for 'snow' turns out to be something of an exaggeration. However, the general notion which it is meant to illustrate is not seriously disputed, and it is quite easily demonstrable without resorting to examples from the frozen north. An example that occurs to me every time I read a nineteenth-century novel relates to horse-drawn vehicles. In the nineteenth century the horse-drawn carriage was highly important both as a means of transport and as a marker of social status; correspondingly there were large numbers of words in use which denoted various aspects of horse-drawn transport – including words denoting different types of vehicle: *barouche*, *brougham*, *chaise*, *landau*, *phaeton* etc. How many English-speakers at the beginning of the twenty-first century would have even the vaguest idea what a barouche or a brougham might be? To take an instance even closer to home, in this case referring to vocabulary associated with a particular academic subculture, the present book contains dozens of terms – from *allophone* to *syllabary* – which refer to absolutely basic distinctions within linguistics, but which simply do not figure (because they do not need to figure) in the lexical equipment available to most non-linguists. Such anecdotal observations have been verified more scientifically; for example, an intercultural study conducted in the 1970s revealed that languages do not have vocabulary for cooking practices that are not used in the cultures with which the languages are associated.

It is, let it be said, always possible to talk about the entities that words denote even if the particular lexical labels do not exist. If we did not have the word *landau*, we could always say something like 'four-wheeled enclosed carriage with a removable front cover and a back cover that can be raised and lowered' (the *Concise Oxford Dictionary* definition), and if we did not have the word *syllabary* we could always evoke the relevant concept with an expression such as 'writing-system whose characters represent syllables'. However, obviously, having the applicable words at our disposal makes life much easier, especially if we are in a society or a profession where landaus or syllabaries have some importance and where we need to speak or write about them relatively frequently. Indeed, if a concept attains significance in the life of a particular group and a term does not exist for the concept in question, then it is very likely that a word will be created to cover the case.

Some chilling illustrations of such lexical innovation are provided by the British linguist Michael Stubbs, who currently works in Germany. Stubbs summarizes an article from a German student newspaper which critically examines the racist lexicon of the political right – items such as: *Fremdenhass* ('hatred of foreigners'), *Scheinasylanten* ('apparent/sham political asylum seekers') and *Überfremdung* ('infiltration by foreigners'); Stubbs cites with approval the article's argument that 'such lexical creations crystallize thoughts, make them easy to refer to, presuppose the existence of such things'. In the realm of love rather than hate, some decidedly more pleasing examples are to be found in the lexical coinages of certain American groups experimenting with new approaches to relationships and who have invented terms such as *polyamory* (to refer to the notion of having responsible, loving, sexual relationships with more than one partner at a time) and *polyfidelity* (to refer to the idea of being sexually faithful to a group of people rather than to just one partner).

Moving on to the question of lexis and thought, whereas, as we have seen, it is possible to represent new thinking by coining new expressions, we do not start from square one in the matter of linguistic representation. When we acquire our first language, that language provides us with one particular set of possibilities of expressing experience and fails to make available other possibilities. For example, English makes available a multitude of words for different colours and thus facilitates the expression of quite subtle distinctions in relation to visual experience; on the other hand, English is much less well-endowed than some other languages with ways of signifying finely graded degrees of distance and intimacy between individuals.

According to some linguists such differences between languages and language varieties determine the way in which we perceive the world and think about it – our *Weltbild* or 'picture of the world'. This idea goes back to ancient times: the early Latin poet Quintus Ennius apparently used to say that because he had three languages, he had *'tria cordia'* ('three hearts'); it also surfaced in the work of the nineteenth-century German linguist Wilhelm von Humboldt, who believed that the *Sprachform* ('language shape') and thought of a people were inseparable. In its more modern manifestation, however, this view is commonly referred to as the Sapir–Whorf hypothesis – after two American linguists, Edward Sapir and Benjamin Lee Whorf, who devoted a great deal of attention to it in the first half of the twentieth century. A quotation from each of these two scholars in turn, starting with Sapir, will give an immediate idea of their standpoint:

> Human beings ... are at the mercy of the particular language which has become the medium of expression for their society ... No two languages are ever sufficiently alike to be considered as representing the same social reality. The worlds in which different societies live are distinct worlds, not the same world with different labels attached.

> The linguistic system of each language is not merely a reproducing system for voicing ideas, but rather is itself the shaper of ideas, the program and guide for the individual's mental activity, for his analysis of impressions, for his synthesis of his mental stock-in-trade ... We dissect nature along lines laid down by our native languages.

The kinds of arguments that have been put against a strongly deterministic interpretation of the Sapir–Whorf hypothesis – the notion that we absolutely cannot escape from the categories imposed by our native language – include the fact that:

- we can learn languages other than our first language and can thus enter into other representations of reality;

- we can talk about and understand categorizations of reality other than those made available by our native language (as Sapir and Whorf both demonstrate!);

- in broad terms at least, the same needs (e.g. for food and drink), problems (e.g. sickness) and existential boundaries (i.e. birth and death) are present in all human societies, so that, again in broad terms at least, we all have common points of reference.

These arguments are persuasive and are supported by the findings of experimental studies which fail to support the notion that language determines perception.

However, it is possible to conceive of a more moderate reading of the hypothesis – the idea that the categories of our native language have a pre-disposing influence on the way in which we deal with the world even if they do not rule out other options. This weaker version of the hypothesis has some evidence on its side. For example, some years ago a study was carried out which investigated whether Navajo-speaking children and English-speaking children differed in the way in which they sorted objects of various shapes and colours. In the Navajo language, unlike in English, the shape of an object involved in the action referred to by a verb has important effects on the form of the verb, and so the hypothesis was that the Navajo-speakers would be more inclined than the English-speakers to sort by shape rather than colour – which indeed proved to be the case. The message of this and other studies with similar results seems to be that, although Sapir and Whorf may have somewhat overplayed their hand, their contention that specific features of languages we know can have an effect on aspects of how we process experience appears to hold water.

7.9   Summary

Chapter 7 began with a brief introduction to the notion of language variation followed by the definition and exemplification of some basic sociolinguistic concepts relative to this phenomenon – notably those of *variety* and *variable*. The chapter then proceeded to consider language variation in relation to geography, social class, ethnicity, gender and context, showing that in each case there was a clear lexical dimension to the variation in question. Finally, reference was made to the possible implications of lexical variation from group to group and community to community – in terms of types and degrees of lexical differentiation in different conceptual spheres – in respect of intercultural distinctions and differences in the perception of reality; the conclusions from this part of the discussion were that differences in vocabulary structure reflect cultural differences, and that, while the specific features of particular languages (including lexical features) do not *determine* perception, they do seem to have some influence on the processing of experience.

Sources and suggestions for further reading

See 7.1. The examples of gender-based variation are taken from Chapter 13 of R. Wardhaugh's book *An introduction to sociolinguistics* (third edition, Oxford: Blackwell, 1998).

See 7.2. The case of the varieties spoken along the Dutch–German border is something of a cliché in sociolinguistics. However, I was fortunate enough to experience it as a fascinating daily reality when, during my undergraduate years, I spent time in the Vorrink household in the German village of Neuenhaus (near Nordhorn). The Norwegian, Danish and Swedish examples in 7.2 were gleaned from the *Collins Scandinavian phrase book* edited by L. Myking (London: Collins, 1959). The reference to Black English is based on p. 333 of R. Wardhaugh's *An introduction to sociolinguistics* (third

edition, Oxford: Blackwell, 1998). The figures on *h*-dropping in British
English are taken from J. Milroy and L. Milroy's article 'Varieties and variation' in F. Coulmas (ed.), *The handbook of sociolinguistics* (Oxford:
Blackwell, 49); the Milroys cite these figures from J. K. Chambers and P.
Trudgill's book *Dialectology* (Cambridge: Cambridge University Press,
1980, 69). The Martha's Vineyard study referred to is W. Labov's 'The social
motivation of a sound change' (*Word* 19, 1963, 273–309).

See 7.4. A. S. C. Ross's article on 'U' and 'non-U' lexis is: 'Linguistic class-
indicators in present-day English' (*Neuphilologische Mitteilungen* 55, 1954,
20–56; reprinted in revised form under the title 'U and Non-U: an essay in
sociological linguistics' in N. Mitford (ed.), *Noblesse oblige*, London:
Hamish Hamilton, 1956). F. Ogden Nash's comment on the Wicked Queen's
non-U status is to be found in *You can't get there from here* (1957). The Fries
study of working-class and professional correspondents' use of English is
referred to in C. C. Fries, *American English grammar* (New York:
Appleton–Century–Crofts, 1940). The study of the language used in inter-
views is reported in L. Schatzman and A. Strauss's article 'Social class and
modes of communication' (*American Journal of Sociology* 60, 1955,
329–38). The account of this study and the Fries study given here is based on
the second section of Chapter 8 in W. P. Robinson's book *Language and
social behaviour* (Harmondsworth: Penguin, 1972). The characteristics of
restricted and elaborated codes presented here are derived from B.
Bernstein's account in his article 'Social structure, language and learning'
(*Educational Research* 3, 1961, 163–76). Studies which appear to validate
Bernstein's lexical claims include those reported in: B. Bernstein, 'Social
class, linguistic codes and grammatical elements' (*Language and Speech* 5,
1962, 221–40); D. Lawton, *Social class, language and education* (London:
Routledge & Kegan Paul, 1968); W. P. Robinson, 'The elaborated code in
working class' (*Language and Speech* 8, 243–52). Critical reactions to
Bernstein's work are to be found in: M. C. Coulthard, 'A discussion of
restricted and elaborated codes' (*Educational Review* 22, 1969, 38–51); W.
Labov, *Sociolinguistic patterns*, (Philadelphia: University of Pennsylvania
Press, 1972); H. Rosen, *Language and class: a critical look at the theories of
Basil Bernstein* (Bristol: Falling Wall Press, 1972).

See 7.5. The definition of ethnicity in the first paragraph of 7.5 is that
offered by J. A. Fishman on p. 329 of his article 'Language and ethnicity: the
view from within' (in F. Coulmas (ed.), *The handbook of sociolinguistics*,
Oxford: Blackwell, 1997). The quotation about Hebrew in the next paragraph is cited by Fishman in the same article (p. 331) from an essay published in 1908 by Yaakov Nakht. The account of the Belgian situation is
based on pp. 295–6 of P. H. Nelde's article 'Language conflict' (in F.
Coulmas (ed.), *The handbook of sociolinguistics*, Oxford: Blackwell, 1997).
The reference to the Turkish community in the Netherlands is informed by
A. Backus's book *Two in one: bilingual speech of Turkish immigrants in the*

Netherlands (Tilburg: Tilburg University Press). Viv Edwards's study of Jamaican Patois is reported in her book *Language in a black community* (Clevedon: Multilingual Matters Ltd, 1986). The article on Puerto-Rican code-switching referred to is S. Poplack's 'Sometimes I'll start a sentence in English *y termino en español*: toward a typology of code-switching', (*Linguistics* 18, 1980, 581–616)'.

See 7.6. The reference to Queen Elizabeth I at the beginning of 7.6 is cited from F. A. Shirley, *Swearing and perjury in Shakespeare's plays* (London: Allen & Unwin, 1979, 10) by G. Hughes in *Swearing: a social history of foul language, oaths and profanity in English* (second edition, London: Penguin, 1998, 103). The Defoe quotations is also borrowed from Hughes's book (p. 209), and the quotation from Lakoff's study (*Language and woman's place*, New York: Harper & Row, 1975) is borrowed from p. 211 of the same source. V. Cook, from whom I have borrowed the reference to *Absolutely Fabulous!* reports the gender-related findings of his informal survey on p. 160 of *Inside language* (London: Arnold, 1997).

See 7.7. C. Ferguson's article 'Diglossia' – referred to at length in 7.7 first appeared in *Word* 15, 1959 (325–40); it is reprinted as Chapter 11 of P. P. Giglioli (ed.), *Language and social context* (Harmondsworth: Penguin, 1972). The example of metaphorical code-switching is taken from p. 425 of J-P. Blom and J. J. Gumperz's article 'Social meaning in linguistic structure: code-switching in Norway' (in J. J. Gumperz and D. H. Hymes (eds), *Directions in sociolinguistics: the ethnography of communication*, New York: Holt, Rinehart & Winston, 1972). J. L. Austin's book *How to do things with words* was first published in 1962 (Oxford: Clarendon Press).

See 7.8. The German examples of lexical innovation cited in 7.8 and M. Stubbs's discussion of these examples are to be found on p. 366 of Stubbs's article 'Language and the mediation of experience: linguistic representation and cognitive orientation' (in F. Coulmas (ed.), *The handbook of sociolinguistics*, Oxford: Blackwell, 1997). The American lexical coinages regarding multiple relationships feature in the publications of, among many others, D. Anapol (see, e.g. her book *Polyamory: the new love without limits*, Initinet Resources Center, 1997). The quotation from E. Sapir is from p. 209 of his article 'The status of linguistics as a science' (*Language* 5, 1929, 207–14), and the quotation from B. L. Whorf is from pp. 212–13 of *Language, thought and reality: selected writings of Benjamin Lee Whorf* (edited by J. B. Carroll, Cambridge, MA: MIT Press, 1956). References to the experimental evidence regarding the Sapir–Whorf hypothesis are informed by pp. 81–125 of R. E. Cromer's book *Language and thought in normal and handicapped children* (Oxford: Blackwell, 1991); the experiment involving Navajo-speakers, summarized on pp. 97–8 of Cromer's book, is reported in J. B. Carroll and J. B. Casagrande, 'The function of language classifications in behaviour' (in E. E. Maccoby, T. M. Newcomb and E. L. Hartley (eds), *Readings in social psychology*, third edition, New York: Holt, Rinehart & Winston, 1958).

The area of sociolinguistics – more than any other area of linguistics in my view – is extremely well served as far as the range of well-written accessible introductions is concerned. The following four titles all fall into this category, and all deal, to a greater or lesser extent, with lexical dimensions of language variation:

> J. Holmes, *Sociolinguistics: an introduction to language and society* (Harlow: Longman, 1992);
> R.A. Hudson, *Sociolinguistics* (second edition, Cambridge: Cambridge University Press, 1996);
> P. Trudgill, *Sociolinguistics: an introduction* (second edition, London: Penguin, 1995);
> R. Wardhaugh, *An introduction to sociolinguistics* (third edition, Oxford: Blackwell, 1997).

Very readable but rather shorter introductions to this topic are to be found in Chapter 8 of V. Cook's *Inside language* (London: Arnold, 1997) and Chapter 10 of V. Fromkin and R. Rodman's *An introduction to language* (sixth edition, New York: Holt, Rinehart & Winston, 1996).

Readers looking wishing to explore further may wish to consult:

> F. Coulmas (ed.), *The handbook of sociolinguistics* (Oxford: Blackwell, 1997);
> N. Coupland and A. Jaworski (eds), *Sociolinguistics: a reader and coursebook* (London: Macmillan, 1997);
> R. W. Fasold, *Sociolinguistics of society* (Oxford: Blackwell, 1984);
> R. W. Fasold, *Sociolinguistics of language* (Oxford: Blackwell, 1990).

With regard to particular aspects of language variation, the following titles are recommended.

Geographical variation:

> J. Cheshire (ed.), *English around the world* (Cambridge: Cambridge University Press, 1991);
> P. Trudgill, *Dialects* (London: Routledge, 1994).

Social variation:

> L. Milroy, *Language and social networks* (second edition, Oxford: Blackwell, 1987);
> P. Trudgill, *The social differentiation of English in Norwich* (Cambridge: Cambridge University Press, 1974).

Ethnic variation:

> V. Edwards, *Language in a black community* (Clevedon: Multilingual Matters, 1986);
> W. Labov, *Language in the inner city: studies in the Black English vernacular* (Philadelphia: University of Pennsylvania Press).

Gender-related variation:

> J. Coates, *Men, women and language: a sociolinguistic account of gender differences in language* (London: Longman, 1993);
>
> S. Mills, *Language and gender: interdisciplinary perspectives* (London: Longman, 1995).

Context-related variation:

> B. Myers-Scotton, *Social motivation for code-switching* (Oxford: Clarendon, 1993).

Lexis, culture and thought:

> J. A. Lucy, *Language diversity and thought: a reformulation of the linguistic relativity hypothesis* (Cambridge: Cambridge University Press, 1992);
>
> A. Wierzbicka, *Understanding cultures through their key words* (Oxford: Oxford University Press, 1997).

Focusing questions/topics for discussion

1. In 7.3 we looked at some differences between American English words and their British English equivalents. Try to find some more examples of lexical differences between American English and British English and/or between any other two subvarieties of a language with which you are familiar.

2. We saw in 7.4 that a number of attempts have been made to identify words or types of words which are particularly associated with particular social classes. Try to come up with some suggestions of your own in this connection – with reference either to English or to any other language you know.

3. In 7.5 Belgium was mentioned as an example of a country where different ethnic groups – defined partly by language – live relatively separate from each other. Can you think of other countries where similar kinds of situations obtain?

4. In 7.6 we noted – with respect to English and French – some words and word-forms which identify the speaker/writer as male or female (e.g. *I'm a monk* (MALE), *Je suis étudiante* (FEMALE)). Try to add further items to the list for either or both of the languages mentioned, or begin a new list of such items for any other language you know.

5. As we saw in 7.7, one of the dimensions of context-related variation is the association of particular words with formal, informal or neutral styles of speech and writing. How would you classify each of the following words in terms of formality, informality or neutrality?

alacrity	*greedy*	*mind*	*snot*
buy	*hyped*	*naughty*	*trouble*
chuck	*inexplicable*	*opulent*	*undergarments*
daft	*jumbo*	*pee*	*vamp*
enervating	*kinky*	*quick*	*watch*
fart	*limpid*	*remuneration*	*yuppy*

6. In 7.8 we considered the different degrees and kinds of lexical differentiation that exist from language variety to language variety. What groups or communities – professional, political, national or international – would you expect to be using linguistic varieties with a high level of lexical differentiation in each of the following spheres (and why)?

beer	*fire*
calligraphy	*horses*
cheese	*pollution*
clouds	*sausages*
cricket (the game)	*tea*

| 8 |

Lexical change

8.1 Language in motion

Chaucer's *Troilus and Criseyde* (1385) contains five lines that often find their way into books about language as well as into general dictionaries of quotations. In these lines Chaucer notes that over the centuries the forms of language are marked by change, to the extent that words of long ago seem strange to us, but that life – in particular, love – goes on whatever the shape of the words in which it is conducted:

> Ye knowe ek that in forme of speche is chaunge
> Withinne a thousand yeer, and wordes tho
> That hadden pris, now wonder nyce and straunge
> Us thinketh hem, and yet thei spake hem so
> And spedde as wel in love as men now do.

Chaucer's philosophical, accepting attitude to language change is mirrored in the comments of Ferdinand de Saussure in his *Cours de linguistique générale* (*Course in general linguistics*, first published in 1916) from which, as was mentioned in an earlier chapter, modern linguistics takes much of its inspiration:

> Time changes all things; there is no reason why language should escape this universal law.

> Every part of language is subjected to change ... The stream of language flows without interruption; whether its course is calm or torrential is of secondary importance.

In fact, linguistics had been looking at language change long before Saussure arrived on the scene. Indeed, for the hundred years or so before the publication of Saussure's major work, linguistics was almost totally preoccupied with comparing different languages and examining particular languages at different historical stages in order to trace the evolution of languages and language families. Saussure's contribution to linguistics, actually, was to broaden its horizons by demonstrating that the *synchronic* study of languages (the study of languages at any given point in their development) was every bit as fascinating as the *diachronic* study of languages (the study of languages in their development through time). This is not to say that diachronic or historical linguistics is a thing of the past. On the contrary, at the present time it is attracting some extremely dynamic researchers, who in their exploration of historical issues are drawing on insights from across the entire spectrum of contemporary linguistics. However, the core methodologies of historical linguistics – the *comparative method* and *internal reconstruction* – have remained substantially unchanged since the nineteenth century. We shall take a brief general look at these methodologies before homing in on language change in the specifically lexical domain.

8.2 The comparative method and internal reconstruction

The comparative method has its origins in the event which launched historical linguistics, namely the beginning of the serious study of ancient Indian language of Sanskrit by Western scholars at the end of the eighteenth century – in the wake of French and British colonization of India. A number of European visitors to India had in earlier times noticed similarities between Sanskrit words and words in European languages, but in 1786 Sir William Jones of the East India Company read a paper to the Royal Asiatic Society in Calcutta in which he provided persuasive evidence and arguments in favour of the notion that Sanskrit was related to Latin and Greek and also suggested that it might be linked to the Germanic languages and the Celtic languages.

Essentially, what Jones did intuitively – noticing resemblances between languages and positing a common source on the basis of such resemblances – the comparative method does systematically. The method can be illustrated by reference to some data from three Romance languages, Spanish, Italian and French:

SPANISH	ITALIAN	FRENCH	
cuerpo (/'kuerpo/)	*corpo* /'kɔrpo/)	*corps*(/kɔʀ/)	'body'
color (/kɔ'lɔr/)	*colore* (/kɔ'lɔre/)	*couleur* (/kulœʀ/)	'colour'
caro (/'karo/)	*caro* (/'karo/)	*cher* (/ʃɛʀ/)	'dear'

Even the casual observer will notice that these are similar forms with similar meanings and will be led by these similarities to speculate that the words in question may be *cognates*, that is, derived from shared origins The historical linguist will go on to look at hundreds of words in each language; will hypothesize, on the basis of finding a constant recurrence of such resemblances, that Spanish, Italian and French are descendants of the same parent language; and will seek to establish what the forms of the parent language might be by examining the correspondences between the forms of the three languages. For example, from the fact that two of the three languages have a *p*-sound in the word for 'body', the inference will be drawn that this *p*-sound probably existed in the original form; and the fact that two of the three languages begin the words for 'dear' with /ka/ rather than /ʃɛ/ will be seen as suggesting that /ka/ rather than /ʃɛ/ was original.

In the above cases it is possible to check the results of this approach, because we know that the Romance languages are all descended from Latin (*daughter languages* of Latin, as the terminology goes), and we know that the Latin words for 'body', 'colour' and 'dear' were, respectively, *corpus*, *color* and *carus*. However, where we have samples of historically related languages but no traces of the parent language, the comparative method is our 'best bet', as far as trying to discover the original forms is concerned. For instance, let us compare the relevant forms of the word for 'father' in Sanskrit, Greek, Latin, Gothic and Old Irish:

Sanskrit:	*pitā*
Greek:	*patēr*
Latin:	*pater*
Gothic:	*fadar*
Old Irish:	*athir*

On the basis of these data, and using the same approach as with Spanish, Italian and French, we can say that in all likelihood the original form from which the above forms are descended had /p/ as its initial consonant (shifted to /f/ in Gothic, lost in Old Irish), that its middle consonant was /t/ (shifted to /d/ in Gothic and to a *th* sound – /θ/ – in Old Irish), and that its final consonant was /r/ (lost in Sanskrit). In fact, historical linguists, having looked at the above examples – and having taken account of data from many other sources – have come to the conclusion that the word from which all of them descended was something like *pətər* (where ə stands for a neutral vowel like the *e* sound in as in *mow<u>er</u>* – and * signifies that the form is 'reconstructed' rather than attested).

Using the comparative method, historical linguists came to the conclusion that not only the languages mentioned by Jones but also a number of other languages across Europe and Asia belonged to the same family – usually referred to as *Indo-European* – all being descendants of a language to which the label *Proto-Indo-European* was attached. *Proto-* comes from a Greek word *prótos* (πρῶτος), which simply means 'first'. It is also applied to the ancestor languages of groups of languages within the Indo-European family; thus, the term *Proto-Germanic* is applied to the (unattested) ancestor of Dutch, German, Swedish etc. The schema below presents a (highly simplified) historical overview of the Indo-European 'family':

PROTO-INDO-EUROPEAN

PROTO-CELTIC	PROTO-GERMANIC	LATIN	GREEK	PROTO-BALTO-SLAVIC	PROTO-INDO-IRANIAN
Old Irish	Gothic	Early	Classical	Early Baltic	Old
Britannic	Early West	Southern	Greek	Early South	Iranian
	Germanic	Romance		Slavic	Sanskrit
	Early North	Early		Early West	
	Germanic	Eastern		Slavic	
		Romance		Early East	
		Early		Slavic	
		Western			
		Romance			
Irish Gaelic	German	Sardinian	Modern	Lithuanian	Persian
Scots Gaelic	Dutch	Sicilian	Greek	Lettish	Kurdish
Manx Gaelic	Afrikaans	Romanian		Croatian	Bengali
Cornish	English	Italian		Serbian	Hindi
Welsh	Icelandic	Spanish		Slovenian	Marathi
Breton	Norwegian	Portuguese		Bulgarian	Gujerati
	Danish	Catalan		Czech	
	Swedish	French		Slovak	
				Polish	
				Ukrainian	
				Russian	

Through the application of the comparative method on a wider scale, similar kinds of 'family-trees' have been arrived at for many other language families.

In the case of language families, such as the Indo-European family, with large numbers of modern representatives and with written records going back thousands of years, the comparative method works well. The more languages that are available, the richer the data to which the method can be applied; and the longer the written record, the easier it is to trace such languages – via their earlier forms – back to a common origin. For example, if the Indo-European family were represented by just two modern languages, French and Modern Irish, linking Modern Irish *athair* to French *père* would be a good deal less obvious than is in fact the case thanks to the availability of other modern forms like Spanish *padre* and English *father*, and thanks also to the availability of older forms such as Latin *pater*. There are, however, cases where the ideal conditions for the comparative method are not in place – cases, for example, where only a few representatives (sometimes just one) of a language family have been discovered and/or a language family is represented by data from just one historical period. In cases like this historical linguists resort to internal reconstruction – that is, they try to infer conclusions about the historical development of the language from internal evidence.

For purposes of illustration, let us consider how internal reconstruction might operate with regard to an aspect of German (about whose history, in fact, we know a great deal). In German, word-final plosive consonants are always voiceless. Thus, the consonant written *b* in *lieb* ('dear') is pronounced /p/ (just like the consonant written *p* in *Typ* – 'type'); the consonant written *d* in *Bund* ('bond', 'federation') is pronounced /t/ (just like the consonant written *t* in *bunt* – 'colourful'); and the consonant written *g* in *Tag* ('day') is pronounced /k/ (just like the consonant written *ck* in *Sack* – 'sack'). When, however, words ending in *b*, *d* and *g* are involved in morphological processes which add vowels to the consonants in question, their final consonants are then voiced. Thus, for instance, *lieber* in *mein lieber Freund* ('my dear friend') is pronounced /ˈliːbər/ (compare *Typen* – 'types' – pronounced /ˈtypən/); similarly, *Bundes* in the expression *die Bundesrepublik* ('the Federal Republic') is pronounced /bundəs/ (compare *bunte* in *bunte Blumen* – 'colourful flowers' – , pronounced /buntə/); and *Tage* in *früh am Tage* ('early in the day) is pronounced /taːgə/ (compare *Sackes* in *des Sackes* – 'of the sack' – , pronounced /zakəs/). This alternation between voiced and voiceless realizations of consonants in certain words is likely to suggest to the historical linguist that at an earlier stage there may have been a single form and that the divergent pronunciations depending on the presence or absence of an additional vowel may have been a later development. In other words, the historical linguist reconstructing the history of the language from which modern German developed on the basis of internal evidence may posit that at an earlier point in the evolution of that language the lexical ancestor of *lieb* would always have been pronounced with a final /b/, the lexical ancestor of *Bund* would always have been pronounced with a final /d/ and the lexical ancestor of *Tag* would always have been pronounced with a final /g/.

In this particular instance supplementary evidence for the proposal in question is present in the spellings of the words concerned, which point to an earlier single form in each case. Thanks to the existence of written forms of Germanic languages over hundreds of years we can also check the plausibility of the internally constructed solution arrived at by looking back to earlier versions of words like *lieb*, *Bund* and *Tag*; with regard to the final consonant of *Tag*, for example, we can note that in Old English the word for 'day' was *dæg*. Given that we know of numerous other modern languages which are closely related to German, we can also check the internally reconstructed solution by examining cognate forms in these languages; for instance we can note that the word for 'day' in Danish, Icelandic, Norwegian and Swedish is *dag*. Such confirmation of the internally arrived at solution by other means in this kind of case encourages historical linguists to have some confidence in internal reconstruction in instances where longstanding orthographic evidence and/or comparative evidence is not available.

As a final comment on the above, it may be worth underscoring the fact that the entire comparative–historical enterprise starts from and is carried forward by a focus on lexis. Linguists hypothesize historical links between languages on the basis of noting large numbers of lexical resemblances; they come to conclusions about the developments within language families and individual languages by comparing, where possible, the details of similar lexical forms across languages thought to be related at different stages of the evolution of those languages; and, where there are limitations on the possibility of cross-language and/or cross-period comparison, they attempt to reconstruct the earlier shape of a language by examining the alternating forms of words which exist in the particular state of the language to which they have access. Whatever a historical linguist's chosen destination – in terms of phonology, syntax, semantics etc. – his/her point of departure and means of transport will inevitably be lexical.

8.3   Changes in lexical form

As we saw in Chapter 6, the view of historical linguists used to be that a given phonological change affected the entire language system at more or less the same time, the same sound in the same environment always shifting in precisely the same way. We also saw that this notion is mistaken. What actually happens is that when a sound change gets under way it spreads on a word by word basis through the lexicon in a process known as *lexical diffusion*. A further example of lexical diffusion comes from Modern Welsh, where words beginning with *chw-* in their written form are increasingly pronounced as if the *ch* (pronounced as in Scots Gaelic – and English – *loch*) were not there. That is, these words, which used to be pronounced with an initial /xw/ sound are now often pronounced with a simple /w/. Interestingly, this shift affected some words before others; thus the word *chwarae* ('to play') was observed to be likely to be pronounced without initial /x/ at an earlier stage than the word *chwannen* ('flea'), and this latter word was observed to be likely to be pronounced without initial /x/ at an earlier stage than the word *chwaer* ('sister').

Another traditional assumption of historical linguistics is that sound changes are regular. If this assumption were not made then the use of correspondences between words in different languages to establish historical relationships would lack any kind of foundation. How, for example, could we be justified in attributing any significance to the correspondences Latin *pater*:Gothic *fadar* ('father'), Latin *pes*:Gothic *fotu* ('foot'), Latin *pellis*: Gothic *fill* ('skin') etc., if we were to assume that a sound like initial /p/ in a given language – Proto-Indo-European, for example – might sometimes change to /f/ in a given daughter language, and sometimes, quite randomly, to entirely different sounds – /g/, /n/, /r/ etc. Clearly, unlike the claim that sound changes affect all relevant contexts in a language simultaneously, the idea that sound changes are regular has to be accepted as a general principle. On the other hand, individual words do sometimes go their own way in phonological terms.

A good example of such individual development is provided by the word *esprit* ('spirit') in French. *Esprit* derives from Latin *spiritus*, a word which, in the days when Latin was the language of the Roman Catholic Church, would have been very widely used and heard in religious contexts – for example, in the invocation of the Trinity ('*In nomine Patris et Filii et Spiritus Sancti*' – 'In the name of the Father and of the Son and of the Holy Spirit') which begins all Catholic services and formal prayers, and in the greeting and response '*Dominus vobiscum – Et cum spiritu tuo*' ('The Lord be with you – And with thy spirit') which figure repeatedly in the mass and other Catholic ceremonies. This – and the fact that in those days people tended to do a great deal of church-attending and praying – probably explains why *esprit* has retained the *s* sound of its Latin forebear in its modern pronunciation (/ɛspri/) instead of losing it in the thirteenth century, as in the case of other French words deriving from Latin words beginning with *sp*: Latin *sparsus* ('scattered') > French *épars* ('sparse'); Latin *spina* ('thorn'). French *épine* ('thorn'); Latin *sponsus* ('bridegroom') > French *époux* ('husband') etc.

Often, the individualized direction of sound changes in particular lexical items seems to be prompted by the need to avoid what is known as *homonymic* or *homophonic clash* – that is a situation where two or more words with totally different meanings end up sounding identical. For example, there is a regular sound change whereby Old English /i/ and /y/ normally converged in Middle English /i/ which in turn developed into Modern English /ɪ/: thus, Old English *brycg* > Modern English *bridge*; Old English *scip* > Modern English *ship*. However, in some cases Old English /y/ developed via Middle English /u/ into Modern English /ʌ/. One such case is that of Old English *scyttan*, from which Modern English *shut* derives. Had *scyttan* undergone the regular sound change it would have resulted in a form identical to Modern English *shit*, which for its part is descended from Old English **scitan* (attested in *besciten*). It has been argued that the way in which *scyttan* evolved represents an instance of development away from unwanted homophony, although not all linguists are convinced by this argument.

The argument is probably strengthened in the particular instance of *scyttan* by the fact that the posited avoidance relates to a word connected with defecation. There seems to be good evidence of phonological (and other) adjustments being triggered by uncomfortable associations with particular body-parts, intimate physical functions, sacred matters, death etc. We saw an example of this in Chapter 6 drawn from Luganda. In English, taboo-induced changes have tended to focus on expletive uses of the taboo words themselves and have tended to lead to the creation of what are

widely thought of as different words, which then co-exist with the original
expletives rather than replacing them, as the following doublets illustrate:

hell!   *heck!*

God!   *gosh!*

Jesus!   *gee(z)!*

As for the more generalized, regular sound changes, these have been
explained in a variety of ways. Some linguists have seen them as originating
in people 'missing the bull's-eye' when attempting to articulate particular
sounds, the idea being that, when a critical mass of mis-hits have been heard,
the position of the 'bull's-eye', as it were, shifts. This kind of explanation
does not, however, take account of the fact that sound changes tend to be
similar in kind in quite unconnected languages and that they do not result in
systemic confusion and chaos, both of which facts seem to be at odds with
the notion that sound change is entirely random. Also somewhat dubious is
the claim that regular sound changes arise from the imperfect acquisition of
sound systems by young children, the idea being that children's 'imperfections' survive into adulthood and are then adopted as norms; unfortunately
for this position, there is little evidence that phonological 'imperfections' of
young children's speech survive into adulthood and exercise this kind of
influence.

Another view is that sound change results from the influence of other
languages or language varieties. This certainly does explain some changes.
For example, in India languages of Indo-European origin (including Indian
English) and historically unrelated languages from the Dravidian family
share a retroflexion feature in certain consonants. That is to say, for
instance, in the Indian pronunciation of a word like *day*, the *d* sound is
pronounced with the tip of the tongue pointing backwards as it makes
contact with the dental ridge. This feature is unusual, and is unlikely to
have arisen spontaneously and separately in each of the languages concerned. Much more plausible is the notion that the feature in question
spread through contact between the different language communities. A
very common phenomenon in this connection is phonological change in
the direction of a variety with high status in a particular community. The
recent and ongoing shift away from the pronunciation of post-vocalic *r* in
words like *car* in the West Country of England towards a London-like,
r-less pronunciation of such words exemplifies this phenomenon. On the
other hand, there are also cases of shifts towards a more local, homely
variety, as we saw in the example of Martha's Vineyard – also referred to in
the last chapter.

A further claim which appears to ring true is that sound changes often
come to pass because of inherent features of the environments in which they
occur. For example, when voiceless plosive consonants such as [p], [t] and
[k] are *inter-vocalic* – situated between two vowels – the quality of the

vowels (voiced, not involving the obstruction of air flow) will tend to influence the consonants, which may become voiced, may cease to involve a complete block of air flow, and in the end may disappear altogether. Let us take, for instance, the case of inter-vocalic Latin /t/ and its development in Spanish and French. In Spanish it first developed into /d/ and then into /ð/ (the voiced *th* sound in English *then*), and so what started out, for example, as Latin *vita* ('life') ended up as Modern Spanish *vida* – pronounced /ˈβiða/. As far as French is concerned, Latin inter-vocalic /t/ travelled the same route in this case, but went further; thus, the word *vita* has an eleventh century French descendant written *vithe*, and its Modern French descendant is *vie*, devoid of all traces of the original /t/. Interestingly, English inter-vocalic /t/ has begun to develop in a similar direction in American English, in many varieties of which the medial consonant sounds of *matter* and *madder* are identical.

With regard to changes in spelling, in sound-based writing systems these often reflect changes in pronunciation. For example, it was mentioned earlier that in French /s/ before /p/ disappeared in the thirteenth century from the spoken form of most words. In fact this was a more general trend than was indicated earlier; /s/ disappeared at this time from all pre-consonantal positions in the pronunciation of most French words. Nevertheless, until the mid-eighteenth century the *s* continued to be written. However, the third edition of the Dictionary of the French Academy finally removed it from words where it was no longer pronounced, replacing it with a circumflex or acute accent; thus *beste* ('beast') began to be written as *bête*, *chasteau* ('castle') as *château*, *escole* ('school') as *école* etc.

On the other hand, there have sometimes been movements in a contrary direction in spelling – that is to say, attempts to make words look more like the forms from which they were assumed to derive – irrespective of the way in which they were pronounced. For example, French scribes of the fourteenth and fifteenth centuries were very concerned to make French look as much as possible like Latin, and so they began spelling *dette* ('debt') as *debte* (cf. Latin *debitum*), *doute* ('doubt') as *doubte* (cf. Latin *dubitum*), *e* ('and') as *et* (cf. Latin *et*), *fevre* ('smith') as *febvre* (cf. Latin *faber*), and *set* ('seven') as *sept* (cf. Latin *septem*). Occasionally their etymology was faulty. For instance, thinking that *savoir* ('to know') was descended from Latin *scire* ('to know'), they introduced a silent *c* and wrote it as *scauoir*; in fact, *savoir* comes from the verb *sapere*, which in formal written Latin meant 'to discern', 'to be wise', 'to think', but which was used colloquially to mean 'to know' (cf. colloquial Modern English 'to be wise to').

Large numbers of these etymological spellings have since been re-simplified: Modern French writes *dette*, *doute* and *savoir*. However, some have 'taken': *et* and *sept* are still in place and, although the word *febvre* has fallen out of use, the surname corresponding roughly to the English surname *Smith* is still often written *Lefebvre*. Interestingly, where etymological spellings have disappeared from French they have sometimes been retained in English – as the above cases of *debt* and *doubt* demonstrate. For English had its own

Latinizers, and Anglo-Saxonizers too. Middle English *iland* ('island'), for example, had an *s* inserted into it because it was wrongly associated with its Romance synonym *isle*, from Latin *insula*; and the word *delit*, which came from Old French *delitier, delit* – deriving from Latin *delectare* ('to delight') – had *gh* 'restored' to it by analogy with the genuinely Germanic *light* (Old English *liht*), *night* (Old English *niht*), *right* (Old English *riht*) etc.

Another dimension of orthographic change is the development of different spellings for different meanings. For instance, many speakers of British English have adopted the American spellings *program* and *disk* for use in the context of computer programs and disks while retaining the British spellings *programme* and *disc* in all other contexts. To take another example, most present-day speakers of English would probably regard the words *flour* and *flower* as totally different words – homophones with entirely unrelated meanings. As a matter of fact they both derive from Old French *flour* ('flower'), flour being seen as the flower – or finest part – of the ground corn and, interestingly, Dr Johnson's *Dictionary of the English Language* (1755) does not distinguish between them in spelling, giving 'the finest part of meal' as one of the meanings of *flower*. However, both before and since Dr Johnson, other writers in English have felt the need to signal the distinction between these meanings orthographically, and so the spellings diverged. It is worth noting also that a concern to differentiate between words with different meanings may sometimes have militated *against* spelling change. Thus, for instance, the words *meet* and *meat* used to be pronounced differently, *meat* rhyming with *great*. In most varieties of Modern English the phonological distinction between them no longer exists. However, there has been no adjustment in the spelling of *meat*, a non-development which possibly has to do with the avoidance of *homographic* clash in the same way that the phonological development of *scyttan* (see above) may have had to do with the avoidance of homophonic clash.

Turning, finally in this section, to changes in the written forms of words in non-sound-based writing systems, these have typically been related to developments in the materials and implements used, the circumstances under which writing proceeded and considerations of learnability. As we saw, for example, in Chapter 6, Sumerian pictograms gave way to stylized cuneiform symbols under the influence of the way in which the writing act came to be performed – involving soft clay and reeds with wedge-shaped 'nibs'. In modern times the Chinese writing system has been simplified: in 1955 the government of the People's Republic of China sanctioned the simplification of 515 characters and 54 particles. The effect of this reform was to reduce the average number of strokes per character from 16 to eight. Its motivation was a concern to give the Chinese population at large easier access to literacy skills, although some of the reductions actually decreased the representational transparency of the characters.

8.4 Changes in lexical meaning

Whereas it is possible – with qualifications (see above) – to talk about general, regular changes in the sounds of a language, notions of generality and regularity have little or no application to changes in meaning. There is absolutely no chance, for instance, that the technological meaning recently acquired by the word *mouse* – 'hand-operated device which controls the cursor on a computer screen' – will be extended to all or most other words referring to rodents – *porcupine, rat, squirrel* etc. On the other hand, the word-specific nature of semantic change does not mean that shifts in meaning are totally arbitrary; there are particular sets of circumstances which are known to favour semantic change, and there are particular processes which are known to recur in semantic development.

One set of conditions for semantic change is the case where knowledge of the world moves on from one point in time to another. Let us take for example the word *world* itself. English-speakers' perception of what the Old English ancestor of *world* (*worold*) signified would have been markedly different from what *world* signifies for present-day English-speakers; in the Old English period *worold* referred to an entity perceived as flat and immobile, whereas (in its literal sense) *world* for us today refers to a spherical object rotating on its axis and travelling at great speed through space. Such changes in conceptualization may, of course, take place within the experience of an individual; thus, when I was a child, the word *whale* denoted for me something like 'huge fish', whereas now I understand it as denoting 'large sea-dwelling mammal'. Linguists and philosophers debate about whether the above kinds of change are really changes in *meaning*, which some wish to define as both socially determined and determined by the actual nature of things rather than simply a matter of the concepts 'in the individual's head'. However, such changes certainly do have consequences in terms of the lexical semantic relations exhibited in an individual's or a group's use of a language. For example, if I think of the whale as a fish, then, clearly, the word *whale* will have a hyponymous relationship with the word *fish* which it will not have if I see the whale as a mammal.

Another situation in which word meanings change is where the realities to which the words are applied change. For instance in any large American city at the end of the nineteenth century it was possible to take a cab from, say, the train station to one's hotel; at the beginning of the twenty-first century that is still true, but the nature of the cab has changed, and so, accordingly, has the meaning of the word *cab*. In the nineteenth century *cab* was applied to a two-wheeled horse-drawn vehicle whereas today it is applied to a four-wheeled motor vehicle. This kind of semantic change can be occasioned by social and political restructuring as well as by technological developments. For example, throughout the Western Roman Empire in the fourth century AD the Latin expressions *princeps* ('foremost (person)') and *dominus noster* ('our master') were applied in legal and administrative texts to the emperor (*imperator*), who also took the title *Augustus*, and to his adjutant and successor designate (the person referred to in the Late Empire as *Caesar*). Despite the kingly trappings of the emperor, the Latin expression for 'king' – *rex* – was never used of the emperor. This latter term had remained something of a 'dirty word' for Roman citizens ever since the proclamation of the Roman Republic in 509 BC and the overthrow of Tarquinius Superbus, the last of the Etruscan (Tarquin) kings of Rome. In the Late Empire *rex* was applied only to these Tarquin kings and to kings of territories outside the Empire. Two hundred years later, the Western Roman Empire having collapsed and Germanic peoples having taken control of erstwhile Western Roman provinces, most of the above words were still in use in legal and administrative texts, but in ways which reflect a totally different social and political reality. Thus in the legal Latin of Merovingian France the expressions *dominus noster* and *princeps* were used synonymously with *rex* (*Francorum*) ('king (of the Franks)'); the terms *imperator* and *Augustus*, on the other hand, were incompatible with *dominus noster* and *princeps*, and were applied (as courtesy titles) exclusively to the emperor of the Eastern Roman Empire, ruled from Constantinople, which was still alive and well but which no longer had any power in the West.

In all of the above cases there is a clear functional continuity between the earlier and the later applications of the terms. Whether horse-drawn or motor-powered, a cab still gets us from the station to our hotel. Whether a Roman emperor or a Frankish chieftain, the man in charge is still our master (*dominus noster*). What happens, then, when a totally new kind of object, animal, social phenomenon etc. appears on the scene of a particular community? One possibility in such a case is to create a descriptive combination of already existing words – as in *traffic-warden* ('a person who takes care of traffic' – cf. *churchwarden, game-warden* etc.) or *group-marriage* ('a long-term committed relationship involving a group of people rather than just a couple'). A variation of this approach is to give the descriptive expression a Greek or Latin form; thus the French word *télégraphe*, from which we get English *telegraph*, was concocted on the basis of Greek τηλέ (*tēlé* – 'far off') and γραφία (*graphía* – 'writing'). Another possibility, as the *télégraphe-telegraph* example shows, and as we shall see later, is to borrow a relevant term from the language of a community already familiar with the concept in question. Yet a further possibility is to press into service a word already present in the language of the community in which the phenomenon concerned makes its appearance by means of some kind of metaphorical extension. The above-cited example of *mouse* is a case in point. Whoever first applied the word *mouse* to the cursor-controller of a computer presumably did so because of some kind of perceived similarity between the technological device and the small rodent – in terms, notably, of shape, size, rapidity of movement, and possession of a 'tail' (the connecting flex in the case of the computer mouse). Other recent computer-related metaphorical extensions include those affecting the words *hardware*, *net* and *window*.

Metaphor is in fact a major factor in semantic change, and not just in relation to new concepts. For example, the word *seethe* comes from an Old English word meaning 'to boil', and this remained the primary meaning of *to seethe* well into the Modern English period. However, these days for most English speakers *to seethe* means 'to be very angry'; few have any idea that this meaning arose from the metaphorical extension of a cooking term. To take another example, this time from French, the word *chef*, which means 'boss' or 'chief' in Modern French, comes from the Latin word *caput*, which meant 'head (of a person, animal etc.)'. This meaning was extended in much the same way that the English word *head* has been (*head of department, head of a company, head of a school* etc.) and in the end the metaphorical meaning eclipsed the erstwhile literal meaning.

A further factor in semantic change is that of context. One dimension of this factor is confusion between meanings of words arising from their frequently occurring in the same kinds of context. For instance, the verbs *to imply* and *to infer* are both associated with contexts where the subject matter is the inexplicit communication of messages. *To imply* refers to the imparting of inexplicit messages – as in: *Susan's absence seemed to imply disapproval* – while *to infer* refers to the extraction of inexplicit messages – as in: *Mike inferred from Susan's absence that she disapproved.* However, this difference of meaning has become blurred in many English-speakers' minds, to the extent that *to infer* is very often used as a synonym of *to imply* – as in: *What are you inferring by saying that?* Similarly with *to deny* and *to refute*, both associated with the negation of claims made by other people, but the meaning of *to refute* carrying the additional element of the demonstration of falsity – as in: *He refuted the accusation by showing that he had been in Stockholm at the time.* Many English-speakers (including many politicians and journalists) no longer observe this distinction and use *to refute* as a synonym of *to deny* – as in: *I refute that!* Sometimes such confusions arising from appearance in similar contexts are reinforced by formal resemblances; thus, *to mitigate* is often used in the sense of *to militate* and *to appraise* is often used in the sense of *to apprise*.

Another contextual element in semantic change is the impact of recurring shared contexts. For example, guests at wine receptions hearing the words *Red or white?* have no difficulty interpreting the question as if it had contained the word *wine*. Such context-induced abbreviations often 'stick'. For instance, in military contexts the word *private* rather than *private soldier* is now the normal way of signifying the lowest military rank, and in the terminology of the professions *undertaker* is now the usual expression for what used to be called a *funeral undertaker*. In the sexual domain too such foreshortenings occur. Thus, *intercourse* is now typically used to mean what previously was denoted by *sexual intercourse*.

The cases of the development of *undertaker* and *intercourse* may well be further influenced by an additional factor – the avoidance of taboo language. It may be significant in these cases that the words that are dropped explicitly evoke topics which are often skirted around – death and sex. The expression *sexual intercourse* actually started out as a euphemism, but, as we have seen, its subsequent evolution has ironically resulted in the word *intercourse* – which used to mean simply 'communication' or 'interaction' – acquiring 'sexual act' as its normal first meaning. Other expressions which now have one foot in the semantic field of sexuality, because of having been deployed as sexual euphemisms, include *jump, the other* and *tumble*. Likewise with words associated with other intimate bodily functions. In earlier times there were even taboos in respect of certain animals, which were accordingly given euphemistic nicknames, which in turn eventually became the normal terms for the animals in question. So it is with the word *bear* in English, which is related to *brown*, and which originally meant simply 'the brown one', and with the word *renard* ('fox') in French, which derives from the personal forename *Reginhard*.

8.5 Changes in lexical distribution

In Chapter 7 we saw that some communities are characterized by the alternation between 'High' and 'Low' linguistic varieties, depending on setting, subject-matter, relations with the addressee etc. We also saw that language use in all communities involves some degree of style-shifting – adjusting one's accent, one's grammar and one's lexis in accordance with the degree of formality of a situation. What needs to be added to this general picture is that items which at one point may figure in the High variety may move into the Low variety – and vice versa – and that items associated with one kind of style may subsequently become associated with a different style.

One of the diglossic situations discussed in the last chapter was that which obtains in Haiti, where Haitian Creole constitutes the Low variety and French the High variety. In fact, this is a simplification. There is a continuum extending from the 'pure' or least French-like creole at one end, through varieties where French influence is stronger, to the 'pure' prestige variety, Haitian French, at the other. Such situations are to be found wherever a creole whose vocabulary mostly comes from a major European language is used in a community where that same European language serves as the High variety. Linguists label the 'pure' creole in such cases the *basilect* (cf. Greek βάσις – *básis* – 'base'), the 'pure' prestige variety the *acrolect* (cf. Greek ἄκρον – *ákron* – 'summit') and the intermediate varieties the *mesolects* (cf. Greek μέσος – *mésos* – 'middle'). There is a tendency in such instances for speakers of basilectal varieties to try to enhance their social standing by including in their speech elements from varieties higher up the continuum, with the result that there is a gradual trend towards decreolization. Thus, to return to Haitian Creole, very close approximations to French expressions – especially high-status technology-related expressions like *radio* ('radio') and *changement de vitesse* ('gear-shift') – have in fact been widely adopted by even 'pure' creole speakers.

The above case represents an example of a situation where words are adopted from a more prestigious into a less prestigious variety. There are also instances of movement in the opposite direction. For example, the word for 'horse' used in Latin in all formal contexts – literary, administrative etc – right down to the end of the Western Roman Empire was *equus* (from which our words *equestrian* and *equine* derive). However, there was another Latin word for horse which was used in less formal contexts. This was *caballus* – from which French *cheval*, Italian *cavallo*, Spanish *caballo* etc. descend. *Caballus* was occasionally used in a jokey, insulting sense in written Latin – to mean something like 'old nag', but in the informal, colloquial Latin of the streets, farms and taverns it became the usual word for 'horse', and in due course it was accepted with this sense into more formal Latin. Thus, in clauses dealing with horses in the sixth-century Salic Law we find the word *caballus*, not *equus*.

Coming back to our own times, we can observe both downward and upward adjustments of lexical distribution in Modern English. For instance, the word *excellent* was, up to less than 20 years ago, rather a formal item – much more likely to be used by schoolteachers at the ends of essays or by wine critics in Sunday newspaper columns than by ordinary mortals having a chat. This same word is now on the lips of every teenager and is applied in every context from sport to sexual attraction. The word *fabulous* underwent a similar fate in the 1960s. As far as upward movement is concerned, we can cite the case of 'bad language'. The extent of the change can be gauged from the fact that, whereas in 1966 the theatre critic Kenneth Tynan was instantly sacked from the BBC for saying on a late-night arts discussion programme that people were no longer shocked by the word *fuck*, these days in Britain one can hear multiple renditions of the word *fuck* in films screened after 9 pm on any channel on any evening of the week. That is not to say that *fuck* is now 'respectable', but it has progressed a considerable distance towards acceptability in public settings. What used to be its French equivalent – *foutre* – has gone much further along this road; for many French-speakers it is simply a slangy synonym of *faire* ('to do') – as in *Qu'est-ce qu'on va foutre cet après-midi?* ('What are we going to do this afternoon?') or *Il y a rien à foutre* ('There's nothing to be done').

Some historical linguists would apply the term *melioration* to the way in which *foutre* has developed in French, by which they would mean that the sense of the word has 'improved' (cf. Latin *melior* – 'better') from being obscene or insulting to being relatively neutral. Likewise for the case of Latin *caballus*, whose meaning in formal contexts 'improved' from 'old nag' to simply 'horse'. The opposite term to *melioration* is *pejoration* (cf. Latin *peior* – 'worse'). This might be applied to the development of the word *excellent*, the force of which ('pre-eminent') has been somewhat diluted in recent years. The terms *melioration* and *pejoration* are applied to meanings rather than distributions of words. The example typically cited of *meliora-tion* is the evolution of *queen*, whose Old English forebear, *cwen*, simply meant 'woman' (cf. Modern Swedish *kvinna* – 'woman'), but which now means 'female sovereign'; as for pejoration, the example often cited in this case is that of *knave*, whose Old English forerunner, *cnafa*, meant 'boy' (cf. Modern German *Knabe* – 'boy'), but which now means 'rogue'. Melioration and pejoration do not always result from changes of distribution in terms of High/Low variety or formal/informal style, but there is clearly often a con-nection between such changes of distribution and the direction of semantic change, as some of the earlier examples demonstrate.

8.6   Lexical changes associated with language contact

What were described as changes in lexical distribution in the last section can, from another perspective, be seen as a kind of borrowing – the High variety borrowing from the Low variety, the informal style borrowing from the formal style etc. Such borrowing is not possible, of course unless the vari-eties in question are in contact in some way. In the above cases the contact was extremely close. However, borrowing between language varieties is cer-tainly not confined to situations where there is this degree of closeness of contact.

For example, Thai has borrowed lexis from both French and English without there ever having been a presence of French-speakers or English-speakers in Thailand remotely comparable to, for example, the French pres-ence in Haiti. An example of a Thai borrowing from French is (in Roman transcription) *pang* ('bread' – cf. French *pain*), and an example of a Thai borrowing from English is *computer*. There is, on the other hand, a common factor between French influence on the development of Haitian Creole and French and English influence on Thai – namely the role of prestige: French and English are both high-status international languages associated with well-respected literature, art etc. and with economically and militarily pow-erful nations.

In the Middle Ages and the Renaissance period in western Europe, the language which served as the most important lexical 'quarry' was Latin, a language which was no longer spoken as a mother tongue in any country, but which, being associated with the past glories of Roman civilization, and as the administrative and liturgical language of the Roman Catholic Church, nevertheless had no shortage of prestige. Such was its power of attraction in lexical terms that even Romance languages, such as French, which had evolved from Latin, began to borrow more pristine or '*learned*' versions of words they already had in less Latin-looking form. The result: a series of lexical doublets, many of which are echoed in English. Some examples follow:

NATURALLY EVOLVED FRENCH FORM	LATER, 'LEARNED' BORROWING	LATIN
chance	*cadence*	*cadentia*
(cf. English *chance*)	(cf. English *cadence*)	
frêle	*fragile*	*fragilis*
(cf. English *frail*)	(cf. English *fragile*)	
poison	*potion*	*potio*
(cf. English *poison*)	(cf. English *potion*)	
sûreté	*sécurité*	*securitas*
(cf. English *surety*)	(cf. English *security*)	

A point worth making in this connection is that prestige of a kind that prompts lexical borrowing is not necessarily dependent on political power. For example, the Romans, who for centuries dominated Greece militarily and who eventually incorporated Greece into the Roman Empire, were nevertheless in constant awe of Greek literature, music and art, and borrowed large numbers of terms from Greek in these domains: *metaphora* (< Greek μεταφορά – *metaphorá* – 'metaphor') *musicus* (< Greek μουσικός – *mousikós* – 'musical'), *poeta* (< Greek ποιητής – *poiētés*– 'poet') etc. Even more dramatic is the case of those Vikings who by force of arms won for themselves (in 911) the territory we now know as Normandy (*Norman* = 'Northman'). So bedazzled, apparently, were these intrepid warriors by the attractions and comforts of their new home that they borrowed not just a few items of vocabulary from their new subjects but an entire language – so that when the Norman invading forces hit the shores of England 155 years later, it was with battle songs in Old French, not Old Norse, on their lips.

Apart from borrowing born of the esteem in which a given language and culture (or aspects thereof) are held, borrowing may also occur as a convenient way of covering lexical gaps in a language. The word *telegraph* has already been briefly discussed. It provides a good illustration of the notion of convenience borrowing. The first electrical telegraph was built in Geneva in 1774 by a French-speaking scientist, Georges Lesage, and so, naturally enough, the first word for this new invention was a French term (though constructed on Greek roots – see above), namely *télégraphe*. When British and American scientists developed the technology further in the nineteenth century, they simply took over the French term and gave it an English form. The Thai borrowing of the English word *computer* – also mentioned earlier – is a further case in point. Actually, not only Thai but other languages as well have borrowed this word – German, for example. Although early calculating machines were invented by the French philosopher Pascal and by the German philosopher Leibniz, the work leading to the development of what we now know as computers was mostly carried out in Great Britain and the United States, and so it is hardly surprising that the English word (coined on a Latin base) came to international prominence and was imported into other languages.

Often though, let it be said, the crucial factor in what word is borrowed in these kinds of instances is not the language of the inventors or the developers of the concept in question, but the language of the group responsible for bringing the concept concerned to a community previously unfamiliar with it. For example, the Christian Church and its theology and practices were not originally invented by Latin-speakers but rather by Aramaic-, Hebrew- and Greek-speakers. However, in western Europe these concepts and activities were mediated and disseminated through Latin, which is why in the languages of western Europe, including the non-Romance languages, so many words relating to churches and what goes on in churches derive from Latin; thus, for instance, in Irish, the words for 'altar', 'blessing', 'chalice', 'consecration', 'introit', 'sacrament' and 'incense' are, respectively: *altóir* (< Latin *altare*), *beannacht* (< Latin *benedictio*), *cailís* (< Latin *calix*), *coisreacan* (< Latin *consecratio*), *intróid* (< Latin *introitus*), *sacraimint* (< Latin *sacramentum*) and *túis* (< Latin *tus*).

8.7   The case of proper names

In the context of a discussion of lexical change it is worth considering the particular case of the development of proper names. Typically, proper names have their origins in expressions which mean something in a general kind of way and which then become attached to specific places, people or things. In a fair number of instances these origins are perfectly obvious even to the casual observer. In relation to towns called *Newcastle*, for example, we can fairly safely assume that at some stage in their history a new castle was erected; indeed, in many cases we can check our assumption by actually inspecting the castle in question. Similarly, a place called *Whitecliffs* is likely to boast or at some stage to have boasted white cliffs, a place called *Foxholes* is likely to be or to have been the abode of foxes, and a place called *Greystones* is likely to feature or to have featured grey stones.

With regard to family names, these originate in nicknames – the original sense of *surname* (cf. French *surnom*) was precisely this. Individuals were identified by, for example, some aspect of their personal characteristics (*Armstrong, Greenhorn, Grey, Long, Short, Sharp, Sweet* etc.), by their profession (*Brewer, Miller, Tanner* etc.) by their family origins (*Johnson, Peterson, Richardson* etc.), or by where they came from. In this last case the name in question might relate to a particular topographical feature (*Field, Mount, Woods* – cf. French *Deschamps, Dumont, Dubois*) or to a particular place-name with its own history (e.g. *Hardcastle, Newhall, Redwood*). Forenames, or 'given names', are for their part assigned to children often on the basis of the impression made by a particular infant or on the basis of aspirations for the child's character (thus, *Bonny*, *Grace*, *Prudence* etc.). Alternatively, a name may be given in honour of some other person (an ancestor, a saint, a current hero etc.) who may – in the parents' fond dreams – perhaps serve as a model for the child. Names given to institutions and products may be similarly aspirational and/or flattering, for example *Golden Wonder* (potato crisps), *Mother's Pride* (bread), *Swiftpost* (express mail system), *The Open University* (university specializing in distance learning), *The Independent* (newspaper).

In all of the above cases, the ordinary meanings of the names in question are transparent to speakers of Modern English. However, in many other cases the original meanings are obscured by historical change and/or by the fact that the items in question have been borrowed from other languages. With regard to the obscuring of the original meaning through historical change, Modern English-speakers will probably recognize *sheep-herd* in the surnames *Shepherd*, *Sheppard* etc. (because *shepherd* still exists as a common noun in English), but will probably not recognize *calf-herd* in *Calvert*, *hog-herd* in *Hoggart* or *sow-herd* in *Seward*. Similarly, on the personal characteristics front, most Modern English speakers no longer connect the surname *Blount* with *blond*, *Gosse* with *goose*, nor *Pennyfeather* with *penny-father* (= 'miser'). As far as borrowing is concerned, this is well illustrated by English forenames, most of which are borrowed from other languages – Hebrew, Latin, Greek, French, Gaelic (both Scots and Irish), Welsh etc. To take a few Latin examples, how many of us know that *Amanda*, *Benedict*, *Cara*, *Dominic*, *Felix*, *Leo*, *Margarita*, *Miranda*, *Paul* and *Septimus* come from words meaning, respectively, 'to be loved', 'blessed', 'dear', 'of the Lord', 'happy', 'lion', 'pearl', 'to be wondered at', 'small', and 'seventh'? Often the origin of a proper name is obscured both by its foreign roots and by the fact that it has undergone change since being borrowed. For instance, I puzzled for many years over my mother's maiden name, *Ayley*; I eventually discovered that this unusual surname is a much-altered version of a Middle French term – *aillier* ('garlic-seller').

In the case of place-names, these may contain elements from languages spoken in the area in question at any time over several millennia. For example, in Great Britain place-names may have Celtic, Latin, Old English, Old Norse or French origins – or may contain elements of two or more of the languages in question. Thus:

- Celtic: all rivers called *Avon* (and the county of that name) derive from a Celtic word which simply meant 'river' (cf. Modern Welsh *afon* – 'river').
- Latin: *Chester* and all -*chester* -*cester* and -*caster* elements in English place-names have their origin in Latin *castra* which meant '(military) camp'.
- Old English: *Hampton* derives from Old English *ham*, meaning 'homestead' and *tun*, meaning 'enclosure'. Similarly with other English place-names containing the elements *ham(p)* and/or *to(w)n*.

- Old Norse: *Normanby* descends from Old Norse *Nor manna býr* – 'enclosure/settlement of the Northmen' ; most English place-names ending in *-by* are Norse in origin (cf. Modern Swedish *by* – 'village', 'hamlet'; Modern Danish and Norwegian *landsby* – 'village').
- French: *Beaulieu* (pronounced /bju:li/ – i.e. as if written *Bewley*) is derived from the French expression *beau lieu* – 'beautiful place'. Other British place-names in which *beau* figures (*Beauchamp, Beaufort, Beaumont*) are also of French origin.
- Examples of blends: *Dorchester* (Celtic element **dor-* or **dur-* (also in *Dorset*) – from the name of the Celtic tribe who inhabited the region (known in Latin as *Durotriges*) – plus *chester* from Latin *castra* – '(military) camp'; *King's Lynn* (English *king* plus Celtic **linn* – 'pool'); *Forde Abbey* (English *ford* plus Old French *abbeie* – 'abbey').

A final point about proper names: while such names, as has been indicated, typically develop from expressions with general denotations into labels attached to particular persons, places etc. in given contexts, sometimes the process operates in the opposite direction. One area where this frequently occurs is the area of taboo language. 'Pet-names' are often created in particular families or groups to refer to entities or actions around which linguistic delicacy is felt to be required. Thus, for example, the penis has been christened, among other things, *Dick, Horatio, Jimbo, Jim Johnson, John Thomas, Micky, Percy, Roger* and *Willy*. Some of these expressions (*dick* and *willy* in the English-speaking world at large, *micky* in Ireland) have evolved into common nouns, and another has given rise to the verb *to roger* ('to have sex with'). A further category of proper names which frequently spawns words of more general application is that of brand-names. Some obvious examples here are *band-aid, biro* and *walkman*, which began as names for particular brands of, respectively, sticking plaster, ballpoint pen and personal stereo, but which later came in each case fairly widely to be used of the whole class of products in question. There is, in addition, a dimension of the question of proper names acquiring more general meanings as a result of the *deliberate* attachment of general denotations to such names. We shall examine this third dimension a little more closely in the next section.

8.8   Lexical engineering

This last section of the chapter deals with language change that is brought about deliberately. We have already touched on this kind of change in our discussion of changes in spelling and in our discussion of the coinage of new terms. We shall return to the conscious creation of new terms in the present section and we shall then home in on the ideological dimension of 'lexical engineering'. This latter aspect involves not only the coining of new expressions but also the modification or in some cases the suppression – or attempted suppression – of existing expressions.

The conscious creation of new terms has already been touched on. We have seen that when a new invention, discovery or idea arrives on the scene, it often occasions the invention in turn of a linguistic label by which the newly developed or observed phenomenon may be identified. We have seen also that the new coinages are often simply descriptive expressions – either in the language of the inventor(s) (e.g. *traffic-warden*) or based on a language, such as Greek or Latin, with ancient pedigree (e.g. *télégraphe, computer*). Another possibility we have noted in such instances is the metaphorical extension of an existing expression – as in the case of *mouse* applied to a cursor-controller in a computing context. It is also clear from earlier discussion that not every new development leads to the creation of new terminology. The example of *cab* – evolving from horse-drawn to motorized but retaining its name – was given earlier.

A dimension of deliberately concocting new expressions which has so far been only briefly mentioned (at the end of the last section) is the incorporation into the new terms of the personal names of individuals closely associated with the inventions, discoveries or ideas in question. Many examples of this phenomenon are to be found in the medical sciences, where there is a tradition of naming diseases after the researchers who identified and/or described them; thus we have *Down's syndrome* – named after the British physician J. L. H. Down (1828–96), *Hodgkin's disease* – named after the British pathologist Thomas Hodgkin (1798–1866) – and *Parkinson's disease* – named after the British physician James Parkinson, (1755–1824). Similarly, engineers have pieces of technology named after them (e.g. *Archimedes' screw*), horticulturists have roses named after them (e.g. *Gibson's Scarlet*), and political philosophers have political movements named after them (e.g. *Marxism*). In some cases an individual's name is used as it stands to supply a very basic term within the discipline in which he/she was prominent; thus in physics the basic unit of measurement of electrical resistance is the *ohm*, which is named after the German physicist Georg Simon Ohm (1787–1854), and the basic unit of measurement of radioactivity is the *becquerel*, which is named after the French physicist Henri Antoine Becquerel (1852–1908).

Overlapping with the deployment of personal names in deliberate lexical innovation is the invention of brand-names. Sometimes, after all, a brand-name is based simply on the name of the founder of the relevant company. So it was with the *Hoover* range of vacuum-cleaners, which took their name from the manufacturer W.H. Hoover – a brand-name so successful that – as in the case of *band-aid, biro* etc. – *hoover* passed into common parlance as a way of referring to all vacuum-cleaners. Brand-names which are not based on a personal name tend to be fashioned so as to evoke associations relevant to the product – technological (e.g. *Technet* – computer network consultants – cf. *technical, technological* etc), washing whiter then white (e.g. *Daz* – washing detergent – cf. *dazzle*), environmentally friendly (e.g. *Ecover* – biodegradable washing-up liquid – cf. *ecology, eco-system* etc.), meaty (e.g. *Oxo* – beef stock cube – cf. *ox*), clean (e.g. *Kleenex* – tissues – cf. *clean*), and so on. Inventors of brand-names, like inventors of other kinds of words, also sometimes borrow elements from other languages; thus, *Bovril* (beef drink – cf. Latin *bos* (genitive *bovis*) – 'ox'), *Lux* (soap – cf. Latin *lux* – 'light'), *Blue Stratos* (aftershave – cf. Greek στρατός – *stratós* – 'army') etc.

Finally let us not forget the contributions of the literary world to the deliberate coinage of new words,. Below are cited two stanzas from Lewis Carroll's 'Jabberwocky' (from *Alice through the looking-glass*, 1872).

> One two! One, two! And through and through
> The vorpal blade went snicker-snack!
> He left it dead, and with its head
> He went galumphing back.

> "And hast thou slain the Jabberwock?
> Come to my arms, my beamish boy!
> O frabjous day! Callooh! Callay!"
> He chortled in his joy.

These two stanzas alone were responsible for the institution of three new words in English – *galumph*, *frabjous* and *chortle* – defined by the *Concise Oxford Dictionary* as follows:

galumph	1 move noisily or clumsily	2 go prancing in triumph
frabjous	delightful, joyous	
chortle	chuckle gleefully	

As with Carroll, so with many other writers, and as with English, so, no doubt, with all other languages possessed of literatures.

The lexicon has also been shaped by deliberate attempts to impose notions of bettering society. These have tended to focus on what have been perceived as sexist, racist, classist and ageist usages and on the lexicalization of sexual orientation and mental and physical handicap. We shall look here at just the first of the above, but this should suffice to exemplify the kinds of approach that are being taken more generally.

Concerning sexism in language, a large number of expressions have been singled out by feminists as demeaning to women. These include terms such as *bird, bitch, cow, chapess, chippy, girl* (applied to an adult female), *popsy, tabby, tootsy, totty* and *wren*. Terms such as these are said to insult women by dehumanizing them (comparing them to other species, e.g. *bird, bitch*), by diminishing them (implying they are immature, e.g. *girl*, comparing them to small creatures, e.g. *bird, wren*, or representing them via diminutives, e.g. *chippy, popsy*) and by classifying them in male terms (representing them as non-males, e.g. *chapess*). On this view, such expressions, as ways of referring to women, should be simply expunged from the language.

In addition, feminists have objected to the fact that certain functions in society have traditionally been signified by words which imply that the person fulfilling that function has to be male: *chairman, fireman, postman, salesman* etc. In this case two options present themselves: one can try to balance things up by creating 'female' versions of the words in question – *chairwoman, saleswoman* etc. – or one can attempt to render the items concerned gender-neutral – *chairperson, chair, firefighter, postal operative* etc. In English, both of these options have been implemented to some extent, but the latter is the one that is clearly favoured by feminists.

In other languages – such as French – the response to the problem of sexism in language has been to feminize rather than to neutralize. For instance, there are in French many words, such as *professeur* ('teacher') and *auteur* ('author'), which are masculine in form and take the masculine articles *le* ('the') and *un* ('a'), but which are applicable to both males and females. Other similar-looking words, such as *chanteur* ('singer') and *acteur* ('actor'), have feminine forms – *chanteuse, actrice* – which are used when the individuals referred to are female. In recent years such feminine forms have deliberately been multiplied. The forms *professeure* and *autrice*, for example, have been coined. There remains the problem that traditionally in French the masculine form constitutes the default form; that is to say, for example, a member of the acting profession whose sex is unknown is referred to via the masculine *acteur*, and a mixed group of male and female members of the acting profession is referred to via the masculine plural form, *acteurs*. Obviously, the creation of forms like *autrice* does not of itself solve this problem.

To return to the basic foundations of attempts to render language less sexist, racist etc., these seem to stand in need of some further exploration and comment. To begin with, who is to decide which terms are insulting and therefore inappropriate? There often seems to be a gap between the perceptions of those abolishing 'offensive' terms and those to whom the terms refer. For example, the 'politically correct' expression *hearing-impaired* is totally rejected by large numbers of deaf people, who dislike the implicit medical perspective on their situation and way of life, and who prefer to identify themselves as *the Deaf* (with a capital D to make the point that they constitute a culture). Even the status of a term like *nigger* is not necessarily as straightforward as it might appear. As Vivian Cook points out, 'the solidarity principle asserts itself and these discriminatory terms become signs of group membership' to the point where a group 'may wear the detested term with pride as a badge of identity'. He cites in this connection the Black rap group *Niggas with Attitude* and the Mikey Smith poem 'Nigger Talk'. Another issue worth considering in relation to conscious endeavours to address socio-politically undesirable features and deficiencies in the lexicon is how far this can *of itself* really change perceptions and attitudes.

8.9 Summary

This chapter began with some general comments on language change and on the fact that during the nineteenth century linguistics was almost exclusively concerned with tracing such change and theorizing about it. A brief account was then given of the two principal research methods developed by historical linguists – the comparative method and the internal reconstruction method, attention being drawn to the importance of the lexical dimension of each of these methods. The chapter went on to describe and exemplify different types of lexical change – changes in lexical form, changes in lexical meaning, changes in lexical distribution and changes associated with language contact. A number of factors were suggested as contributing to the causation of such changes, including concern with social prestige, cross-linguistic influence, avoidance of homonymic clash; avoidance of taboo words (and words resembling taboo words) and the need to provide labels for new technology, institutions etc. In the final two sections of the chapter some discussion was devoted to the origins and development of proper names (typically from expressions with more general application) and to the issue of deliberate intervention in lexical change – on the one hand the conscious invention of new terms and, on the other, attempts to shape the lexicon in a socio-politically more acceptable direction.

Sources and suggestions for further reading

See 8.1. The Chaucer quotation is from *Troilus and Criseyde*, Book 2 (lines 22–6). The two quotations from Ferdinand de Saussure's *Course in general linguistics* are cited from Wade Baskin's translation (revised edition, Glasgow: Fontana/Collins, 1974); the first quotation is to be found on p. 77 of this volume and the second on p. 140.

See 8.2. The discussion of the origins of comparative–historical linguistics owes much to chapters 6 and 7 of R. H. Robins's book *A short history of linguistics* (second edition, Harlow: Longman, 1979), and the content of both 8.2 and 8.3 is informed by (and borrows some examples from) J. A. Anderson's book *Structural aspects of language change* (London: Longman, 1973).

See 8.3. The Modern Welsh examples relative to lexical diffusion are cited by J. Aitchison in her book *Language change: progress or decay* (London: Fontana, 1981, 95–6) from M. Chen's article, 'The time dimension: contribution toward a theory of sound change' (*Foundations of Language* 8, 457–98). Aitchison's book (especially chapters 7, 8 and 11) is one of the sources for the discussion of the causes of language change; other sources for this discussion include Chapter 9 of R. Antilla's book *An introduction to historical and comparative linguistics* (second edition, New York: Macmillan,

1988) and Chapter 10 of W. P. Lehmann's *Historical linguistics: an introduction* (London: Routledge, 1992). The exceptional status of *esprit* is referred to by A. Ewert in his book *The French language* London: Faber & Faber, 1933, 286–7) and by P. Rickard in his book *A history of the French language* (second edition, London: Unwin Hyman, 1989, 65). This latter work (especially Chapter 4) in addition supplies many of the examples relative to changes in French orthography. The *scyttan/shut* example is taken from A. M. S. McMahon's *Understanding language change* (Cambridge: Cambridge University Press, 1994, 332–3). The *iland/island* example is borrowed from S. Potter's book *Our language* (revised edition, Harmondsworth: Penguin, 1966, 45), on p. 72 of which is also to be found Dr Johnson's definition of *flower* in the sense of *flour*. The *delit/delight* example is borrowed from E. Weekley's *The romance of words* (new edition, London: John Murray, 1961, 103, fn. 6). The information about the simplification of Chinese characters is taken from L-J. Calvet's *Histoire de l'écriture* (Paris: Plon, 1996, 101).

See 8.4. The case against seeing changes in conceptualization as changes in meaning is put by (for example) H. Putnam in his article 'Meaning and reference' (in A.W. Moore (ed.), *Meaning and reference*, Oxford: Oxford University Press, 1993). The Late Latin examples are based on research I undertook many years ago in connection with my doctoral thesis (*A structural survey of the vocabulary denoting social status in Late Imperial and Early Merovingian Latin*, University of Cambridge, 1976). The *bear* and *renard* examples are borrowed from p. 41 of R. L. Trask's *Historical linguistics* (London: Arnold, 1996).

See 8.5. The source of the idea of the creole continuum and the attendant terminology is D. Bickerton's book *The dynamics of a creole system* (Cambridge: Cambridge University Press, 1975). The Haitian Creole examples are borrowed from p. 53 of Hélène Seligman's unpublished undergraduate dissertation *Haitian Creole: a sociolinguistic and sociocultural exploration* (Dublin: Trinity College, Department of French, 1988).

See 8.6. The Thai examples were provided by Jennifer Pariseau. The remarks about later Latin borrowings in French follow Chapter 8 ('The Latinizing tendency') of my little book *French: some historical background* (Dublin: Authentik Language Learning Resources, 1992).

See 8.7. The discussion of family-names draws on the examples given in Chapter 12 of E. Weekley's *The romance of words* (new edition, London: John Murray, 1961). The treatment of place-names was in general informed by a visit to the *UK English Place Name Database*, which may be consulted at the following website: http: //www.connections.ndirect.co.uk/pnamesdb.html The *Normanby* example was borrowed from p. 28 of S. Potter's *Our language* (revised edition, Harmondsworth: Penguin, 1966). The treatment of the evolution of proper names into common nouns etc. was generally informed by

A. Sholl's interesting and amusing book *Bloomers, biros and Wellington boots: how the names became the words* (Oxford: Past Times, 1999).

See 8.8. The discussion of deliberate lexical innovation owes some of its inspiration to Chapter 7, Section 3, of A. M. S. McMahon's *Understanding language change* (Cambridge: Cambridge University Press, 1994). Cook's astute comments on the use of discriminatory terms as badges of identity are to be found on pp 244–6 of his book *Inside language* (London: Arnold, 1997).

Accessible introductions to language change and historical linguistics include:

- J. Aitchison, *Language change: progress or decay* (London: Fontana, 1981);
- R. Antilla, *An introduction to historical and comparative linguistics* (second edition, New York: Macmillan, 1988);
- T. Crowley, *An introduction to historical linguistics* (Oxford: Oxford University Press, 1992);
- W. P. Lehmann, *Historical linguistics: an introduction* (third edition, London: Routledge, 1992))
- R. L. Trask, *Historical linguistics* (London: Arnold, 1996).

Readers wishing to deepen their understanding of language change would do well to go on to consult:

- W. Labov, *Principles of linguistic change, I: internal factors* (Oxford: Blackwell, 1994);
- W. Labov, *Principles of linguistic change, II: external factors* (Oxford: Blackwell, forthcoming);
- A. M. S. McMahon, *Understanding language change* (Cambridge: Cambridge University Press, 1994);
- S. Romaine, *Bilingualism* (Oxford: Blackwell, 1989).

Readers with a reading knowledge of French who would like to know more about the development of the different language-groups and languages in Europe would have much to gain by consulting:

H. Walter, *L'aventure des langues en Occident: leur origine, leur histoire, leur géographie* (Paris: Robert Laffont, 1994).

Focusing questions/topics for discussion

1. In 8.2 we briefly looked at various branches of the Indo-European family of languages (Celtic, Germanic, Romance, Slavic etc.). Can you say to which branch each of the following languages belongs (and where it is/was in use)? If in doubt, consult an encyclopedia or other reference materials.

Avestan	Occitan
Faroese	Old Church Slavonic
Frisian	Punjabi
Galician	Pictish
Macedonian	Yiddish

2. Consider the following set of cognates from Dutch, English, Swedish and Standard German. Can you – on the basis of these data – say something about the changes in the pronunciation of consonants which separated German off from the rest of the Germanic family? (NB in German *ch* following *a*, *o* or *u* is pronounced /x/, and *z* is always pronounced /ts/).

DUTCH	ENGLISH	SWEDISH	GERMAN
boek	*book*	*bok*	*Buch*
eten	*to eat*	*äta*	*essen*
haat	*hate*	*hat*	*Hass*
hopen	*to hope*	*hoppas*	*hoffen*
koken	*to cook*	*koka*	*kochen*
peper	*pepper*	*peppar*	*Pfeffer*
pijp	*pipe*	*pipa*	*Pfeife*
tien	*ten*	*tio*	*zehn*
tand	*tooth*	*tand*	*Zahn*

3. Try to come up with explanations as to how the following underlined expressions acquired their meanings:

The specialist he went to has diagnosed the <u>big C</u>.

A pint of <u>bitter</u> please.

We've saved all the data on <u>floppy</u>.

He'll need some help at first because he's a bit <u>green</u>.

Does this watch have a second <u>hand</u>?

Shall we go and fly your new <u>kite</u>, Chris?

You can open up the <u>throttle</u> a bit on this stretch of the road.

Dad's father <u>passed away</u> when I was nine.

He always wears <u>shorts</u> in July and August.

There is an emergency exit adjacent to each <u>wing</u> of this aircraft.

4. The following expressions are all included in *The Oxford Dictionary of Slang* (compiled by J. Ayto, Oxford: Oxford University Press, 1998) in the section dealing with the area of fear. Are all of these expressions in fact equally 'slangy'? If not, which of them have begun to move out of the slang category, and which of them are definitely still tied to highly informal contexts?

blue funk	*shake in one's shoes*
cold feet	*shitless*
get the wind up	*spooked*
hairy	*sweat blood*
put the fear of God into	*the creeps*
run a mile (from)	*the shits*
scaredy-cat	*white-knuckle*
scary	*yikes*

5. On the basis of what was said about place-names in 8.7, what would you deduce about the history of the following places in Great Britain and about features that may be or may have been associated with them:

Avonmouth	Gatenby
Beauly	Greenham
Cirencester	Kirkby
Clifton	Littleton
Fordham	Sevenoaks

6. Try to create your own brand-name for each of the following; in each case explain why you decided on the name you are proposing (and why you rejected any other names you may have thought of).

a chocolate bar containing pistachio nuts;

an ice-cream flavoured with exotic fruit;

a dandruff shampoo;

a highly perfumed luxury soap;

a garage specializing in fast repairs;

a hypermarket with very low prices;

a record label specializing in light classical music;

a record label specializing in heavy rock music;

a men's magazine;

a women's magazine.

|9|

Acquiring and processing lexis

9.1   The 'mental lexicon'

Up to this point in the book we have been treating the lexicon as an important dimension of language that needs to be addressed in any description of the phenomenon of language or indeed in the description of any particular language. In the present chapter we shall be looking at the lexicon which each speaker carries around 'inside his/her head', that is to say the lexical knowledge, or *mental lexicon*, upon which all use of any given language heavily depends. We shall look at the process by which lexical knowledge is internalized in the course of the acquisition of the mother tongue, we shall explore some ideas about how the mental lexicon is organized and how it functions, and we shall also examine some of the questions that arise in situations where more than one language is known by an individual.

A question that immediately arises when we start to talk about lexical knowledge is: what does it mean to know a word? We can make a fairly reasonable attempt at answering this question just by observing ordinary language use and noting what aspects of a word's profile we need to be familiar with in order to be able cope with it in such ordinary language use. On this basis we can straightaway say that knowing a word involves:

- knowing what it sounds like – so that we can recognize it and produce it in speech;
- (at least in literate societies) knowing its written form – so that we can recognize it and produce it in writing;
- knowing what it means – so that we can understand it and deploy it appropriately;
- knowing how it behaves morphologically – so that we can recognize and use its different forms (singular, plural etc.);
- knowing how it behaves syntactically – so that we can identify its function in phrases and sentences and so that we can use it in different roles in phrases and sentences.

All of the above are fairly obvious. However, conclusions emerging from discussion in earlier chapters would lead us to go further. Thus, what was said in Chapter 4 about the various effects which accrue when a given word participates in specific compounds, collocations, fixed expressions and idioms strongly suggests that we cannot really be said to know a word unless we know about 'the company it keeps' and the different impacts on its meaning and usage which result from participation in particular combinations. Context and meaning were dealt with in a more general way in Chapter 5, and this discussion reinforces the notion that knowing a word must include knowing how its interpretation shifts in accordance with the different contexts in which it may occur. Finally in this connection, the discussion of the association of particular words with particular social groupings and contexts in chapters 7 and 8 implies that knowing a word must involve knowing its social associations and knowing the kinds of social contexts in which it would and would not be likely to occur.

9.2   Meeting the lexical challenge

Some linguists claim that language is such a vast and complex phenomenon and the language input supplied to the infant by his/her caregivers so limited in nature that no child could ever acquire language if it were not for the fact that every human being is born with an inbuilt language faculty – a subsystem of the mind/brain which has evolved to deal specifically with the processing and acquisition of language. This contention is known as the *poverty of the stimulus argument*. According to this view, the inborn or innate language faculty enables the young child to distinguish linguistic from non-linguistic data and provides a guiding framework for the organization of linguistic information so that language development may proceed swiftly and systematically. Customarily this line of argument is applied in respect of the acquisition of syntax. However, a similar argument can be, and has been, applied to lexical acquisition.

Whatever may be the truth of the matter regarding an innate language faculty, it is possible to point to other facilitating factors which have to do with the nature of the input encountered by the child. It has been observed that in many cultures adults behave differently towards children in linguistic terms from the way in which they behave towards each other. They talk to children more slowly, using shorter utterances, in a higher pitch, and with repetition of key elements. It is thought by many language acquisition researchers (though not all) that such features of what is variously called *motherese, parentese, caretaker-talk* and *child-directed speech* make it easier for children to identify the units out of which utterances are composed. One aspect of child-directed speech that seems to be particularly relevant in this connection is *ostensive definition* – the definition of single words by pointing at what they refer to and naming them; in this case individual word-units are ready-isolated for the child by the caregiver, as well as being explicitly connected to particular meanings.

This latter semantic aspect of the lexical challenge is obviously vitally important. Extracting word-units from the speech stream would be of little benefit to the child in communicative terms without the attachment to the units in question of appropriate meanings. A further feature of speech directed at very young children which is relevant in this connection is that such speech is largely focused on the 'here and now'. Obviously, with or without explicit ostensive definition, it must be easier for the child to make links between words and meanings where these meanings relate to his/her present and immediate environment than would be the case if the reference were to objects, people, events etc. not accessible to the child's senses at the time of the interaction.

With regard to later stages in children's lexical development, further major lexical challenges await them during their school years. With the acquisition of literacy skills, they are required to add an orthographic dimension to the entries already present in their mental lexicons and to all entries acquired subsequently. While mastering the orthographic aspects of lexis is no easy matter, it does yield a certain pay-off in lexical-developmental terms. Once literacy skills have begun to be acquired, this significantly increases the range of opportunities for word-learning – both via ostensive routes and through the use of context. With regard to ostension, this is provided by a whole gamut of combinations of pictures and written words and by all the written definitions of words in terms of other words that teachers and textbooks provide from the earliest stages of schooling. As for use of context, the precise extent of its role in reading has been a matter of some controversy. However, research certainly does show that pre-readers and beginning readers rely heavily on context, and the general assumption is that the process of decoding unfamiliar words in context – in reading as in the handling of spoken language – leads to lexical acquisition.

9.3   Before the first words

Children begin to produce recognizable words around the age of 12 months. However, before that point a number of phenomena can be observed which appear to be relevant to lexical development. These include: the capacity of even new-born babies to discriminate between particular speech sounds, the development of concepts well before the onset of word production, and the gradual drift of the child's pre-lexical 'babbles' towards incorporating features of the language of the environment.

With regard to speech sound discrimination, the results of a number of experiments suggest that that new-born infants are sensitive to critical *voice onset time (VOT)* differences. VOT refers to the point at which the vocal cords begin to vibrate relative to the release of the closing off of the flow of air in voiceless plosives such as [p] and in voiced plosives such as [b]. In the case of a voiceless plosive there is a clear delay before the vocal cords begin to vibrate, whereas in the case of a fully voiced plosive the vocal cords vibrate throughout. Even if vocal cord vibration does not begin immediately, however, a sound will still be perceived as voiced if the time-lapse between the release of the stop and the beginning of vocal cord vibration falls within certain limits.

It is possible to investigate infants' sensitivity to speech sound differences via a technique based on the fact that the longer human beings (and indeed other species) are exposed to a particular sensory input the less it stimulates them. This is known as the *habituation effect*. In the experiments in question the child is given a 'blind nipple' to suck on and is exposed to certain sounds. As long as what the child perceives as the same sound continues to be played, his/her rate of sucking gradually decreases. If then an adjustment to the sound triggers an increase in the rate of sucking, this is interpreted as indicating that the child has noticed the change, and that the habituation effect has thus been disrupted. According to evidence yielded by this kind of technique, infants of just one month can discriminate between synthetically produced sounds which in terms of their VOT values would be categorized as voiced and voiceless plosives respectively, while failing to distinguish between sounds whose differences failed to cross the voiced–voiceless boundary.

Such results have been interpreted by some researchers as indicating the presence of a biological endowment specifically related to the particularities of the phonology of human language and part of an innate language faculty unique to humankind. Unfortunately for this point of view, it has been shown that other species, such as chinchillas and rhesus monkeys, are also able to discriminate between voiced and voiceless speech sounds, and so it is unlikely that this ability represents a specifically linguistic mechanism. Nevertheless, it seems fair to assume that the general capacity of very young children to distinguish between different types of sound does constitute an aid to language development – including, of course, lexical development.

With regard to concept development, there is no doubt about the existence of concepts in the child's mind before the first words begin to appear, but it is not so easy to answer the question of where such concepts come from and that of how early conceptualization relates to later lexical development. Research in this area – as in the case of research into sound discrimination in young children – often uses techniques which rely on the habituation phenomenon. For example, it is well known that infants who have been familiarized with a particular visual stimulus and who are then offered a choice between the familiar stimulus and a new stimulus will usually opt for the novel experience on offer and will look longer at the new stimulus.

Further evidence of conceptualization prior to word production is provided by the observation of interaction between babies and their caregivers. For example, it appears that by around 8–9 months infants fairly consistently look in the same direction as their caregivers, a phenomenon which researchers interpret as *shared reference*, involving a deliberate endeavour on the part of the child to locate the referent of the caregiver's gaze. Such behaviour is taken to indicate not only some understanding on the infant's part of the fact that attention typically refers to something but also a general conception of the range of likely objects of the attention in question.

With regard to the origins of concepts, as we saw in the last section, some researchers have suggested that concepts are innate. If this were the case, what might be the level of specificity and detail of such concepts? Would they be rich and well-developed or elementary and highly general? The first proposition runs up against the problem of finding a plausible explanation as to how such a fulsome concept-structure might have evolved, and the second runs up against the problem of appearing to fly in the face of evidence that children's first concepts are of a moderate level of generality rather than being elementary and universal in nature. Although neither of these points necessarily rules out the notion of innate concepts, both demonstrate that the innateness solution to the question of where concepts come from is by no means a straightforward one.

It is, on the other hand, possible to envisage a contribution of innate mechanisms to concept development without actually taking the view that the concepts themselves are innate. Thus, for example, the Swiss psychologist Jean Piaget claimed that concepts were the result of, on the one hand, the nature of the biological 'hardware' with which the infant comes equipped into the world (e.g. the particular characteristics of the human senses) and, on the other, the interaction between the child's innate mode of general intellectual functioning and the environment. According to this view, the development of concepts about objects are, as John Harris puts it, 'closely linked to the child's growing understanding of space, spatial relations and the notion of objects and people being located in a common space', this understanding being arrived at through the child's exploration of the world in terms of actions and their effects. Another proposal regarding the role of innate factors in concept development is that of the American psychologist Jerome Bruner, who suggests that there may be 'some special features of human action and human attention' which are inborn and which help the child to decode various kinds of communicative behaviour and thus facilitate the establishment of concepts such as *agent, effect, location* etc.

Turning now to the question of the relationship between the child's late 'babbles' and first words, our first step in this context must be to situate *babbling* in the general scheme of things. Babbling is the second of the four early developmental milestones which are most consistently referred to in accounts of child language. These four milestones are:

- *cooing* (onset 1–4 months, characterized by vocalizations with a vowel-like quality);
- *babbling* (onset 4–8 months, characterized by combinations of vowel-like and consonant-like sounds, including reduplications such as *baba, mama*);

- *one-word utterances* (onset around the end of the first year);
- *two-word utterances* (onset 18–24 months).

Babbling thus immediately precedes what is sometimes called 'true speech', that is, meaningful one-word utterances. A question that fairly obviously arises, therefore, is whether the babbling stage and the one-word utterance stage blur into each other or are entirely separate developments.

One perspective on this question is that there is a *babbling drift* (otherwise known as *babbling shift*) under the effects of which the children's babbles gradually take on more and more of the characteristics of the language to which they are being exposed. Evidence in favour of the idea of babbling drift includes that which shows that adults are able to distinguish French, Arab and Chinese children of eight months on the basis of their babbles. Linguists who take a strongly nativist approach to language acquisition, on the other hand, tend to dismiss the notion of continuity between babbling and early utterances. Their dislike of this suggestion has to do with their distrust of any attribution of an important role to environmental factors, which they see as running counter to their theoretical stance assigning an overwhelmingly predominant role to innate mechanisms. It is noteworthy in this connection that one of the earliest publications of the arch-nativist Noam Chomsky was a virulent attack on the view of language acquisition propounded by behaviourist psychology, according to which language acquisition is a process whereby early vocalizations are gradually shaped into communicative 'verbal behaviour' through the 'selective reinforcement' of responses appropriate to particular stimuli.

It must be admitted that not all of the evidence in this area supports the babbling drift idea. It is also interesting to note that that the more persuasive evidence of babbling drift in the period prior to the onset of word production – including the evidence mentioned above – comes from studies of intonation. For evidence of drift at the level of sound segments we have to go to studies of children in their second year and who have thus already begun to produce meaningful one-word utterances. It may well be that babbling drift affects only intonation during the period prior to word production, and that segmental patterns begin to shift in the direction of the language of the environment only after the onset of word production.

The babbling drift/shift debate addresses the question of continuity of babbling and 'true speech' with reference to phonetic/phonological form. However, there is also a dimension to the continuity issue which has to do with meaning. For example, it is clear that from an early stage, particular types of babbling may be associated with particular activities, emotions and needs. Examples to be found in the literature include an indicator of pleasure at seeing something come into view ([ji i i]) and a vehement protest sequence ([nə nə nə nə nə]). Babbling – 'true speech' continuity is supported in the meaning domain by the fact that when adult-like forms begin to be used they also seem to have – in the main – situational, general pragmatic rather than labelling functions. Such forms seem often to start as imitations in specific contexts. For example, one child being studied by researchers was observed to imitate her mother saying 'Uh oh, where'd it go?' as the mother dropped rings into a jar; later the child spontaneously produced a version of *uh-oh* when she dropped a comb and to perform a version of *where'd it go* when her mother dropped a brush and said 'Uh-oh'. It appears, then, that the early adult-like forms used by the child often become attached in a quasi-ritual manner to specific actions or action-sequences (in this case the dropping of objects) in much the same way that particular types of babbling do at a slightly earlier stage.

9.4   First words and beyond

An oft-cited instance of the early use of an expression which is associated with a very particular set of circumstances, is the use by a 12-month-old child of the utterance *dut* ('duck'), which he produced excitedly as he knocked a toy duck off the edge of the bath at bathtime but which he never uttered when the duck was actually floating in the water. Not *all* early uses of lexis are context-bound, however. A minority of the expressions deployed by children at the beginning of the one-word utterance stage are used to refer context-flexibly to particular objects or classes of objects. An example of such context-flexible use of an expression would be where the word *shoes* might be used by a child as a comment on a picture of shoes, on a real pair of shoes or on the shoes of a doll. It is also worth noting, perhaps, that not all of the items deployed in a clearly meaningful way by children at the one-word utterance stage are derived from adult input; sometimes they are the child's own creations.

With regard to the way in which lexical development proceeds once the first words have appeared this seems to be a process in three phases: (1) a phase during which the child is working out what words are, how they can be used to refer to things, people etc. and which words go with which entities, actions etc.; (2) a 'vocabulary explosion' phase, during which very large numbers of words are acquired very rapidly; and (3) a phase during which lexical knowledge is consolidated, revised and reorganized.

In Phase (1) – up to the point where about 30 words have been acquired – progress tends to be quite slow. There is, however, significant variation among children as far as the rate of early vocabulary acquisition is concerned. A factor that has been identified as relevant to later vocabulary development is variation from child to child in the degree of efficiency with which they are able to create short-term memory codes for lexical forms they hear. For example, the degree of accuracy with which children show themselves to be able to repeat unfamiliar phonological word-shapes correlates significantly with the quantity of vocabulary they subsequently acquire, and phonological short-term memory has been discovered to be a greater factor than either non-verbal intelligence or age in certain language disorders in children. It seems reasonable to assume that phonological memory variation is also a contributory factor in relation to individual differences in respect of the very early stages of lexical acquisition.

Four (not incompatible) kinds of statement are to be found in the literature about word meanings at this early stage:

- that such meanings are *vague and fluid*;
- that they are *over-extended* relative to the meanings of the words in question as used by adults;
- that they are *under-extended* relative to the meanings of the words in question as used by adults;
- that they reflect a '*basic*' level of categorization.

An example of the vagueness and fluidity of early word meaning comes from a study conducted by the French researcher P. Guillaume of his own son's language development in the 1920s. The form under scrutiny here is *blablab*.

> 'blablab' refers to the act of making the lips vibrate with the finger, then the mouth, especially that of a child's in a picture, then any picture of a person, any drawing, illustrated cards . . . any piece of paper with writing or printing on it, a newspaper, a book, but also expresses the act of "reading" or the desire to read.

In relation to over-extension, common instances are: the use of the term *apple* to refer to oranges, peaches, pears etc. as well as apples; the use of the term *dog* or *doggy* to refer to cats, rabbits and even cows and horses as well as dogs; and the use of the term *sweet* or *sweety* to refer to absolutely anything with a sugary taste – cake, ice-cream, syrup etc. There is clearly a connection between the notion of over-extension and vagueness and fluidity of meaning. It is precisely because the meaning of an item is still vague as far as the child is concerned that he/she uses it across a wider range of situations than an adult would – on the basis, it seems, of perceptual cues such as shape, colour, feel, taste, sound etc., functional characteristics (e.g. pears, like apples, are things one eats) and situational factors (e.g. ice-cream and sweets may be associated with similar kinds of situation – reward, relaxation etc.).

Under-extension has already been alluded to with reference to cases where expressions are used by the child in very specific sets of circumstances. Under-extension is not, however, confined to this sort of instance. There is a second sort of under-extension which is not situation-bound, and which has rather to do with narrowness of reference. Thus, for example, Margaret Harris reports 'early uses of "clock" to refer only to wall clocks, "music" to refer only to a hi-fi system in the child's home, and "light" to refer only to ceiling lights with a conventional shade.' Some researchers have suggested that, typically, a child will begin by under-extending the meaning of a word and then apply it to an increasingly wide range of phenomena – in some instances over-extending its application. This kind of scenario is, once again, entirely compatible with the notion that the child's early understanding of word meanings is uncertain and changeable.

Concerning the notion of a 'basic' level of categorization, the claim is that in coming to grips with the world around him/her, the child begins by classifying objects in such a way that: (i) the attributes of each category are predictable; (ii) items belonging to the category in question behave or are used in the same way; (iii) items belonging to the category can be readily identified; (iv) each category is easy to image; and (v) the categories concerned have a high utility value. Such categories are designated as 'basic'. For example, the category *flower* is seen as basic, whereas the category *plant* is not. Flowers by and large share a large number of characteristics in terms of what they look and smell like and what people do with them; it is easy to identify and to form a mental image of a flower; and knowing what a flower is will be extremely useful across a range of situations and interactions. The *plant* category, on the other hand, is highly heterogeneous in nature (including as it does seaweed, climbing creepers, grasses etc. as well as flowers), and for this reason poses more problems in respect of identification and imaging than the *flower* category; and the higher level, more inclusive *plant* tends to be less frequently referred to in most situations than the more concrete *flower*. Empirical evidence supports the suggestion that basic categories come first in the child's lexicon.

Moving on to Phase 2, the particular characteristic of the stage beginning from the point where the child has acquired upwards of 30 words is what is sometimes called a 'vocabulary explosion' – that is to say, a very marked increase in the rate at which new words are acquired. The 'explosion' in question is attributed by some researchers to the arrival by the child at a particular developmental landmark, a 'naming insight', that is to say, a sudden realization on the part of the child that the world is composed of things that have names. This is a controversial claim, but it is noticeable that this phase is characterized by a rapid acquisition of one particular type of word – nouns which name objects. A further dimension of this last point has to do with imageability. Some research suggests that nouns are generally easier to 'picture' than other grammatical categories and that this may be why they are more easily learned. There is certainly evidence from other sources in favour of the notion that words around which images are created are more readily retained.

Two features which accompany the acceleration in lexical development during Phase 2 are, on the one hand, a sort of naming obsession and, on the other, 'fast mapping', a capacity to learn new words after minimal exposure. This is the time when children go around asking for the names of virtually everything and everyone they encounter – the *'what's that'/'who's that'* phase, as it is sometimes known. Remarkably, there is evidence to suggest that at least as far as objects and colours are concerned new items may be acquired by the child at this stage after just one occasion of exposure. The child's hunger for naming data during this period appears, in other words, to be correlated with an extraordinary capacity to digest and retain such data both rapidly and efficiently.

A few words, finally, on Phase 3. This period of consolidation and revision seems to have its onset in the pre-school period, but some of the reorganizing processes that begin at this point clearly continue through the years of primary schooling and, indeed, into adulthood. One aspect of the re-organization process is the clustering together of related words, which allows the child to represent information about links between lexical items. What eventually emerges from the clustering of related words in the mental lexicon is a set of classificatory hierarchies. The child starts by associating words from the same semantic area ever more closely (e.g, *dog, cat, rabbit* etc.) and then starts putting such groups of words under the headings of superordinate terms (e.g. *pet, animal etc.*). These hierarchies gradually build upwards to the point where the superordinate expressions become quite abstract (e.g. *something that's alive, living thing*). Evidence for such development comes from word-association tests, which show a shift from a predominance of *syntagmatic* (i.e. combinatory) associations (of the kind *Daddy – working, dog – barks, red – apples*) in the early stages to a later predominance of *paradigmatic* (i.e. substitutional) responses (of the kind: *Daddy – Mummy, dog – cat, red – green*).

Finally in this section it is perhaps worth emphasizing that lexical development does not come to a halt at the end of childhood, or indeed, it seems, at any stage prior to our last exit. Two American researchers, John Carroll and Karl Diller concluded some years ago – on the basis of having examined a range of lexical studies – that lexical acquisition continues through adulthood. Carroll drew from his reading of the relevant research the message that vocabulary tends to increase significantly up to at least the age of 40 or 50 while Diller reported research suggesting that there is no point before death at which lexical acquisition can be predicted to cease.

9.5   Models of lexical processing

Having considered various aspects of lexical development, we come now to the vexed question of how lexical knowledge is organized and retrieved once it has been acquired. A distinction is sometimes made between direct and indirect models of the processing of lexical information. The indirect type of model assumes that the processing of lexical knowledge follows the same kind of pattern as looking up a word in a dictionary – or extending the metaphor slightly – finding a book in a library. This kind of model sees lexical access as involving more than one component or step. Direct models, on the other hand, portray accessing lexical knowledge as a one-stage process; a metaphor which has been used in this connection is that of a computer software package which allows items stored by name to be accessed simply by the typing in of as many letters as are sufficient to distinguish the relevant name from all other stored names. Two much-discussed representatives of the direct kind of model are the *logogen model* and the *cohort model*, whereas an oft-cited representative of the indirect type of model is the so-called *search model* of lexical access. We shall look at each of these in turn, go on to examine W. Levelt's highly influential 'blueprint for the speaker', which has much to say about lexical processing, and finally focus briefly on two general (but lexically relevant) perspectives on language processing – the *modularity hypothesis* and *connectionism*.

The logogen model

The logogen model – the brainchild of the British psychologist John Morton – began as an attempt to account for the fact that words are recognized more quickly in contexts where they are very likely to occur than in contexts where they are less likely to occur. For example, the word *station* will be more quickly recognized in a context such as *He waved a railway ticket at me and asked the way to the station* than in a context like *The three-star seafood restaurant was a splendidly converted station*. Morton postulates that when an item is accessed in the mental lexicon there is an 'event' in a part of the nervous system which, in his early writings, he labels simply as *neural unit* and to which he later applies the term *logogen*.

The essential components of Morton's model are: the *logogen system*, the *cognitive system* and the *response buffer*. The term *logogen* is concocted from Greek *lógos* (λoγoς – 'word') and the Greek and Latin root *gen* (as in Greek *génesis* – γένεσις – 'birth'; Latin *generare* – 'to bring to life'). The logogen system is conceived of as a set of mechanisms – one for each word in a given individual's lexicon – specialized for collecting perceptual information and semantic evidence concerning the presence of words to which the logogens correspond. When the information, including contextual information, pointing in the direction of a particular word reaches a critical threshold, the relevant logogen 'fires', and the word concerned is 'born' or 'brought to life', i.e. either recognized in the incoming signal or identified as the appropriate item to be used for productive purposes. The cognitive system is envisaged as a collection of semantic information of various kinds, including information relating to context and contextual probabilities. As for the response buffer, this is the component in the model to which responsibility for generating spoken or written word production is attributed.

A basic principle of operation of the model is that a given piece of input will in most cases supply evidence to more than one logogen. For example, in the case of the processing of the printed word *rat*, the output from the visual analysis will include such attributes as <three letter word>, <tall letter at the end> etc. Such information is relevant not only to *rat* but to other words too. Accordingly, the attributes <three letter word> and <tall letter at the end>, for example, will be expected to excite not only the logogen for *rat* but the logogens for all three-letter words ending in tall letters (*cat, cut, eat, eel, red, rod* etc.). Hence the need for the model to incorporate thresholds: it is necessary that, of all the logogens stimulated by a particular piece of input, one logogen should – on the basis of all the available data – reach such a level of excitation that it 'fires', in order that the appropriate word should be selected.

The cohort model

One criticism which has been levelled at the logogen model is that some of the concepts on which it is based – such as 'threshold' and 'activation level' are difficult to be precise about. The cohort model, developed by the British psycholinguist William Marslen Wilson, offers a possible answer to this problem, since it aspires to specify for each word exactly where the critical activation level occurs.

The cohort model postulates a set of word-detectors which are activated by input from a spoken word and which start operating as soon as someone within earshot begins to produce a word. As soon as the first sounds of the incoming item are processed, all the detectors for words beginning with that particular sequence of sounds – otherwise known as the relevant *word-initial cohort* – are fully activated. Each of the detectors in this cohort then continues to monitor subsequent input. Mismatches are in this way progressively removed from the running, until a single word-candidate finally corresponds precisely to the input. In contradistinction to the varying levels of activation posited by the logogen model, the early version of the cohort model allows for just two states of activation for a particular item: *on* (for as long as it forms part of a cohort of word-candidates) or *off* (when it fails to be selected for the word-initial cohort or is eliminated from the cohort). However, later versions of the model envisage that, instead of immediately eliminating themselves, non-matching members of a cohort will go into an activation decline in the absence of further support from incoming data.

In principle, the cohort model identifies the *uniqueness point* for word recognition, that is, the precise point at which a word is recognized. To illustrate this, let us take the word *elephant* (/ˈɛlɪfənt/). On the basis of the incoming data from the uttering of the first two syllables of this word – /ˈɛlɪ/ – the cohort of word-candidates would include words such as *elevate* and *element*. However, at the point where the /f/ sound occurs the cohort will have only *elephant* and its inflectional variants (*elephants, elephant's, elephants'*) left, since no other word in English begins with the sequence /ˈɛlɪf/. This then is the uniqueness point for *elephant*. Such a system would appear to be maximally efficient. A system which plumped for *elephant* before the occurrence of /f/ would run the risk of generating erroneous identifications, whereas a system which delayed identification beyond that point would increase processing time without increasing accuracy levels. The cohort model also defines the point at which non-words are recognized. This is the point at which the sequence of phonemes uttered fails to correspond to any word in the language in question. For instance, in English, the non-word recognition point in *tnot* will be the occurrence of /n/, since no English word begins with /tn/, while in the case of *daffodip* the critical point will coincide with the very last sound /p/, since until this is uttered the possibility of a match still exists.

There is a fair amount of experimental evidence in favour of notion that word recognition proceeds as the cohort model suggests – at least in broad terms. To take one example of a relevant finding from among many, it has been shown that the time taken to recognize non-words is shorter where recognition points come early in words and longer where recognition points come late. On the other hand, it is most unlikely that things happen quite as neatly as is suggested by the cohort model. We know, for example, that sound segments do not reach the ear as separate entities, but are to an extent interwoven with each other, so that any given point in the speech signal will show evidence of preceding and succeeding elements. Accordingly, the idea that the perception of the speech signal revolves around precise judgments about points at which particular elements occur is not particularly plausible. However, this does not undermine the model in any crucial way.

Context was mentioned as important preoccupation of Morton's in relation to his development of the logogen model. Marslen-Wilson's interest in context effects is no less strong. The cohort model, like the logogen model assumes that available contextual information assists lexical processing. However, whereas the logogen model suggests that context effects are the result of information passing through the cognitive system, which is separate from, though connected to, the logogen systems, the cohort model posits that each and every entry in the mental lexicon is equipped with a set of procedures for determining which, if any, of the meanings of a word are applicable in any given context. However, the model does not represent contextual information as *pre*-selecting words, Marslen-Wilson's view being that context-driven pre-selection would be highly inefficient in the open-ended, unpredictable circumstances of everyday language use.

The search model of lexical access

The most widely discussed search model of lexical access is that which was elaborated by the American psychologist Kenneth Forster. In this model the process of accessing an item in the mental lexicon is represented as a series of steps, involving first a search for a matching from a phonological, orthographic, grammatical/semantic starting point and then a guided retrieval of the full word. As has already been noted, such a two-stage process is comparable to what happens when we look up a word in a dictionary or look for a book in a library.

Obviously, we come to the task of lexical access from different points of departure on different occasions – depending on whether we have heard the word, read it, or have a meaning and category that we wish to express – just as we approach the task of, for example, finding books in a library on the basis of different kinds of information available to us at different times (author, title, subject area etc.). In Forster's model the initial search is represented as proceeding with the help of a number of *peripheral access files*, one organized along phonological lines, one organized according to orthographic properties, one organized on a syntactico–semantic basis etc. These correspond to the different library catalogues. The peripheral files are envisaged as containing listings of entries in the respective modes and also pointers (corresponding to shelf-marks) to the precise location of each entry in its complete form in a *master file* (corresponding to the library shelves).

According to the model, if one is listening to speech, one processes each spoken word by going first to the phonological access file; if one is reading written language one goes first to the orthographic access file; and if one is producing language on the basis of particular meaning intentions, one goes first to the syntactic/semantic access file. The access file in question then facilitates access to the master file, and once this has been accessed, it supplies whatever is necessary for any kind of further operations on the word in question – whether this be in the realm of speaking, writing or understanding.

With regard to the master file, this is seen as a collection of individual (fully specified) lexical items and is envisaged as having to contain some provision for meaning connections between the items in question. Any lexical model needs to account for the fact that, for example, when we hear the word *doctor* we process any subsequent occurrence of the word *nurse* more rapidly than if we had not heard the word *doctor*. The logogen model deals with this phenomenon of *semantic priming* via the cognitive system; the cohort model deals with it via word-specific context-sensitive procedures; Forster's model, for its part, posits cross-references in the master file between words that are related in meaning. Thus, in relation to the above example, the idea is that calling up *doctor* in the master file will cause *nurse* to be processed via a direct link within the master file without the necessity for a return to the relevant peripheral access file. However, experimental studies have failed to produce any really convincing evidence that this is how things work. Such lack of experimental support has led to doubt being cast on the whole idea of a distinction between access files and master file and thus the very notion of two-stage lexical processing.

Levelt's 'blueprint for the speaker'

Up to this point we have been looking at models which are wholly focused on the mental lexicon. The model which we now come to is different, insofar as it seeks to address language processing in a more general way. However, its lexical dimension is particularly highlighted by its creator, the Dutch psycholinguist, Willem Levelt, who has a particular interest in lexical processing. The work in which the model is elaborated is entitled *Speaking: from intention to articulation*, and, true to this title, the primary perspective of Levelt's 'blueprint' is a productive one, although receptive aspects of processing are not entirely left out of the account.

The model comprises two categories of component, *declarative knowledge* and *procedural knowledge*. The former is conceived of as 'knowledge that', knowledge as facts, whereas the latter is conceived of as 'knowledge how'. Declarative knowledge required for language processing, according to Levelt, includes general information about the world (*encyclopedia*), information about particular situations (*situational knowledge*), and information about stylistic appropriacy relative to specific circumstances (*discourse model*). Also included under the heading of declarative knowledge is lexical knowledge, both semantico-grammatical (*lemmas*) and morphophonological (*forms*). As far as the procedural components are concerned, these include: the *conceptualizer* (responsible for message generation and monitoring), the *formulator* (responsible for giving the pre-verbal message a syntactic and phonological shape), the *articulator* (responsible for executing as overt speech the phonetic plan emerging from the formulator), the *audition* component (responsible for analysing the incoming speech sounds) and the *speech comprehension system*, responsible for making sense of the phonetic strings received).

As far as the lexical component is concerned, this, as has been mentioned, is represented as containing, on the one hand, lemmas and, on the other, forms. According to the model, a word's lemma specifies its basic meaning, its syntactic category, its conceptual argument structure, its grammatical profile (e.g. in the case of a verb, whether or not it takes a direct object), and its 'diacritic parameters' of variation (tense, aspect, mood etc.). The lemma also includes a 'lexical pointer' to the precise place in the lexicon where morphological and phonological information about the word in question is located. The implication here is that lexical search happens in two stages, which means that Levelt's model is in this respect comparable with Forster's model. With regard to lexical forms, these are seen as specifying the precise morphological information that is necessary in order for phonological encoding to be able to take place.

The role of the lexicon in speech production is seen by Levelt as central; for him the entire set of formulation processes is lexically driven, the particular syntactic, morphological and phonological properties of an activated lexical item triggering the grammatical, morphological and phonological encoding procedures underlying utterance generation. This designation of the lexicon as the mediator between conceptualization and grammatical and phonological formulation – referred to as the *lexical hypothesis* – sits well with the evidence discussed in chapters 1 and 2 of the interpenetration between lexis and grammar. On the other hand, the separation posited by the model between lexical meaning and encyclopedic knowledge is problematic; many linguists are highly dubious about the possibility of making a distinction of this kind. A further issue arises in relation to the representation of lexical knowledge as purely declarative. This appears to fly in the face of evidence relating to such phenomena as word formation, lexical change and context effects which suggest that the lexicon is a highly dynamic rather than a static entity.

The modularity hypothesis

We turn now to a view of language processing – the *modularity hypothesis* – which claims that the entire language faculty is a fully autonomous *module*. The hypothesis can be summarized as follows:

> The mind is not a seamless, unitary whole whose functions merge continuously into one another; rather, it comprises – perhaps in addition to some relatively seamless, general-purpose structures – a number of distinct, specialized, structurally idiosyncratic modules that communicate with other cognitive structures in only very limited ways.

The kinds of systems that are seen as modular within this perspective include input systems, such as certain components of the perceptual and the language-reception systems, and output systems, such as aspects of motor control and language production.

The modular view of the mind has two very influential advocates in the persons of the theoretical linguist Noam Chomsky and the psycholinguist Jerry Fodor. Between these two, however, some differences exist: whereas Chomsky discusses modularity essentially in relation to language acquisition (in connection with his notion of an innate language faculty – see above), Fodor's concerns are largely processing-oriented. Since in the present section we are concerned with language processing, we shall focus on Fodor's account.

The cornerstone and the most controversial aspect of Fodor's conception of modularity is the notion that modules are 'informationally encapsulated' – the notion that, with regard to language processing, for example, general knowledge, contextual information etc. play no part in the operations of the module while those operations are in progress. The claim in this regard is that any connections between modular processing and other knowledge take place beyond the operating domain of the module. In the case of language reception, for example, the idea is that general and contextual information interact with linguistic information only at the point where the linguistic forms in question have been fully processed and analysed by the mechanisms of the language module. One of Fodor's arguments for the informational encapsulation of modules takes the line that such encapsulation is necessary to the efficient operation of the modules. One example he uses in this connection is drawn from the realm of visual perception; this is the case of someone catching sight of a 'yellow stripey thing' in New York and having to decide very rapidly whether what they are seeing is a tiger. Fodor argues that in such circumstances a perceptual system that took account of contextual expectations while perceptual processing was actually going on would not process information quickly enough to avoid disaster, and that therefore modular processing needs to be immune to online penetration by anything which is extraneous to the specific focus of the module in question.

Against this line of reasoning it is easy enough to find instances of people not believing and therefore not reacting appropriately to the evidence of their senses. Thus, in relation to language, the following example, related by a native speaker of Finnish, is not untypical:

> My sister, while studying in France, was once addressed on the street in Finnish. Only after several attempts by the speaker did she understand her own native language, the point being that she was expecting French. I have had a very similar experience trying to make Finnish out of something that was easy enough to understand when I realized it was English.

Fodor's position is further undermined by what we know about the effects of deep hypnosis. At the hypnotist's suggestion, a hypnotized subject may fail to perceive objects or persons which are present and/or perceive and interact with objects and persons which are not present. Even reflexive responses may, apparently, be affected by hypnosis. For instance, hypnosis can suffice to anaesthetize patients undergoing surgical operations, and even to arrest salivation and bleeding. If something as fast and as automatic as a physiological reflex can be influenced by information or pseudo-information implanted by an external source, there has to be a question-mark over the notion of informational encapsulation in language processing.

In any case, as Fodor himself acknowledges, the idea of informational encapsulation does not appear to sit very happily with the findings of psycholinguists – notably from experiments involving reduced-redundancy procedures like cloze (where subjects have to fill in the blanks in a gapped text). It is universally recognized that in cloze tasks the more predictable the target items in relation to the blanks in the given context, the more successful will be the attempts of those performing the task. For example, of the two sentences below, the first is a great deal easier to complete than the second.

I was so thirsty that I absolutely had to have something to _____.

I was so happy that I absolutely had to _____.

This looks like strong evidence of the mechanisms involved in such tasks having access to subjects' expectations based on general knowledge and context. To attempt to deal with evidence of this kind Fodor deploys two lines of argument. His first is to question whether the mechanisms involved in the 'highly attentional' process of reconstructing degraded linguistic stimuli are the same as those involved in the 'automatic and fluent' processes of everyday language use; and his second is to suggest that what looks like interference by general and contextual knowledge with the processes of the language module could in fact be explained in terms of lexical forms activating other forms to which they are linked without any involvement of considerations of contextual meaning. Thus, in the case of the first sentence above, he would say that the forms *thirsty* and *drink* are connected in the lexical network and that, accordingly, when *thirsty* is activated, *drink* is too, irrespective of meaning and context.

The advantage for Fodor of limiting his conception of the language module to that of a formal processor with no semantic role is that it does not confront him with the problem, discussed above, of where to draw the line between linguistic and non-linguistic meaning. However, his attempts to explain away context effects are less than persuasive. Regarding his non-standard processing argument, there is in fact nothing especially abnormal about having to process language which is incomplete in some way. Who has not from time to time, for example, had to work hard at understanding someone with an unfamiliar accent, strained to catch what was being said over a crackly telephone line, pored endlessly over a letter penned in the handwriting from hell, or struggled to read a blotchy or faint photocopy? With regard to what Fodor says about the excitation of complexes of lexical forms, this seems plausible enough as a non-semantic account of what looks like a meaning-related phenomenon until we stop to consider the nature of the links it presupposes. There is certainly plenty of evidence that such inter-lexical links exist (as we have already seen), but what is interesting to note is that they are (in the proficient language user) primarily based on semantic relatedness. Indeed, if the excitation posited by Fodor were not assumed to proceed along pathways linking semantically related items then the 'mimicking' of contextual-semantic effects of which he writes would remain unaccounted for. This must cast doubt on his suggestion that it is possible to explain away apparent context effects in terms of purely formal processes. A much more straightforward, and therefore more plausible, position is that what look like online context effects *are* actually online context effects.

Connectionism

Finally in this discussion of models of lexical processing, we turn to an approach which, like the modularity hypothesis, encompasses mental operations in general, but which, unlike the modularity hypothesis, draws no essential distinction between language processing and the processing of other kinds of information. This is the perspective known as *connectionism* or *parallel distributed processing*. The term *connectionism* relates to the fact that this approach takes its inspiration from neurophysiological activity in the brain – with its network of interconnected neurons sending signals to each other. The connectionist model takes the analogy of brain-style neuronal interactions as its metaphor for the workings of the mind, although in this case the suggestion is that the analogy in question may be more than just a metaphor. The alternative label, *parallel distributed processing,* refers to the claim made by connectionists that different portions of information are simultaneously processed independently of one another ('in parallel') on different levels ('distributed').

The connectionist view of mind is usually taken to be incompatible with the modular position discussed above. However, some linguists posit different networks of connections for the parallel but totally autonomous processing of different types of information, which they see as a merely a connectionist translation of the modularity idea. It is worth noting that connectionism belongs to a much broader *parallel processing* perspective which stands in opposition to the *serial processing* perspective. The issue here is not strictly about simultaneity versus sequentiality. Sequences of operations are found within parallel models, where successively presented aspects of the language to be dealt with obviously have to be dealt with as they arise; and simultaneity of operations is found in serial models, where different levels of operation may be simultaneously active though working on different domains – for example, the processing of item *x* may be beginning at one level while the processing of item *y* is nearing completion at another. The real distinction between the parallel perspective and the serial perspective is that the former posits the independence of the different processing operations which are triggered by particular events and stimuli, whereas the latter sees processing as organized in stages, with each stage dependent on the output of the previous stage. The notion of independence of different processing operations in parallel models such as the connectionist model is not, however, in any real sense comparable to the idea of informational encapsulation. Independence of processing in parallel models refers to micro-operations, and is not to be identified with a barrier between, for example, 'higher level' semantic processes and 'lower level' formal processes. On the contrary, parallel processing models are usually interpreted as envisaging a high degree of interactivity between semantic and formal processing.

A further respect in which connectionism has been seen to pose a challenge to the Chomskyan/Fodorian view of language and mind (and to most others) lies in its rejection of what is sometimes called the *symbolic paradigm,* the idea that mental operations involve the manipulation of symbols. So far in this chapter the entire discussion has been based on this notion, assuming, with regard to language that there are entities stored in the mind referring to external phenomena which can be retrieved from memory and combined according to rules or patterns which are also stored. The *connectionist paradigm* calls all of this into question, representing knowledge in terms of connection strength rather than in terms of rules or patterns.

According to connectionists it is not the patterns that are stored – not even the patterns of features that make up what we know as words, morphemes and phonemes – but rather the connection strengths between elements at a much lower level that allow these patterns to be recreated. Computer simulations have provided some evidence in favour of such a view by showing that quite simple networks can be trained to supply appropriate morphological and phonological structure on the basis of frequency of occurrence of the relevant configurations, without any kind of rules being involved in the training process. There are sharply differing views about significance of such findings, and the debate which has developed around them has been quite fierce.

However, there have also been attempts to reconcile the symbolist and the anti-symbolist positions. In any case, it is clear that there is significant overlap between some features of connectionism and other models of language processing. For example, the cohort model also relies on the notion of parallel processing. Moreover, the influence of connectionism is now so wide and powerful that other models are increasingly evolving in a connectionist direction. It has to be said also that connectionism is itself evolving; whereas in its early versions it was focused purely on formal aspects of language, there are now signs of a connectionist concern to take account of semantic issues.

9.6　L2 dimensions

We end this chapter with a brief exploration of the issue of how the mental lexicon is constructed and organized when more than one language is in question. Such a situation arises not only in cases of early bilingualism/multilingualism, where a child acquires more than one language from infancy onwards but also in cases where an individual acquires languages in addition to his/her first language at a later stage – whether at a subsequent stage of development during childhood or in adolescence or adulthood.

As far as early bilingualism/multilingualism is concerned, the phases passed through are, broadly speaking, the same for each language as described in 9.3 and 9.4 in respect of a single language. On the other hand, where languages are acquired later in childhood or beyond the childhood years there is no question of the individuals in question having to revisit the various 'milestones' that are associated with speech development in infancy. Such learners do not coo or babble, and when they begin producing utterances in their target languages such utterances are from the outset mostly comprised of combinations of meaningful elements. Accordingly, most of the discussion in 9.3 and 9.4 *vis-à-vis* the relationship between pre-verbal development and 'true speech' and much of what was said about lexical development after the onset of word production is irrelevant to the acquisition of additional languages beyond infancy. However, there are some points of contact, since the lexical challenge faced by the later learner of additional languages in crucial respects resembles that which confronts the infant, involving as it does the isolation of lexical units in the speech stream and the making of connections between such units and the meanings they are intended to communicate

With regard to the phonetic/phonological domain, just as the infant has to struggle to come to grips with the sound-shapes of the language of his/her environment from a starting-point – babbling – which is not necessarily very helpful phonetically, so the later acquirer of additional languages has to deal with sounds of these languages that may differ markedly from those of his/her first language. Also, while later learners have internalized the principle of phonemic distinctions and its role in differentiating between lexical items, they, like the infant, still have to work out which phonetic differences are phonemic and which are not. Moreover, the fact of having one phonological system already in place can be a source of hindrance as well as of help in this matter. It is also interesting to note that the relative efficiency of phonological working memory is as important in determining the rate of second language lexical development as it is in determining the rate of first language lexical development, and that therefore processing of phonological form is particularly crucial in the early stages of acquiring a new word.

In relation to the conceptual/semantic domain, learners of additional languages are obviously at a more advanced stage of concept development than infants acquiring their mother tongue. Indeed, many of the meanings and meaning hierarchies that have already been internalized in the course of the acquisition of first language will be re-applicable with only minimal adjustment in other languages. However, whatever the extent of the conceptual overlap between two language communities, there will always be areas of meaning in which the languages in question differ. In some instances the difference is such that totally new concepts need to be mastered; more often (and perhaps more problematically) the meanings of the two languages – reflecting the cultural particularities of the respective language communities – are differently structured and distributed. It is hardly surprising, in such circumstances, that lexical fluidity, over-extension and under-extension, familiar from what is observed in first language development, also occur in lexical development when additional languages are learned. Another meaning-related feature shared by first and second language lexical development is that easily imageable words tend to be more readily acquired than words with meanings that are less easy to 'picture'. Finally in the context of meaning-related aspects of lexical development observable in both first and second language development, we can note that, in the latter case as in the former, as the acquisition of a word proceeds, the manner in which its meaning is integrated changes. Initially it is primarily associated with the meanings of words with which it collocates (this being reflected in syntagmatic word associations – see above – such as *blue – sky*). Subsequently this kind of association tends to give way to a more hierarchical organization, with words covering the same broad area of meaning becoming linked in networks based on paradigmatic relations as synonymy (e.g. *little – small*), oppositeness of various kinds (e.g. *fat – thin*) hyponymy (e.g. *carrot – vegetable*).

Despite such similarities between first language lexical development and lexical development in additional languages, there is a quite widely held view that the second language mental lexicon is qualitatively different in structure from the first language mental lexicon. This view claims that, whereas in the first language mental lexicon the connections between the lexical units are predominantly semantic, in the second language mental lexicon they are predominantly phonological. Evidence in favour of this claim has been cited from word-association test data, which, so it is claimed, indicate the predominance of phonological links in the second language mental lexicon, the source of the response being in each case a word which is phonologically connected to the stimulus.

The opposite point of view – namely, that the first language mental lexicon and the second language mental lexicon function in essentially the same manner – is also advocated and supported. According to this perspective, whether on a given occasion the processing of a lexical item relies predominantly on meaning-based links and associations or on phonological relationships will depend not on the status of the language in which the item occurs (whether or not it is a first language or an additional language), but rather on the degree of familiarity of that particular word to that particular speaker at that particular time. This latter position assumes that newly encountered items tend to trigger form-focused processing because they have not yet – because of lack of relevant evidence – become connected up to the speaker's internal semantic schemata, whereas very familiar items are predominantly handled in terms of their meaning. Evidence in favour of this point of view comes from studies which show that as second language proficiency increases so does the proportion of semantically motivated responses produced in word-association tests, and that advanced second language learners confronted with second language vocabulary which is more or less within their grasp, will, in word-association tests and tests involving gapped texts, produce very small numbers of responses that are not semantically motivated.

A further issue is whether the second language mental lexicon is separated from or integrated with the first language mental lexicon. One indication of separateness comes from cases of language loss due to brain damage where one language is recovered before another. One very interesting instance of this phenomenon reported in the literature is that of a native speaker of Swiss German who first recovered French, a language he had learned imperfectly as an adult, who then recovered Standard High German, which had been the language of his formal education, but who failed to recover his L1, Swiss German. A not dissimilar case is that of the British Classics scholar who recovered Ancient Greek, Latin, French and English (his native language) in that order. Obviously, if languages – including the lexicons of these languages – can be recovered one by one in this kind of way then it is diffi-cult not to infer that they are separately stored and organized.

Integrationist arguments are not difficult to find either. The British lin-guist Vivian Cook who has for some years been putting the case for 'multi-competence' – i.e. the notion that language competence is unitary, no matter how many languages are involved – cites lexical evidence such as the fol-lowing:

- reaction time to a word in one language is related to the frequency of its cognate in another known language;
- morphemic similarities between two known languages influence transla-tion performance;
- bilinguals consult the lexical stores associated with both their languages when taking vocabulary tests in one of their languages.

Such evidence certainly supports the notion that the first language mental lexicon and the second language mental lexicon are connected, but it does not necessarily argue for total integration of the first language and second language lexical operations. A position which takes account of this evidence but also the evidence noted earlier of sequential language recovery is one which sees the first language and the second language mental lexicon as neither completely disconnected from each other nor totally integrated with each other.

Some interesting suggestions in this connection are to be found in the rel-evant research literature. One such suggestion is that pairs of translation-equivalents with concrete meanings in the two languages known to an individual and pairs of words perceived as cognates across the two lan-guages are stored in a 'compound' manner (i.e. as two forms with a shared meaning), whereas pairs of abstract non-cognate translation-equivalents in the respective languages are stored in a 'co-ordinate' manner (i.e. as distinct items in both their formal and their semantic aspects). Another suggestion is that second language forms which are perceived as related to first language words (e.g. French *table* – English *table*) are stored as variants of the first language vocabulary. The kind of evidence that is used in support of these ideas includes, for example, the fact that translating between cognates is much faster than translating between non-cognates (e.g. English *table* will tend to be translated as French *table* more rapidly than *armchair* will be translated as *fauteuil*). There is also some evidence of a learning environ-ment factor and a proficiency factor in the degree to which the first language and second language lexicons are integrated; that is to say, it seems to be the case that the more the first language is involved in the environment in which the second language is learned, the greater will be the degree of integrated-ness between the two mental lexicons, and that, as second language profi-ciency increases, the second language mental lexicon becomes less and less dependent on and more and more separate from the first language mental lexicon. In sum, the precise relationship between a given entry in the second language mental lexicon and a given entry in the first language mental lexicon probably appears to depend on how the words have been acquired, how well they are known, and to what extent formal and/or semantic similarity is perceived between them

9.7   Summary

Chapter 9 has been concerned with the internal or mental lexicon. It has examined some aspects of the acquisition of the mental lexicon in the course of first language acquisition; it has addressed some proposals regarding ways in which the mental lexicon might be organized and accessed; and it has explored some of the lexical issues that arise when more than one language is acquired and used by a given individual. Under the heading of lexical acquisition, topics dealt with included: the challenge posed for the language acquirer by the problem of isolating lexical units in the speech signal and connecting them with relevant content, the relationship between the first meaningful words produced by the child and everything that precedes this milestone, and the different phases of lexical development which follow the onset of word production. With regard to lexical processing, the chapter has summarized and assessed various psycholinguistic models concerning the organization and functioning of the mental lexicon – Morton's logogen model, Marslen-Wilson's cohort model, Forster's lexical search model, and Levelt's 'blueprint for the speaker' – and has also given consideration to modular and connectionist perspectives on lexical processing. Concerning the second language dimension, the chapter has noted a number of similarities between first language and second language lexical development, as well as some differences, and it has also looked at the issues of similarity/difference and integration/separation in respect of first language and second language lexical organization and processing.

Sources and suggestions for further reading

See 9.2. The poverty of the stimulus argument is rehearsed widely in publications by Chomsky and Chomskyans. It is accessibly discussed by N. Chomsky in his book *Language and problems of knowledge: the Managua lectures* (Cambridge, MA: MIT Press, 1988, Chapter 1) and by V. Cook and M. Newson in their volume *Chomsky's Universal Grammar: an introduction* (Oxford: Blackwell, 1996, 81ff.). The sources for the treatment of child-directed speech include: O. Garnica's article 'Some prosodic and paralinguistic features of speech to young children' (in C. Snow and C. Ferguson (eds), *Talking to children*, Cambridge: Cambridge University Press, 1977); M. Harris, D. Jones and J. Grant's article 'The non-verbal context of mothers' speech to children' (*First Language* 4, 1983, 21–30),

J. McShane's book *Cognitive development: an information processing account* (Oxford: Blackwell, 1991, 140ff.); E. Markman's article 'Constraints children place on word meanings' (in P. Bloom (ed.), *Language acquisition: core readings*, Hemel Hempstead: HarvesterWheatsheaf, 1993); and C. Snow's article 'Conversations with children' (in P. Fletcher and M. Garman (eds), *Language acquisition: studies in first language development* (second edition, Cambridge: Cambridge University Press, 1986). The comments on the different kinds of challenge posed by different kinds of writing system draw on relevant discussion in M. Clark's book *Young fluent readers* (London: Heinemann, 1976) and O. Tzeng and W. S.-Y. Wang's article 'The first two R's' (*American Scientist* 71, 1983, 238–43). The source for the remarks about early readers' use of context is A. Biemiller's article 'The development of the use of graphic and contextual information as children learn to read' (*Reading Research Quarterly* 6, 1970, 75–96).

See 9.3. An overview of experimental evidence regarding sound discrimination in infants is to be found in P. Eimas's article 'The perception of speech in early infancy' (*Scientific American* 252, 1985, 46–52). The studies dealing with sound discrimination in chinchillas and rhesus monkeys are reported in P. Kuhl and J. Miller, 'Speech perception by the chinchilla: voice–voiceless distinction in alveolar plosive consonants' (*Science* 190, 1975, 69–72); P. Kuhl and J. Miller, 'Speech perception by the chinchilla: identification functions for synthetic VOT stimuli' (*Journal of the Acoustical Society of America* 63, 1978, 905–17); and P. Morse and C. Snowdon, 'An investigation of categorical speech discrimination by rhesus monkeys' (*Perception and Psychophysics* 17, 1975, 9–16). A much-cited experiment relating to pre-linguistic concepts is that reported by P. Bomba and E. Siqueland in their article, 'The nature and structure of infant form categories' (*Journal of Experimental Child Psychology* 35, 1983, 295–328). Evidence of pre-linguistic concepts from infant–caregiver interaction is discussed by M. Scaife and J. Bruner in their article, 'The capacity for joint visual attention in the infant ' (*Nature* 253, 1975, 265–6). The discussion of the level of generality of innate concepts is based on R. Campbell's article 'Language acquisition and cognition' (in P. Fletcher and M. Garman (eds), *Language acquisition: studies in first language development*, second edition, Cambridge: Cambridge University Press, 1986). The quotation from J. Harris is from his book *Early language development: implications for clinical and educational practice*. (London: Routledge, 1990, 82). The quotation from J. Bruner is to be found on p. 2 of his article 'The ontogenesis of speech acts' (*Journal of Child Language* 2, 1975, 1–19). Some of the evidence in favour of babbling drift is summarized by M. L. Moreau and M. Richelle on p. 50 of their volume *L'acquisition du langage* (Brussels: Pierre Mardaga, 1981). Typical of the representatives of the nativist anti-babbling drift position is H. Goodluck – as indicated by remarks on p. 21 of her book *Language acquisition: a linguistic introduction* (Oxford: Blackwell, 1991). N. Chomsky's much-cited early attack on behaviourism is his review of B. F. Skinner's *Verbal behavior* (New York: Appleton–Century–Crofts, 1957), which was published in the journal *Language* (1959, 35, 26–58). The [i i i]example is borrowed from p. 54 of M. L. Moreau and M. Richelle's book *L'acquisition du langage* (Brussels: Pierre Mardaga, 1981) and the [nə nə nə nə nə] example from p. 90 of L. Bloom's book *One word at a time: the use of single word utterances before syntax* (The Hague: Mouton, 1973). The 'Uh oh, where'd it go?' example is taken from p. 158 of M. Vihmann and R. Miller's article 'Words and babble at the threshold of language acquisition' (in M. D. Smith and J. Locke (eds), *The emergent lexicon: the child's development of a linguistic vocabulary*, London: Academic Press).

See 9.4. The *dut* example comes from M. Barrett's article 'Early semantic representations and early semantic development' (in S. Kuczaj and M. Barrett (eds), *The development of word meaning*, New York: Springer, 1986). The co-existence of context-bound and context-flexible usages in the very early stages of word production is reported and discussed by M. Harris in her book *Language experience and early language development: from input to uptake* (Hove & Hillsdale, NJ: Lawrence Erlbaum, 1992, 77ff.). Harris also discusses and advocates – in the same book (pp. 69ff.) – the three-stage view of early lexical development. The importance of phonological working memory in vocabulary development emerges from studies reported in S. Gathercole and A. Baddeley's articles 'Evaluation of the role of phonological STM in the development of vocabulary in children: a longitudinal study' (*Journal of Memory and Language* 28, 1989, 200–13) and 'Phonological memory deficits in language-disordered children: is there a causal connection?' (*Journal of Memory and Language* 29, 1990, 336–60). The P. Guillaume quotation is cited (in my translation) from p. 8 of his article 'Les débuts de la phrase dans le langage de l'enfant' (*Journal de Psychologie Normale et Pathologique* 24, 1927, 1–25). Over-extension is very much a *leitmotiv* of the work of E. Clark and is much discussed in her book *The lexicon in acquisition* (Cambridge: Cambridge University Press, 1993). The M. Harris quotation about under-extension is to be found on p. 71 of her 1992 volume (see above). An advocate of the 'under-extensions first' position is P. Griffiths – see, for example his article 'Early vocabulary' (in P. Fletcher. and M. Garman (eds), *Language acquisition: studies in first language development*, second edition, Cambridge: Cambridge University Press, 1986). 'Basic' categories are primarily associated with the work of E. Rosch and her colleagues – see, for example, E. Rosch, C. Mervis, W. Gray, D. Johnson and P. Boyes-Braem, 'Basic objects in natural categories (*Cognitive Psychology* 8, 1976, 382–439). Evidence in support of the notion that basic categories come first in lexical development summarized by S. Waxman in her article 'The development of an appreciation of specific linkages between linguistic and conceptual organization' (in L. Gleitman and B. Landau (eds), *The acquisition of the lexicon*, Cambridge, MA: MIT Press, 1994). The naming insight in relation to the 'vocabulary explosion' is discussed by J. McShane in his book, *Cognitive development: an information processing approach* (Oxford: Blackwell, 1991, 143ff.). The notion that imageability is a factor in word retention is treated by N. Ellis and A. Beaton in their articles 'Factors affecting the learning of foreign language vocabulary: imagery keyword mediators and phonological short-term memory' (*Quarterly Journal of Experimental Psychology: Human Experimental Psychology* 46A, 1993, 533–58) and 'Psycholinguistic determinants of foreign language vocabulary learning' (in B. Harley (ed.), *Lexical issues in language learning*, Ann Arbor/Amsterdam/ Philadelphia: Language Learning/John Benjamins Publishing Company, 1995). Evidence in favour of 'fast mapping' is cited by S. Carey and E. Bartlett in their article 'Acquiring a new word' (*Papers and Reports on Child Language Development* 15, 1978, 17–29) and by K. Nelson and J. Bonvillian in their article, 'Early language development: conceptual growth and related processes between 2 and 4½ years' (in K. Nelson (ed.), *Children's language. Volume 1*, New York: Gardner, 1978). The principal sources for the discussion of the development of hierarchical relations are J. Anglin's books, *The growth of word meaning* (Cambridge, MA: MIT Press, 1970) and *Word, object and conceptual development* (New York: Norton, 1977). J.B. Carroll's conclusion is to be found on p. 124 of his article 'Development of native language skills beyond the early years' (in C. Reed (ed.), *The learning of language*, New York: Appleton–Century–Crofts, 1971); K. Diller's comment is on p. 29 of his book, *Generative grammar, structural linguistics and language teaching* (Rowley, MA: Newbury House, 1971).

See 9.5. The distinction between direct and indirect access models of the lexicon is made by, for example M. Garman in his book, *Psycholinguistics* (Cambridge: Cambridge University Press, 1990, 260ff.). The term 'neural unit' is used as a forerunner of the term *logogen* in, for example J. Morton's article, 'A preliminary functional model for language behaviour' (in R. Oldfield and J. Marshall (eds), *Language: selected readings*, Harmondsworth: Penguin, 1968; originally published in *International Audiology* 3, 1964, 216–25). The classic cohort model is outlined in W. Marslen-Wilson and A. Welsh's article, 'Processing interactions and lexical access during word-recognition in continuous speech' (*Cognitive Psychology* 10, 1978, 29–63); a modified version of the model is presented in W. Marslen-Wilson's article 'Functional parallelism in spoken word recognition' (*Cognition* 25, 1987, 71–102). The evidence concerning the recognition of non-words was presented in W. Marslen-Wilson's paper 'Sequential decision processes during spoken word-recognition' at the Psychonomic Society meeting, San Antonio, Texas, 1978. The argument about the interwoven nature of speech sounds is put by M. Garman on p. 288 of *Psycholinguistics* (cited above). The cohort model's account of context effects is dealt with in W. Marslen-Wilson and L. Tyler's articles 'The temporal structure of spoken language understanding' (*Cognition* 8, 1980, 1–71) and 'Against modularity' (in J. Garfield (ed.), *Modularity in knowledge representation and natural-language understanding*, Cambridge, MA:

MIT Press, 1987). The account of K. Forster's search model is based on his article 'Accessing the mental lexicon' (in R. Wales and E. Walker (eds), *New approaches to language mechanisms*, Amsterdam, North-Holland, 1976). The account of W. Levelt's model is a simplified summary of what he has to say in his book, *Speaking: from intention to articulation* (Cambridge, MA: MIT Press, 1989). The quotation summarizing the modularity hypothesis is to be found on p. 1 of J. Garfield's editorial introduction to the above-cited collection of essays entitled *Modularity in knowledge representation and natural-language understanding*. The account of J. Fodor's perspective on modularity is mostly based on his book, *The modularity of mind: an essay on faculty psychology* (Cambridge, MA: MIT Press, 1983). The 'yellow stripey thing' example is discussed in his article 'Why should the mind be modular?' (in A. George (ed.), *Reflections on Chomsky*, Oxford: Blackwell). The example relating to Finnish in France figured in a personal communication to me some years ago from the Finnish psychologist Elisabet Service. The material on hypnosis was culled from M. Orne and A. Hammer's article 'Hypnosis' (in *Macropaedia*, Volume 9, *Encyclopedia Britannica*, 1974) and L. Chertok's book, *Hypnose et Suggestion* (Paris: Presses Universitaires de France, 1989). The account of connectionism given here is derived principally from D. Rumelhart, J. McClelland and the PDP Research Group (eds), *Parallel distributed processing: explorations in the microstructure of cognition. Volume 1: Foundations* (Cambridge, MA: MIT Press, 1986) and J. McClelland, D. Rumelhart and the PDP Research Group (eds), *Parallel distributed processing: explorations in the microstructure of cognition. Volume 2. Psychological and biological models* (Cambridge, MA: MIT Press, 1986)). Further insights were gleaned from J. Elman's articles, 'Finding structure in time' (*Cognitive Science* 4, 1990, 179–211) and 'Representation and structure in connectionist models' (in G. Altman (ed.), *Cognitive models of speech processing* (Cambridge, MA: MIT Press, 1990)). An example of an attempt to reconcile connectionism with modularity is to be found in M. Tanenhaus, G. Dell and G. Carlson's article, 'Context effects in lexical processing: a connectionist approach to modularity' (in the above-cited 1987 volume edited by Garfield). A version of connectionism with a semantic dimension is sketched in for example, B. MacWhinney and J. Leinbach's article 'Implementations are not conceptualizations: revising the verb learning model' (*Cognition* 48, 1991, 21–69).

See 9.6. The role of cross-linguistic influence is very widely discussed in the literature of second language acquisition – see, for example T. Odlin's *Language transfer: crosslinguistic influence in language learning* (Cambridge: Cambridge University Press). Specifically lexical dimensions of cross-linguistic influence are dealt with by B. Laufer in articles such as 'Words you know: how they affect the words you learn' (in J. Fisiak (ed.), *Further insights into contrastive linguistics*, Amsterdam: John Benjamins, 1990) and 'Appropriation du vocabulaire: mots faciles, mots difficiles, mots impossibles' (*Acquisition et Interaction en Langue Etrangère* 3, 97–113).

Evidence of the importance of the role of phonological working memory in second language acquisition is presented in, for example, A. Baddeley, C. Papagno and G. Vallar, 'When long-term learning depends on short-term storage' (*Journal of Memory and Language* 27, 1988, 586–95); C. Papagno, T. Valentine and A. Baddeley, 'Phonological short-term memory and foreign-language vocabulary learning' (*Journal of Memory and Language* 30, 1991, 331–47); E. Service, 'Phonology, working memory and foreign-language learning' (*Quarterly Journal of Experimental Psychology* 45A, 1992, 21–50). The syntagmatic–paradigmatic shift in second language lexical development is documented by T. Söderman in her article, 'Word associations of foreign language learners and native speakers: the phenomenon of a shift in response type and its relevance for lexical development' (in H. Ringbom (ed.), *Near-native proficiency in English*, Åbo: Åbo Akademi, English Department Publications, 1993). The point of view that the second language mental lexicon is qualitatively different from the first language mental lexicon is advanced by P. Meara in 'The study of lexis in interlanguage' (in A. Davies, C. Criper and A. P. R. Howatt (eds), *Interlanguage*, Edinburgh: Edinburgh University Press). Meara's position is challenged in, for example, D. Singleton and D. Little, 'The second language lexicon: some evidence from university-level learners of French and German (*Second Language Research* 7, 1991, 61–82). The Swiss case of language recovery is reported by F. Grosjean in *Life with two languages: an introduction to bilingualism* (Cambridge, MA: Harvard University Press, 1982, 260); the British case of language recovery is reported by H. Whitaker in 'Bilingualism: a neurolinguistics perspective' (in W. Ritchie (ed.), *Second language acquisition research: issues and implications*, New York: Academic Press, 1978, 27). V. Cook pleads the case for multicompetence in 'Evidence for multicompetence' (*Language Learning* 42, 1992, 557–91). The suggestions regarding different factors in the precise ways in which entries in the first language and the second language mental lexicon are to be found in A. De Groot 'Determinants of bilingual lexicosemantic organisation' (*Computer Assisted Language Learning* 8, 1995, 151–80); K. Kirsner, E. Lalor and K. Hird, 'The bilingual lexicon: exercise, meaning and morphology' (in R. Schreuder and B. Weltens, *The Bilingual Lexicon*, Amsterdam: John Benjamins, 1993); U. Weinreich, *Languages in contact*, New York: Linguistic Circle of New York, 1953).

An excellent first introduction to child language acquisition in general is:

S. Foster-Cohen, *Language development in children* (London: Longman, 1998).

Another title which, though not strictly introductory, is accessibly written and well worth consulting in this connection is:

M. Harris, *Language experience and early language development: from intake to uptake* (Hove/Hillsdale, NJ: Lawrence Erlbaum, 1992).

Good introductory works on language processing include:

A. Ellis and G. Beattie, *The psychology of language and communication* (London: Weidenfeld & Nicolson, 1986);

M. Forrester, *Psychology of language: a critical introduction* (London: Sage, 1996);

M. Harris and M. Coltheart, *Language processing in children and adults* (London: Routledge & Kegan Paul, 1986).

The best introduction to all aspects of the mental lexicon is:

J. Aitchison, *Words in the mind* (second edition, Oxford: Blackwell, 1994).

In a somewhat less introductory mode, the mental lexicon is also fairly comprehensively dealt with in:

M. Garman, *Psycholinguistics* (Cambridge: Cambridge University Press, 1990).

On the topic of second language mental lexicon readers may wish to consult:

D. Singleton, *Exploring the second language mental lexicon* (Cambridge: Cambridge University Press, 1999).

Focusing questions/topics for discussion

1. Imagine that in the room with you is a two-year-old child and imagine yourself talking to this child about the various features of the room and the objects in it. Write down the dialogue you imagine and then compare what you have written with the description in 9.2 of typical features of child-directed speech. If there is a young child in your family or home environment observe the way in which adults (including yourself) actually do talk to this child and assess how far what you observe corresponds to what is suggested in 9.2.

2. In many cultures words like *baba* and *mama* are used by adults when talking to young children. Why do you think this might be, and how do you think it might complicate the task of sorting out the relationship between babbling and later language development?

3. Suggest some likely responses to the following word association stimuli from (i) a pre-school child acquiring English as his/her first language and (ii) an adult native speaker of English:

ask	*go*
cake	*hot*
mummy	*sweet*
doll	*two*
eat	*water*

4. Give a brief account of how the cohort model would deal with the receptive processing of the words *bottle, egregious, endeavour, policy* and *sterility*. What is the 'uniqueness point' in each case?

5. Write down the translations of the following English words into any other language you know:

apple	quality	kiosk	totality
beautiful	red	lamp	unbelievable
charity	real	meaning	vary
desk	seat	note	vapour
kindness	terrible	piety	wash

In the light of the discussion in 9.6, which of the pairs of translation-equivalents you now have before you (if any) would you expect to have a particularly close relationship in terms of the organization of the mental lexicon – and why?

|10|

Charting and imparting the lexicon

10.1 Dictionaries and didactics

Having explored the lexicon in its various linguistic dimensions – syntactic, morphological, phonological etc., having looked at its social and historical dimensions, and having examined some aspects of lexical development and lexical processing in the individual, we turn now to two time-honoured ways in which the individual's lexical proficiency is supported and advanced – namely, through the elaboration of dictionaries and through the promotion of vocabulary learning in the context of formal education.

Dictionaries have a long history, and dictionary-making, or lexicography has been through a succession of changes in its orientation and its methodology. What has remained stable amidst all this flux is the status of the dictionary, which remains high. Indeed, the fact that dictionaries are increasingly based on vast computerized corpora of language data derived from real instances of language in a variety of uses has, if anything, enhanced their authority. In the first part of this chapter we shall trace the evolution of lexicography from ancient glossaries down to dictionaries on the web – with particular (though not exclusive) reference to dictionaries of English, and we shall note the ways in which the impossibility of seeing lexical phenomena in isolation from other aspects of language has challenged lexicographers.

With regard to lexis in the classroom, it is also true to say that language teaching is a practice and a profession with a past. Like lexicography, it has been through many different forms. In the second part of the chapter we shall explore some different approaches to the lexical learning and teaching in the context of formal language education, and we shall consider, in the light of all that has been said in previous chapters, to what extent it is possible to conceive of lexical instruction as separable from the teaching of other dimensions of language.

10.2   Lexicography: a potted history

As we saw in Chapter 8, the forms and meanings of words evolve over time
– sometimes, as we saw, over a relatively short period of time. This presents
a problem when it comes to understanding and interpreting texts which may
be decades or centuries old and which reflect a no longer current state of
affairs as far as lexical forms and meanings are concerned. This problem is
especially acute when the texts in question are of great significance to a given
community. One option in such cases is to update the texts – to 'translate'
them into the contemporary idiom. However, factors such as the fear of
destroying the aesthetic integrity of a text or taboos around the altering of
'the word of God' often militate against revisions of this kind. The alternative route is to provide commentaries on and explanations or *glosses* of the
forms and senses which are no longer current. In the modern world this is
what we see in, for example, school editions of the works of Shakespeare. In
earlier times the same principle was applied, for example, in first century AD
Greece to older Greek literary texts, and in northern France of the eighth-
century AD to the Latin version of the Bible (the Vulgate).

With regard to the Greek case, by the first century AD much of Homer's
language, and that of writers such as Plato, was opaque to users of the Greek
of that time. Accordingly, glossaries of the difficult elements in such texts
were compiled from this time onwards by commentators such as Pamphilus
of Alexandria, Diogenanius and Zopyrion. As far as the eighth-century
Latin glosses are concerned, these are to be found in a document now known
as the *Glosses of Reichenau*, and what they do is to explain a number of
Latin words, chiefly from the Vulgate, in terms that an educated user of the
'Latin' or Romance used in that region at that time would understand. Some
examples of such glosses are:

Ager: campus	('field')
Cecenit: cantavit	('he/she/it sang')
In foro: in mercato	('in the marketplace')
In ore: in bucca	('in the mouth')
Semel: una vica	('once')

Explanations of the above kind are essentially translations between words
used at one stage in the development of a language and words used at a subsequent stage. However, in other cases translations between two distinct languages were involved. For example, in Ancient Mesopotamia, when the
Sumerian language began to die out as a mother tongue (around 2000 BC),
giving way to the group of Semitic varieties known as Akkadian, it nevertheless remained an important vehicle of important elements of Mesopotamian
culture – rather like Latin in western Europe in the middle ages. Accordingly,
it was formally taught in the schools so that important texts could continue

to be understood, and one element used as an aid in this context was a large corpus of Sumerian–Akkadian vocabulary-lists and treatments of Sumerian morphology. A little closer to our own era, in early Anglo-Saxon times it was common practice in the monasteries to insert Old English equivalents of difficult Latin words between the lines of Latin manuscripts. As a time-saver, the custom subsequently arose of providing the relevant glosses either in lists in the margins of pages or in pages appended to the manuscripts. These kinds of collections of Latin–Old English translation-equivalents go back as far as the eighth century AD.

None of the above would constitute what we nowadays call a dictionary, but we can see in all of them the beginnings of the dictionary idea. As glossaries grew in size and scope the question of how to organize the material started to loom large – a question which continues to challenge lexicographers even today. One solution was to group words according to topic; so, one list of words might comprise Latin names of plants with English (French, German etc.) equivalents, another might be focused on names of animals, another on parts of the body etc. Such specialized classifications – forerunners of today's technical dictionaries – were known as *nomenclatores* – the Latin word *nomenclator* having originally been applied to a slave who told his master the names of the persons he met. Some *nomenclatores* were not just bilingual but multilingual – notably the sixteenth-century work by Hadrianus Junius, *Nomenclator omnium rerum* ('*Namer of all things*') (1567) which gave equivalents in Latin, Greek, French and English. Thematic dictionaries are still with us. For example, the *thesaurus* type of dictionary, such as *Roget's Thesaurus* or the *Oxford Thesaurus*, provide collections of words under entries such as *border (edge, margin, hem . . .) nimble (agile, lively, active . . .), scatter (spread, diffuse, shower . . .)* etc. and some dictionaries are organized on rather broader thematic lines; for example, the *Oxford Dictionary of Slang* is arranged in sections with headings like 'People and Society', 'Money Commerce and Employment', 'Behaviour, Attitudes and Emotions', each of which is divided up on the basis of subtopics.

The other approach to arranging the content of glossaries in cultures using an alphabetic writing system was to sequence items according to their written form and following the conventional sequence of letters in the relevant alphabet. Embryonic Latin–English dictionaries of this kind appear as early as the fifteenth century. After the invention of printing rather larger alphabetized Latin–English dictionaries became available, and in due course a printed dictionary appeared with the Latin words placed after the English words. This was the *Abdecedarium Anglico Latinum* compiled by Richard Huloet (1552). It has to be said that alphabetization was somewhat approximate in these early glossaries and dictionaries. Thus, for instance, in the fifteenth-century *Catholicon Anglicum'* to *Nee as a horse* ('neigh') and *Negligent* come before *a Nede* ('need').

The first monolingual dictionaries devoted to modern vernaculars began to appear in Europe in the sixteenth and seventeenth centuries. This was, of course, at a time of when interest in the languages of Ancient Greece and Rome was extremely high. Paradoxically, this led scholars and writers in various European countries to wish to bring their own languages and cultures to the point where they could begin to emulate Classical Greek and Latin in terms of richness, orderliness, stability etc. Hence the efforts to codify, regularize and enhance the vernacular languages of Europe through the production of not only dictionaries but also treatises on various aspects of the languages in question. With regard to dictionaries, the fact that the dictionaries which had been around prior to vernacular dictionaries had focused on Latin, and the fact that there was a tradition – going back to the medieval glossaries – for such dictionaries to concentrate on difficult words had a strong influence on what was included in and excluded from the content of early vernacular dictionaries. Thus, the first monolingual English dictionary, *The Table Alphabeticall* (1604), compiled by Robert Cawdrey, set itself the task of defining 2560 'hard vsual English wordes gathered for the benefit & helpe of Ladies, Gentlewomen, or any other vnskilfull persons'. Examples of such 'hard usual words' can be seen in the first eight entries under O in Cawdrey's work – *obdurate, obeisance, object, oblation, oblectation, obliged, oblique, oblivious* – all of which are derived from Latin and French, and most of which would have been 'usual' only in learned discourse. Of less hard words such as *oaf, oak, oar, oath, oats* or *obey, The Table Alphabeticall* has nothing to say whatever.

Other English dictionaries based on the 'hard word' policy swiftly followed; these included John Bullokar's *English Expositor* (1616) and Thomas Blount's *Glossographia* (1656). Indeed, the 'hard word' tradition in dictionary making continued through many centuries, and its influence persists even into modern times. However, some lexicographers, even in the seventeenth and eighteenth centuries, had a wider perspective. Thus, for example, Henry Cockeram's *English Dictionarie* (1623) listed 'vulgar' terms and glossed them with more refined equivalents and also included everyday items such as *hair, tavern* and *yellow*. A dictionary published anonymously some decades later, the *Gazophylacium Anglicanum* (1689) was even broader in scope. At the beginning of the eighteenth century a fairly explicit break with the 'hard word' approach came with John Kersey's *New English Dictionary* (1702), which included a larger number of 'ordinary words' than any previous dictionary.

Nathaniel Bailey's *Universal Etymological Dictionary* (1721), which became the standard dictionary of its time, continued with the policy of including everyday words, and also included illustrative quotations. This latter practice was familiar from ancient times. It was to be found in limited form in bilingual and multilingual dictionaries such as Cotgrave's *Dictionarie of the French and English Tongues* (1632), and in very fulsome form in continental dictionaries such as that of the Académie Française (1694). Illustrative quotations had also figured in Blount's *Glossographia* (see above) and were very much a feature of the best-known English dictionary of the eighteenth century, Samuel Johnson's *Dictionary of the English Language* (1755).

Johnson's dictionary set out to encapsulate the 'best' usage of the period, while rendering certain older usages accessible to the eighteenth-century reader. To this end it incorporated earlier senses of words as well as the then current senses, supporting its definitions with more than 100,000 quotations. Johnson's manner of proceeding was in fact a forerunner of the 'historical approach' later adopted by the compilers of the *Oxford English Dictionary*. However, Johnson's insistence on focusing exclusively on what he considered the best usage and his exclusion of authors which did not meet his approval meant that the histories of many of the items he dealt with were somewhat incomplete. Incidentally, some of the authors excluded by Johnson were ruled out not on linguistic or stylistic grounds but because Johnson disagreed with them. Thus, for example, Johnson did not cite the philosopher Thomas Hobbes because he did not like his ideas.

Other English dictionaries produced in the eighteenth century tended to take a rather different line, principally focusing on spellings, correct usage and, increasingly, pronunciation. On the other hand, lexicographers interested in the historical method continued to make their presence felt. John Jamieson, for instance, in his *Etymological Dictionary of the Scottish Language* (1808), gave the earliest authority for every sense specified for each headword. Jamieson was, indeed, more adventurous than Johnson in his wide-ranging use of sources, and was in fact criticized by his reviewers for the lowliness of some of his authorities.

Across the Atlantic Johnson's method was only partially taken on board by the father of American lexicography, Noah Webster. He thought that Johnson had expended too much space on the 'useless' illustration of well-known words by quotations. He was also highly prescriptive in his outlook, which was out of keeping with an approach that was prepared to take account of variation and development in meaning. Webster's own *American Dictionary of the English Language* (1860) focused on etymologies and definitions, with quotations being assigned a relatively minor role.

The last great landmark in lexicography in respect of English up to the advent of information technology was a dictionary which explicitly declared itself in its title to be based on an historical approach. This was *A New English Dictionary on Historical Principles* (1884–1928), more popularly known as the *Oxford English Dictionary* or the *OED*. The chief originator of the dictionary, Richard Cheveix Trench, believed that it was possible to make judgments about given lexical usages, but, on the other hand, he did not believe in excluding what he considered less acceptable usages from the dictionary. As we have seen, 'historical principles' figured in earlier English dictionaries, including Johnson's, and so it is possible to see the *OED* as the culmination of an already established tradition in English lexicography. However, there was a further very important – perhaps crucial – influence on the shaping of the method used in the preparation of this dictionary –

namely the work of the German lexicographer Franz Passow, who in 1812 published an essay in which he strongly advocated the provision of chronologically arranged citations in the service of showing forth the history of each word. Passow's approach had a major impact on the work of H.G. Liddell and R. Scott, compilers of *The Greek–English Lexicon Based on the Work of Franz Passow* (1843). When the first editor of the OED, Herbert Coleridge, wished to explain the approach he and his team had adopted, he simply quoted from the Preface of Liddell and Scott's lexicon the proposition that every word 'should be made to tell its own story'. A second edition of the dictionary began to be prepared in 1983 under the administrative direction of Timothy Benbow and under the editorship of John A. Simpson and Edmund S.C. Weiner, and was published in 1989.

The great leap forward in dictionary making in very recent times has been the use of information technology in both lexicographical research and the production and presentation of lexicographical material. On the research front, as was mentioned in Chapter 4, there has been a massive investment since the 1980s in the construction and exploitation of computerized corpora of naturally occurring language, both spoken and written. As was indicated earlier, the leader in the field in this connection was the *COBUILD* (*Collins Birmingham University International Language Database*) project, involving a partnership between the Collins (now HarperCollins) publishing house and the School of English of the University of Birmingham, which has assembled a corpus of naturally occurring English data, now known as the *Bank of English*, running to more than 300 million words. A number of reference works – aimed primarily at advanced non-native learners and users of English – have been based on this corpus, including the *Collins COBUILD English Language Dictionary* (Glasgow: Collins, 1987), the *Collins COBUILD English Dictionary* (Glasgow and London: HarperCollins, 1995), the Collins COBUILD Dictionary of Idioms (Glasgow and London: HarperCollins, 1995) and the *Collins COBUILD English Words in Use* (Glasgow and London: HarperCollins, 1997).

Other previously mentioned corpora which have informed recent dictionary production – again especially, though not exclusively, in the area of dictionaries intended primarily for advanced non-native learners of English – are the *British National Corpus* (90 million words of written British English and 10 million words of spoken British English), the *Longman–Lancaster Corpus* (30 million words of spoken and written British and American English), and the *Cambridge International Corpus* (95 million words of written English plus a spoken language annexe, comprising five million words, known as the *Cambridge and Nottingham Corpus of Discourse in English*). The *British National Corpus* was used in the preparation of such dictionaries as the *Longman Dictionary of Contemporary English* (third edition, London: Longman, 1995) and the *Oxford Advanced Learner's Dictionary* (fifth edition, Oxford: Oxford University Press, 1995), and recent dictionaries published by Longman, including the *Longman*

Dictionary of American English (second edition, London: Longman, 1997) have also been informed by the *Longman–Lancaster Corpus*. The *Cambridge International Corpus*, for its part, was drawn on in the preparation of the *Cambridge International Dictionary of English* (Cambridge: Cambridge University Press, 1995).

Advantages of using corpora in dictionary making include the following. First, the existence of such vast amounts of attested English means that examples are readily available for citation in respect of every usage of the word to which the lexicographer wishes to refer. Corpus-based dictionaries tend to follow 'historical principles' to the extent that they rely exclusively on 'real' rather than made-up examples in support of their definitions; they differ from dictionaries such as the *OED* in this connection only insofar as they focus on just one historical phase of development (current usage) rather than tracing development over several centuries and insofar as the examples they deploy draw on sources which extend beyond 'serious' writing. Second, the fact that the databanks in question are computerized means that it is extremely easy to extract information from them about the frequency of occurrence of any given item in any given variety (spoken, written, British English, American English etc.) and generally. Even more interestingly, using concordancing techniques, it is a straightforward matter to obtain information about the combinations in which any given word appears, and with what frequency, in different varieties and generally. Accordingly, lexicographers using corpora no longer have to rely on their own intuitions and impressions when making decisions about which items and usages are 'mainstream' and which are more peripheral. Data emerging from frequency counts and concordancing procedures can also be used in decision-making about the ordering of information provided in association with any given entry – whether, for example to present and illustrate more typical usages earlier than less typical usages. Finally, the kind of information made available by computerized corpora enables the lexicographer to provide accurate and useful profiles of the discourse marking functions of words like *well* and *right* which were largely ignored in traditional dictionaries for example, the use of *right* to signal drawing a line under one point or topic and moving on to another, as in:

> *That's how Descartes saw the matter. Right. Now let's have a look at what the Empiricists had to say about this issue.*

Turning now to the use of information technology in the production and presentation of lexicographical material, the reference here is, essentially, to dictionaries on CD-ROM and dictionaries on the Internet. In principle, electronic dictionaries of this kind could solve large numbers of the problems faced by lexicographers over the centuries – specifically those having to do with the question of the amount of material to be included and that of the ordering of material. With regard to the former, a traditional book-type dictionary obviously presents severe constraints on how much information can be included under any given entry. Electronic dictionaries are not subject to such constraints, and, with their capacity to offer links to other entries and to other sources of information, may indeed be virtually limitless in respect of the quantity of information they can make available. As far as the ordering of material is concerned, since in an electronic dictionary it is possible to provide search facilities which operate instantly on more or less whatever information the user has at his/her disposal to key in (word-form, definition, common collocates etc.), the quest for a self-consistent and user-friendly way in which to sequence lexical material – whether on a formal basis (e.g. alphabetically) or within a thematic framework – is no longer such a major issue in this context.

An example of a dictionary which has recently appeared in a CD-ROM version is the above-mentioned *Oxford Advanced Learner's Dictionary*. The CD-ROM version can be used in a book-like fashion – to the extent that it can be scrolled though as continuous text. However, it can also be instantly searched by inputting various kinds of information. Moreover, the searching facilities provide instant access to usage notes, to maps, illustrations and photographs, and to tens of thousands of corpus-based examples. A further dictionary from the Oxford stable with a CD-ROM version is the *Oxford American Wordpower Dictionary* (Oxford: Oxford University Press, 1999). This is a dictionary aimed at intermediate students of American English as a second language which sets out to bridge the gap between basic survival vocabulary and a broader lexical range. In this connection, as well as containing the usual kind of information that one might expect to find in a dictionary (plus special sections on American culture and appendices dealing with areas such as irregular verbs, numbers and place-names), it includes 'study pages' presenting information on, for example, collocations, phrasal verbs and study skills in a schematic, uncluttered way. It thus begins to blur the distinction between dictionary and learning materials. The CD-ROM version goes much further in this direction; as well as providing a search facility giving instant access to any part of the text, it makes available hundreds of pictures, video clips illustrating the use of difficult words, audio elements modelling pronunciation, grammar and vocabulary exercises, and educational games.

With regard to dictionaries available on the Internet, many of these are quite disappointing in terms of their failure to use the extraordinary possibilities offered by the technology, some being little more than rather crude glossaries with very limited search facilities. Other online dictionaries present large amounts of flexibly searchable information but without really going beyond the book form of the texts in question in terms of types of information available. There are, however, a number of dictionaries on the Internet which take fuller advantage of the technology and which adventure beyond traditional formats. One such is the *Newbury House Online Dictionary*, available at http://nhd.heinle.com/. This is an electronic version of the *Newbury House Dictionary of American English* (third edition, Boston: Heinle & Heinle, 2000). The major addition to the online version is a database of 50,000 photographs, which can be accessed by clicking on a

'Related Photograph' button in respect of any given entry. More impressive still is the *Larousse Multimédia Encyclopédique sur CompuServe*, a subscription encyclopedic dictionary to be found at http://larousse.compuserve.com, which offers, alongside definitions and other information which one might expect to find in a normal dictionary, the possibility of accessing not only relevant visual displays but also articles on related topics.

10.3   The lexicon – lexicographer's bane!

The clear message of earlier chapters of this book has been that the lexicon is a great deal more complex, a great deal broader in scope and a great deal more bound up with other areas of language than has traditionally been acknowledged. What this means from the lexicographer's point of view is that the material he/she has to try to organize presents many more problems than are ever imagined by the 'dictionary-user in the street'.

We can begin to explore some of these problems by looking at those aspects of the dictionary which are often thought of as its basic functions – the provision of the accepted spelling of a given entry and the definition of its meaning. With regard to spelling, despite the fact that there is a popular demand for prescriptiveness in this area – one 'correct' spelling for any given item – dictionary makers often find it difficult to meet this demand. For example, with regard to English, as we saw in Chapter 7, within the English-speaking community, different spellings are accepted in different countries. Accordingly, lexicographers aiming their work at the entire population of English speakers have no choice but to note spelling variants associated with different parts of the English-speaking world.

Even within a given country more than one spelling may be accepted in respect of particular words. Thus, for example, in the current standard English of Britain and Ireland each of the following pairs represents an acceptable spelling of the word in question:

connection: *connexion*

jail: *gaol*

publicize: *publicise*

wagon: *waggon*

yogurt: *yoghurt*

Similarly with the following (identically pronounced) pairs in current 'metropolitan' French:

bistrot: *bistro* ('bistrot')

essaie: *essaye* (first and third-person singular present of the verb *essayer* – 'to try') *paiement*: *payement* ('payment')

remerciement: *remercîment* ('thanks')

serre-freins: *serre-frein* ('brakesman', 'brake adjuster').

Again, the dictionary maker has to take account of such variation in the forms he/she includes.

With regard to non-alphabetic writing systems, these are also subject to variation. To take an example already referred to (in Chapter 8), in the 1950s the government of the People's Republic of China decreed the simplification of the forms of several hundred Chinese characters. However, the simplifications in question were not implemented in Singapore or Taiwan and were not accepted in the Chinese diaspora. Accordingly, any account of the written forms targeted in the above-mentioned reform which aspired to completeness would have to include the 'classic' as well as the reformed versions of the characters involved.

Moving on now to the definitions of meaning supplied by dictionaries, two major problems which arise for the lexicographer in this area are the question of how much information to provide and the question of how many meanings to specify. It is not at all clear that there is a straightforward theoretical way of setting up a strict demarcation between the 'basic' sense of a term and a fuller account of its meaning. Looking at the issue in a more practical perspective, presumably what the lexicographer has to aim for is a definition which (at least within the constraints of a book-type dictionary) is maximally economical while supplying enough information for dictionary-users to be able to understand the item in question and indeed to use it appropriately themselves. The problem is that, as far as traditional formats are concerned, there is a price to be paid for a more 'encyclopedic' approach to definitions, either in terms of a significant increase in the length of the dictionary or in terms of a reduction in the number of entries. In principle, however, there is no reason why dictionaries and encyclopedias should not blur into each other. The long-standing existence of 'encyclopedic dictionaries' demonstrates this point quite clearly. An example of such a dictionary is the *Dictionnaire Encyclopédique Général* (published by Hachette), which includes proper names as well as common nouns (and other parts of speech), which runs to 1587 pages of text, incorporating some 3500 graphic illustrations, and contains in addition a number of appendices (neologisms, Anglicisms, an atlas etc.). As we saw in the last section, the new technologies have the potential to develop the encyclopedic dictionary idea much further than could have been envisaged in traditional book mode.

The encyclopedic approach has been notably absent from bilingual dictionaries. The definition of meaning in such dictionaries tends to be in the form merely of the provision of translation-equivalents in the other language. On the other hand, as we have seen, some of the monolingual dictionaries produced with advanced non-native learners in mind have begun to move in a more encyclopedic direction. The *Oxford Advanced Learner's Dictionary* (see above) is a case in point. Again, information technology may in the end transcend the above categories, having the potential to provide access via a single set of search facilities to translations into other languages, traditional monolingual dictionary-type definitions, more accessible advanced learner dictionary-type definitions and/or more encyclopedic information – according to the demands of particular users at particular times.

Concerning the question of multiple meaning, one part of the traditional solution to this has been, following the distinction made by semanticists between homonymy and polysemy, to distinguish between cases where the meanings attaching to a particular form are connectable in some way and cases where they are wholly unrelated. In the latter cases, the different meanings are seen as betokening different words, which are handled as quite separate dictionary entries, whereas in the former cases the different but related meanings are seen as belonging to the same word and are handled within the framework of a single entry. A good illustration of the above is the treatment of the meanings associated with the form *kip* in *The Concise Oxford Dictionary*. This form is treated in four separate entries, where the respective definitions given are as follows:

kip[1] 1 a sleep or nap. 2 a bed or cheap lodging house. 3 a brothel.

kip[2] the hide of a young or small animal as used for leather.

kip[3] the basic monetary unit of Laos.

kip[4] a small piece of wood from which coins are spun in the game of two-up.

Whereas the three meanings listed under *kip*[1] can all be seen as interrelated insofar as they all denote things that happen in or customarily require the presence of beds, the meanings of *kip*[2], *kip*[3] and *kip*[4] appear to have no obvious connection with sleeping, lodging or fornicating – or with each other.

One problem that arises in making the above kind of distinction is that meanings of a word arrived at by metaphorical extension – and therefore linked to other, earlier or more 'central', meanings of the word in question – may nevertheless be as far removed from these other meanings as 'nap' is from 'small piece of wood'. For example, the English word *cool* means something like 'fairly cold'. By extension, in the emotional realm it means 'calm' or 'unexcited'. By further extension, it has come to refer to a relaxed style of playing music (especially jazz) and by further extension still it is used as a term of praise – roughly equivalent to 'excellent'. The question for lexicographers is whether *cool* meaning 'fairly cold' should be treated together with *cool* meaning 'excellent' or whether these meanings are now so divergent as to warrant separate entries under *cool*[1] and *cool*[2]. There is no easy answer to questions such as this.

Even where it is clear that a set of meanings is linked, a further question that needs to be attended to is to what extent the meanings involved need to

be specified and to what extent they can be taken to be supplied by context.
In some instances, almost all the meaning of a particular expression seems to
derive from the context in which it is used. A good example of this is the way
in which the word *nice* is used in current English (cf. Chapter 4) as an indicator of approval. The precise sense associated with the approval in question
is a function of the particular combination in which it occurs, the particular
type of entity being referred to and the nature of the utterance – as the following sentences demonstrate:

> *She has nice hair.*   ('attractive')
>
> *He's a very nice man.*   ('kindly')
>
> *Nice shot, my son!*   ('well-executed')
>
> *Nice girls don't kiss on first dates.*   ('morally sound')
>
> *He said some very nice things about you.*   ('complimentary')

In this sort of case it would be not only impractical and superfluous but also
misleading to include every possible contextual interpretation of *nice*.
However, it would also misleading to give too limited an account of the possible contextual interpretations. What is in fact required in this kind of
instance is a general indication that *nice* in this sense 'adds a plus sign', as it
were, to anything to which it is attached, and some representation through
examples – clearly labelled as selective illustrations – of the great variety of
contexts in which it may fulfil such a role.

Having discussed the difficulties presented to lexicographers by even the
types of information which have traditionally been thought of as basic to the
content of the dictionary, let us now range a little more widely over other elements of information that are found in dictionary entries. One such element,
which we explored in some depth in chapters 1, 2 and 3 is grammar – both
syntax and morphology. We saw in these earlier chapters that syntax is very
largely determined by word-choice and that morphology, in both its derivational and its inflectional dimensions, is quintessentially a lexical issue.
Accordingly, any description of lexis – including the practically oriented
kinds of description to be found in dictionaries – cannot avoid grammar, the
proof of this particular pudding being that dictionaries always do include
grammatical information – to a greater or lesser extent. One of the problems
faced by lexicographers in this connection is precisely whether the extent of
their treatment of grammar is to be greater or lesser. If they decide to opt for
a fairly fulsome treatment of grammar, a further problem arises: how to
present grammatical information in such a way that it is as complete as possible while remaining reasonably economical (in book-type dictionaries) and
accessible.

An example of a minimalist approach to grammar in the dictionary is
provided by the *Oxford Learner's Pocket Dictionary: English–Greek,
Greek–English*, edited by D.N. Stavropoulos (Oxford: Oxford University

Press, 1990). In the English–Greek section of this dictionary the basic grammatical categories of the entries are given – noun (*n*), adjective (*adj*), adverb (*adv*), preposition (*prep*) etc. and in addition in the case of verbs information is supplied as to whether a verb is transitive (*vt*) or intransitive (*vi*) or both (*vti*), and as to whether a verb is irregular (*irreg*). The Greek–English section follows exactly the same pattern except that Greek nouns are specified for gender – masculine (*nm*), feminine (*nf*) or neuter (*nn*). The advantage of such a system is that it is highly transparent, with no very specialized knowledge being required to make sense of the labels in question. The disadvantage is that it leaves a large gap between the information on offer and what the learner actually needs in order to interpret or deploy a given word in context. For example, labelling the verb *give* as *vt irreg* does not prepare the user for the fact that this item is actually ditransitive, typically requiring an object and an indirect object; nor for the fact that its objects may be configured in different ways – thus: *I gave the cat to my sister – I gave my sister the cat*; nor for the specificities of its irregularity: *give, gave, given.*

An example of more ambitious approach to grammar can be seen in the third edition of the *Oxford Advanced Learner's Dictionary* (1974). Here a complex coding system was adopted for the representation of syntactic patterns. Thus, for example, the first two meanings given for the verb *determine* are defined and illustrated as follows in this dictionary:

decide; fix precisely; to ____ the meaning of a word; to ____ a date for a meeting

calculate; find out precisely; to ____ the speed of light/the height of a mountain by trigonometry

In the first case the codes VP6A and VP10 are specified, and in the second case, VP6A. These codes are explained elsewhere in the dictionary in the following terms:

VP6A   Subject + vt   noun/pronoun

VP10   Subject + vt   dependent clause/question

Obviously, the information provided by codes in question, indicating as they do the kinds of objects that come into the frame in relation to particular usages of this verb, is extremely useful – especially to non-native users of English. The problem is that, in order to profit from the encoded information, the dictionary user has to invest time and effort either in learning the (not very transparent) codes or in constantly consulting the key to the codes. It is not by any means evident that most dictionary users are prepared to make this kind of investment.

The latest (fifth) edition of the *Oxford Advanced Learner's Dictionary* (1995) tacitly recognizes this last point by incorporating a coding system which is rather easier to master. Thus, the coding for verbs is based on the letters, words or parts of words which can be related to their syntactic profile in a fairly straightforward manner. For example:

[V], [Vpr], [Vadv], [Vp]

Intransitive verbs do not take an object. When used alone after a subject they are coded [V]:

- *A large dog **appeared**.*

Some intransitive verbs are often used with a prepositional phrase, an adverb or an ADVERBIAL PARTICLE (an adverb like **down, out** or **over**). The codes and examples show which type of word or phrase can be used with a particular verb:

- **[Vpr]** (verb + prepositional phrase)

  *He doesn't **care about** other people's feelings.*

- **[Vadv]** (verb + adverb)

  *Well done, you **guessed right**!*

- **[Vp]** (verb + particle)

  ***Sit down** and tell me all about it.*

Similarly, transitive verbs are coded as **[Vn]** (verb + noun phrase), ditransitive verbs are coded as **[Vnn]** (verb + noun phrase + noun phrase), and copulas (linking verbs) are coded as **[V-adj]** (verb + adjective complement – as in *Her voice sounds hoarse*) or **[V-n]** (verb + noun phrase complement – as in *Elena became a doctor*).

This dictionary succeeds fairly well at providing a large amount of grammatical information in an economical fashion in its entries, using abbreviations and codes which are readily associable with what they refer to and which therefore do not over-tax the dictionary user's memory or patience. As in other dimensions, the new technologies, with the possibilities they make available for multi-media cross-links, have the potential to improve the grammatical aspects of dictionaries still further; in an electronic dictionary instant access from within a given entry can be provided to full grammatical explanations, to large numbers of examples – including audio and video illustrations, and indeed to relevant grammatical exercises.

Since, as we saw in chapters 1 and 6, words are sound shapes as well as being semantic, grammatical and orthographic entities, it is natural enough that dictionaries should attempt to give some account of how they are pronounced. Two major difficulties that stand in the way of this enterprise are that (i) within any language community there is likely to be variation – across geographical areas etc. – in the ways in which particular lexical items sound, and (ii) most users of dictionaries are not familiar with systems of phonological transcription, and so the lexicographer working in print is faced with a real challenge when it comes to representing pronunciation.

With regard to (i) even if there is a recognized standard variety of the language being dealt with, this is almost bound to be characterized by acceptable alternative pronunciations. For example, as far as English is concerned, in standard North American, Irish and Scottish varieties, the words *bar*, *fear*, *hire* etc. are pronounced with a final *r*-sound, whereas in the standard English, Australian, New Zealand and South African varieties words such as these are pronounced without an *r*-sound (except where they appear immediately before a word beginning with a vowel – as in *Let's hire another van*). The *Concise Oxford Dictionary* tries to cope with this by giving a transcription of hire – /haɪə(r)/ – which simply allows for possibility of the occurrence of the 'post-vocalic *r*'. This is a neat solution from one point of view, since it also encompasses the case of occurrence of the 'post-vocalic *r*' before following vowels in English, Australian, New Zealand and South African varieties. On the other hand, it fails to inform the dictionary user which pronunciation is typical of which parts of the English-speaking world.

As in the case of orthography, even within a given geographical area, more than one pronunciation may be acceptable as standard. For example, within the standard English of south-east England the word *controversy* may be acceptably pronounced with its main stress either on its first syllable (<u>contr</u>oversy) or on its second (cont<u>ro</u>versy). Similarly, the word *either* may be pronounced as either /'aɪðə/ or /'iːðə/, the word garage may be pronounced /'gærɑːdʒ / or d /'gærɪdʒ /, and *scone* may be pronounced as either /skɒn/ or /skəʊn/. In these sorts of instances lexicographers have to give an account of all the relevant possibilities.

Turning to the question of representation of pronunciation, a fairly common device which has been used by lexicographers over the years has been to take the most common pronunciations of particular letters or sets of letters in the dictionary users' orthographic system and to use these as the basis for a pronunciation guide. For example, the 1969 edition of the *Hugo Pocket Dictionary: Dutch–English, English–Dutch* represents Dutch pronunciations to English-speaking users of the dictionary in precisely this way – thus:

blad, blɑt ('leaf')

huis, howss ('house')

This kind of system looks as if it might be readily accessible. However, in fact, explanation of the conventions it adopts is still necessary, for example:

a indicates a sound similar to the English a in 'was'

ow to be pronounced as **ow** in '**now**'

Moreover, a pronunciation guide based on this kind of approach will necessarily provide only approximations – sometimes rather inadequate

approximations at that. For example, the pronunciation of English *ow*
resembles the pronunciation of Dutch *ui* (/œy/) only if the English being
spoken is that of certain parts of Ulster; the standard pronunciation of *ow*
(/əʊ/) elsewhere in the English-speaking world is fairly distant from that of
the Dutch diphthong. For these kinds of reasons, most dictionaries now
represent pronunciation by means of the symbols of the International
Phonetic Alphabet, the reasoning being, presumably, that if one has to
provide a key to symbols anyway, why not use symbols which are capable
of providing a really accurate account of the relevant sounds and which
have international currency?

Once again the new technologies are in principle able to resolve more or
less all of the above difficulties relative to the phonological dimension of lexicography. An electronic dictionary has the potential to provide instant
access from within a given entry to a key to the symbols used in the relevant
phonological transcription and also, at the click of a button, to model the
pronunciation of any given word in audio mode. Indeed, an electronic dictionary could supply a whole range of audio models of the pronunciation of
any specific item, signalling whether the pronunciations are in free variation
or labelling the provenance of each pronunciation (American, Australian
etc.) as appropriate.

Another important dimension of the lexicon treated earlier in the book
(especially in Chapter 4) is the whole area of collocation. This aspect of things
poses a number of challenges to the lexicographer, of which we shall look here
at just two: (i) the arbitrariness of identifying combinations of words which
warrant their own entries and (ii) the difficulty of communicating how fixed or
flexible a given combination may be. Concerning (i), we saw in Chapter 4 that
there was no principled way of distinguishing between fixed expressions and
compound words, and that the rule of thumb applied in this connection was a
highly arbitrary orthographic one – so that, for example, *greenfinch, school-
teacher, teapot* are treated as compound words, while *blue whale, bus driver*
and *tea caddy* are treated as fixed expressions. In lexicographical terms what
this tends to mean is that – for no very good reason – the former are accorded
their own separate dictionary entries, whereas the latter are not. There is no
real sign in recent printed dictionaries of any attempt to move beyond the limitations of orthographic conventions in this connection. Electronic dictionaries, in allowing for non-linear search and, in providing the possibility of
using collocates as a trigger for search mechanisms, offer the best chance of
transcending such limitations, but they will not entirely solve the problem,
since some kind of judgment will always have to be made as to whether or not
a particular combination occurs frequently enough to constitute a partnership
to be included in the category of collocations/fixed expressions.

As far as specifying the degree of openness or fixedness of fixed expressions in dictionaries is concerned, again the discussion in Chapter 4 is relevant. There we saw that some fixed expressions are more fixed than others.
Thus, whereas in expressions such as *seeing is believing* and *the more the*

merrier only minimal changes are admissible, in other cases, such as *the other side of the coin*, changes in the syntax and in the actual components of the expression can be made without any resultant undermining of the force of expression. Dictionaries can easily enough indicate when expressions are absolutely invariable, but, in the case of expressions which allow for some degree of flexibility, indicating what kinds of variations are possible and where precisely the limits of flexibility are is highly problematic. Some interesting developments in this context came out of the compilation of *The Oxford Dictionary of Current Idiomatic English* (1975/1983), in which, for example, the kinds of subject and object that a verb is likely to take are specified, and in which severe collocational restriction is marked with a warning exclamation mark. For example, the expression *blow up*, in the sense of 'make bigger', is shown as taking objects (O) applying only to images:

O: ! negative, photograph, picture, snap

However, this kind of device, useful as it is, has to be seen as merely a modest beginning in the light of the bewildering array of collocational probabilities and improbabilities associated with expressions of different degrees of fixity – often without any discernible rhyme or reason. Technology can help to a certain extent both in terms of establishing what are and are not the usual combinatorial patterns and in terms of providing ready access in electronic dictionaries to relevant commentary and sets of examples, but even with such technological support, the task is a daunting one.

Reference has been made in the foregoing to variation of spelling and pronunciation. As we saw in Chapter 7, however, variation affects other areas of language too. For example, the very occurrence of a particular lexical unit may be more likely in some regional, social, ethnic etc. varieties of a given language than in others; and/or it may be more likely occur at one or other end of the formal–informal continuum in terms of style. The obverse of such sets of probabilities is that a given expression may be characterized by a set of associations or connotations in respect of the categories of speakers/writers who are likely to use it and the typical circumstances of its use. Lexicographers have traditionally made some kind of effort to communicate such associations to dictionary users. Unfortunately, the classification that has traditionally been used in this context has been rather crude: the geographical labels ('British', 'American' etc.) take no account of variation within the areas in question; little attention is given to variation associated with social class, gender or ethnicity; and the usual stylistic indicators ('colloquial', 'poetic', 'obscene' etc.) suggest categories with hard and fast boundaries rather than points along a scale. On the other hand, very recent dictionaries are tending to provide more finely differentiated information in these areas, and the possibilities of electronic dictionaries in this connection regarding contextualized exemplification are beginning to be usefully exploited.

Meanings and grammatical patterns associated with particular expressions are also subject to variation. For example, as we saw in Chapter 5,

meanings may vary from context to context. Thus, the word *note*, which in
the context of correspondence means 'short letter' in the context of music
means 'sign representing pitch and duration of a musical sound'.
Dictionaries have traditionally indicated this kind of context-related
semantic variation by labelling meanings – e.g. with *Mus.* for 'musical'.
Other kinds of context-related variation in meaning – those having to do
with the developing context of the discourse – e.g. whether *kick the bucket* is
interpreted literally as 'strike the pail with one's foot' or as 'die' (see Chapter
5) – have been addressed in dictionaries only insofar as different meanings
have been illustrated by examples. Semantic differences are also associated
with variation related to geography, social class, ethnicity and gender as well
as with stylistic variation. Again, dictionaries have taken account of such
variation to some extent, using lables such as *slang, colloquial, poetic* etc.
With regard to grammar, an obvious example of variability is the different
morphological patterning of a verb like *get* in the English of the United
States (*get – got – gotten*) as compared with its patterning in most other
parts of the English-speaking world (*get – got – got*). Here too, dictionaries
have traditionally coped with such variation by the application of labels like
Brit., US. etc. In all these cases, much the same kinds of comments could be
applied as in the previous paragraph in respect of the deficiencies of most
lexicographical practice, and also in respect of the opportunities offered by
technological advances.

Finally in this section, let us look very briefly at the question of how
lexical change (see Chapter 8) is reflected in dictionaries. Many widely used
dictionaries (such as the *Concise Oxford Dictionary*) include brief treatments of the etymological origins of the items they contain – giving the
forms from which the words in question derive in Old English, Old French,
Latin, Ancient Greek etc. with the meanings of these ancestor forms. As we
saw in the last section, a number of other dictionaries – such as the *OED* –
adopt a more general 'historical approach' to the words with which they
deal, tracking and illustrating the evolution of their usage over the decades
and indeed centuries. This latter aspect of the lexical change dimension of
dictionary entries is a good deal more problematic than the former, requiring
as it does, a decision on the part of lexicographers as to how far back to go
in their attempts to take account of and illustrate changes in the lexicon that
relate to the needs of the current user of the language concerned. It also
involves decision-making about how quickly to incorporate new lexical
developments.

With regard to how far the lexicographer should reach back into the
history of the language being treated, a complicating factor is that forms and
meanings which may not have been current for hundreds of years may still
be of relevance to dictionary users who may be reading Cervantes, Dante,
Luther, Rabelais, Shakespeare etc. Moreover, an expression or usage which
may no longer be current amongst one group of speakers may still be
extremely common amongst other groups. For instance, the word *press* was

once widely used in English to mean 'large cupboard'. It is no longer used with this meaning in the everyday English of England, but in Ireland is still very frequently used in this sense. Dictionaries typically deal with forms and meanings which may be encountered in reading but which are no longer in current use by labelling them as 'archaic' or 'dated', but determining which to include and which to exclude is no straightforward matter. Nor does such labelling address the kind of variability that was noted above in relation to *press*.

As for the question of how quickly to recognize new coinages or new meanings in dictionary entries, this is, if anything, an even thornier issue. An example of a new meaning becoming fairly rapidly associated with an existing form is provided by the instance of the English word *hopefully*, which in the late 1960s was beginning to be widely used in the sense of 'it is hoped' in addition to continuing to be used to mean 'in a hopeful manner'. How were lexicographers to know whether the new usage of *hopefully* was a mere passing fad or whether (as has turned out to be the case) it was going to be a development of a more lasting kind? In fact, lexicographers tend to bide their time, to 'wait and see', before including such innovations. Such conservatism no doubt yields benefits *vis-à-vis* the authority of dictionaries, insofar as it reduces the chances of incorporating forms and meanings that are truly ephemeral. On the other hand, it does no service to the dictionary user, whose need for information about unfamiliar words and usages he/she encounters is not dependent on their pedigree or longevity, and whose lexical gaps may well principally relate to precisely those very recent lexical innovations which the lexicographer spurns.

10.4   Approaches to lexis in the language classroom

We turn now to the topic of lexical dimensions of language instruction in the first language. As was mentioned in Chapter 9, a major focus of teaching as far as the first language lexicon is concerned is on enabling children to read and write words which they are already able to understand and use in speech. However, as Chapter 9 also makes clear, the introduction of new vocabulary in various ways is also a concern of first language lexical instruction. With regard to classrooms where languages other than the first language are being taught, the typical scenario in this case is that when learners begin to be exposed to a second language in a formal educational setting, all aspects of the words they encounter are new to them, which clearly presents those responsible for designing and teaching the lexical component of second language programmes with a challenge of some magnitude.

In both the first language and the second language classroom the approach to lexis – across virtually the entire gamut of methodologies – has typically involved a combination of, on the one hand, instruction and/or activities focused on particular expressions and, on the other, reliance on the assumption that a certain amount of new vocabulary will be picked up 'incidentally' through simple exposure to dialogues, reading passages etc. containing the new items in question, whether or not teaching is specifically focused on them. Interestingly, there seem to be arguments in favour of this general perspective from what we know about naturalistic lexical acquisition by young children, which as we saw in Chapter 9, appears to proceed on the basis of both a certain amount of special teaching – notably via 'ostension' – and acquisition from context.

A visit to almost any early primary school class during a reading lesson will provide copious illustration of the above-sketched combination of approaches. Around the walls of the room there are likely to be brightly coloured posters and charts with pictures of animals, plants and other natural phenomena, with individual items lexically labelled. Also likely to be hung up in prominent positions are ordered lists of words referring to sequences such as the days of the week, the months of the year and the four seasons. All of these constitute instances of pedagogic focus on particular words. There may in addition be wallcharts with pieces of texts on them – poems, short sayings etc. These can be seen as relevant to the more context-based, incidental dimension of lexical instruction. With regard to the actual reading activities, whether the teacher is working 'frontally', involving the whole class collectively in such activities, or whether the activities are happening on a groupwork, pairwork or individual basis, they will include both the challenge of decoding the meaning of the text being read – that is to say, attention to the overall developing context of the passage – and also a frequent homing in on specific expressions. Guiding and reflecting this two-pronged strategy, reading textbooks will typically contain not only commentaries on and questions about the message being communicated by the passage but also explanations, definitions, illustrations and perhaps exercises relating to individual words and phrases. Furthermore, the nature of the teacher's input will usually assist contextual learning by being 'tuned down' to the lexical level of the pupils, which allows new items to be interpreted with the help of more familiar expressions in its environment. The teacher's input will more often than not address specific lexical units too – offering definitions either explicitly (e.g. 'This means X') or implicitly by intonation (e.g. 'a triangle?' 'It's got three sides').

At later stages in the educational process some elements of the above change: as the pupils' mother-tongue lexical proficiency comes closer to adult levels, the brightly coloured wallcharts disappear, the number of explanations of specific expressions declines, and the teacher's input becomes less obviously 'tuned down'. Nevertheless, the dual approach is still discernible. As time goes on there may be much more emphasis on the individual pupil's interaction with texts, but unfamiliar words and phrases still need occasionally to be focused on – in particular, when their context is an insufficient guide to their meaning, their syntactic profile etc. As previously, such focusing may happen in teacher talk, in classroom activities and/or in the commentaries of textbooks.

With regard to second language lexical instruction, basically the same pattern emerges. Again, a visit to more or less any second language classroom would confirm this. Second language teachers also make use of labelled wallcharts and posters. Another device sometimes used in second language teaching areas – especially where beginners are being taught – is the labelling of features of the room and items of furniture (the window, the door, the cupboard, the teacher's desk, the blackboard etc.) with the relevant words in the target language. On the other hand, connected texts in the target language, such as poems and song-lyrics, are also frequently on display in such areas. As far as class activities are concerned, the input for these typically comprise audio-recorded dialogues, printed texts, video-clips, songs and other similar 'chunks' of language in use from which an overall meaning is derivable and which require different parts of a context to be related to each other in order to be interpreted. However, as in the case of mother-tongue teaching, individual expressions are often drawn from such 'chunks' for particular attention – whether explanation or exercises – and indeed, especially in the early stages of a second language course, single words may be focused on for definition and practice in complete isolation from any context. The content of second language textbooks is also typically characterized by a mixture of context-based and atomistic approaches in terms of their exposition of linguistic material. In addition, instructed second language learners, like pupils undergoing mother-tongue teaching also seem to be in receipt of input-tuning on the part of teachers. Second language speech addressed by teachers to pupils tends to be more standard-like in terms of pronunciation, to contain more lexical items with general meanings, to include fewer idiomatic expressions and to be syntactically simpler than discourse addressed to adult native speakers – all of which features clearly add up to an attempt (whether conscious or unconscious) to enhance the comprehensibility of what is said and the possibility of incidental acquisition. Finally, second language teachers, no less than first language teachers, frequently home in on specific words or phrases for 'ostensive definition' whether by reference to visual, aural or tactile data (a picture, an object in the room, a sound, a texture etc.), to other words in the target language, or to a translation-equivalent in the learners' first language.

It may be worth pausing at this point to observe that both incidental learning and learning based on ostension have their place in naturalistic lexical acquisition, and that, as we shall see in what follows, both context-based and individual word-focused approaches are efficacious in formal instructional settings also. Concerning the role of context in lexical acquisition, research suggests (i) that words are acquired incidentally from context in the normal course of reading and oral interaction, although the number of words acquired from any given context on any given occasion is likely to be rather limited; (ii) that the relevance of an unknown word to the informational needs of the learner is a determining factor in relation to the amount of attention the learner gives to that word; and (iii) that making an effort to derive the meaning of unknown words from contextual and formal clues improves such words' chances of being retained. A further sidelight on this question is cast by research looking at the differential effects on vocabulary acquisition of (a) reading plus comprehension exercises plus further reading and (b) reading plus comprehension exercises plus further related exercises involving selective attention to words: word (form and meaning) recognition, morphosyntactic manipulation of words and word-parts, interpretation of words in context, production of words in context (the same amount of time being taken up by either set of activities). The results of such research indicate that, while both treatments resulted in considerable gains in vocabulary, the gains of the groups who did the further exercises were significantly greater than those of the groups who did not. It appears from these results that, in terms of lexical gains, contextualized activities focused on individual expressions can improve on processing for meaning unaccompanied by such activities.

With regard to atomistic approaches, the time-honoured way of dealing with individual expressions in the classroom has been to require pupils to learn lists of words together with their definitions (or, in the second language context, together with their first language translation-equivalents). Another atomistic technique much discussed in the literature is the encouragement of learners to make semantic–associative links between new words they encounter and other words they know already and/or images. Again, there is evidence that such processes happen naturally in lexical acquisition. Thus, while language acquisition is certainly not reducible to mere imitation, imitation and rehearsal (whether aloud or subvocally) have nevertheless been demontrated to be important aspects of the process of constructing memory codes for the phonological form of new items encountered by children acquiring language – but also by older learners of both first and second languages. Interestingly, from some of the very studies that show the importance of rehearsal in the creation of faithful replications in short-term memory of the phonological form of the target items, it also emerges that success in learning new words also depends on the exploitation, where possible, of semantic associations between the target words and words already internalized.

There is also a long and venerable tradition in verbal memory research which indicates, on the one hand, that recall of memorized items is improved by a 'longer opportunity for rehearsal' and that 'more extensive processing ... may increase the durability of a memory code', and, on the other, that verbal input is made more memorable by ' "deep processing" in which a variety of relations are established between the newly learned and the pre-existing knowledge'. Some verbal memory research suggests – rather like the above-cited research relating to incidental lexical acquisition – that a combination of strategies yields the best results; thus, for example, it seems that the rote-learning of lexical forms pure and simple is less effective than attending to meaning as well as to form. Especially interesting in this connection in the light of what was noted earlier regarding the relevance of individual needs in incidental vocabulary acquisition is the finding that in verbal memory experiments accurate recall of verbal material is more likely in relation to 'statements with personal significance for the participants'.

A particular mnemonic technique which has been found to work well in both first language and second language lexical learning is the so-called keyword technique. This involves the learner in constructing a mental image which links the newly encountered word with a word which is already known, whether in the same language or some other language. The vocabulary acquisition and testing researcher Paul Nation exemplifies this technique as follows for the case of an Indonesian learner of English trying to learn the English word *parrot*.

> First, the learner thinks of an Indonesian word that sounds like *parrot* or like a part of *parrot* – for example, the Indonesian word *parit*, which means 'a ditch'. This is the keyword. Second, the learner imagines a parrot lying in a ditch! The more striking and unusual the image, the more effective it is.

In fact, while the keyword technique is certainly to be classed as an atomistic strategy, the use of image as a general approach is applicable to longer stretches of language too – with very beneficial effects in terms of what is retained. Thus, research has shown that visualization in the course of reading – whether in a first or a second language – greatly enhances the impact of the text in question not only in terms of comprehension but also in terms of the retention of specific content (including lexical content). Visualization appears to be less frequent among second language readers than among first language readers, but the second language readers who do visualize are those who do best in recalling the text. Such research indicates that encouraging readers to visualize while reading for comprehension and pleasure is likely to boost incidental lexical acquisition, which in turn means that the construction of mental images is a strategy whose effectiveness transcends the atomistic–incidental divide.

A particular feature of second language learning and teaching in formal educational settings is that it has been through some fairly radical changes even in the past five or six decades. Three methodologies have successively dominated the second language education scene during that period: the *grammar-translation* method, the *audio-lingual* method and the *communicative* approach. These are not the only methods which have been on offer, but they do constitute the landmarks by reference to which other approaches can generally be situated.

The grammar-translation method essentially attempted to apply to living languages the same approach that had for centuries been used in the teaching of classical languages (notably Latin and Ancient Greek). That is to say, much emphasis was laid on the conscious memorization of grammatical paradigms (noun declensions, verb conjugations etc.) and rules (word order in various types of phrase and clause etc.), and these memorized forms and rules were then practised largely by translating sentences and longer passages into and out of the target language (usually in writing). The goal of this approach was primarily to give learners access to the literary treasures of the language in question.

The audio-lingual method had its origins in objectives which were fairly remote from the accessing of literary treasures. It started life as the 'army method', that is to say, an approach developed in the United States during the latter years of the Second World War which was designed to prepare American military personnel for duties in mainland Europe. Consequently its goals belonged to the realm of the concrete and practical rather than that of the aesthetic, and its orientation was in the first instance towards the oral–aural aspects of the languages in question. It was created in large measure by structuralist linguists rather than members of departments of modern languages and literature, and it was heavily influenced by the prevailing psycholinguistic model of the time – namely, the application of behaviourist psychology to language acquisition and use. We have seen that American structuralist linguistics was particularly interested in observable forms (phonology, morphology and syntax) and tended to disregard meaning because of its perceived resistance to scientific analysis (cf. Chapter 5). We have also noted that behaviourist psychology viewed language acquisition as habit formation via selective reinforcement and imitation (cf. Chapter 9). In view of these givens, it is hardly surprising that the methodology arrived at by the linguists involved focused especially on the manipulation of form and involved large amounts of repetition and structural 'drilling'. After the war this methodology became known as *audio-lingualism*, and, as more visual aids (such as slides and filmstrips) began to be used in classrooms, it formed the basis of the approach of many of the so-called '*audio-visual*' courses that were used in second language classrooms around the world in the 1960s and 1970s and indeed into the 1980s.

The original motivation for the development of the third of the above-mentioned approaches, the communicative approach, was also very practical in nature – namely the need to equip the more mobile members of the European workforce with linguistic skills which would enable them to meet their professional and personal requirements in countries and languages other than their own. Out of this situation arose a whole set of ideas relating to the analysis of learners' communicative needs, the definition of course objectives in terms of the meanings that would need to be understood and/or expressed in order to meet such needs, the early exposure of learners to authentic samples of the target language, and the development of pedagogical activities which were clearly related to activities associated with real-life needs. In other words, the concern of the early theorists of the communicative movement was to connect language teaching and learning in the classroom as transparently and as closely as possible to the likely uses of the target language that learners would be called upon to make. When such ideas began to be applied to second language learning in primary and secondary schools, a broader view had to be taken of needs, since – in contradistinction to the case of migrant workers attempting to survive far from home – it was not at all clear to most pupils beginning to learn a second language at school (nor indeed to their teachers) what such pupils' real-life needs in the target language might be. Accordingly, the notion of needs was given a broader interpretation in respect of the school context, so that interests and expectations could be included in the picture. Also, attention began to be paid to the needs of learners relative to their life within the language classroom as well as their life beyond its walls. Despite such adjustments, the essential features of the communicative approach have not changed; it remains committed to founding the entire language teaching enterprise on an analysis of what the learner needs, wants or expects to be able to do with the target language, and it takes as given not only the proposition that the mediation of meaning is the core function of language but also the proposition that it is principally through the experience of the meaning–mediating dimension of language that language acquisition progresses.

Let us consider now how each of these three methodologies relates to the different dimensions of lexical acquisition that were discussed earlier. With regard to the grammar translation method, the typical composition of a lesson taught within this framework is: an introductory passage in the target language for reading and translation, glosses for new words introduced in the passage, explanations of grammatical points exemplified in the passage, grammatical exercises, exercises involving translation into the target language, and supplementary activities such as the learning of poems, songs etc. in the target language. By way of illustration, let us explore a chapter of textbook conceived within a grammar-translation perspective. One such textbook is a volume entitled *Heute Abend* ('This Evening'), intended for English-speaking learners of German as a foreign language, which was first published in 1938 but which continued to be used into the 1950s and beyond. The content of Chapter 15 of this book (picked more or less at random) includes the following.

- a four-page text to read and translate entitled '*Am Bahnhof*' ('At the station');
- a list of vocabulary which appears in the text plus English translation-equivalents and some information about the grammatical profiles of the words in question (e.g. gender specification through the provision of the appropriate form of the definite article and plural markers in the case of nouns, irregular third person singular forms in the case of verbs, irregular comparative forms in the case of adjectives etc.);
- a vocabulary revision section in the form of a list of numbered German items and a separate list of English equivalents tagged with numbers corresponding to those of their German counterparts;

- grammar exercises focusing on the morphology of verbs, pronouns, articles, adjectives and nouns;
- comprehension questions in German relating to the text (which learners are required to ask each other);
- a passage to translate from English into German (about a holiday in the Bavarian Alps);
- a short song to learn.

If we examine this material in the light of opportunities it presents for incidental vocabulary learning, we can see that the text which opens the lesson provides just such an opportunity. The lexis is embedded in a context with an overall meaning which, presumably, learners endeavoured to work towards in their exploration of the text. Other possibilities for incidental learning include the instructions and examples associated with the exercises, most of which are in German and indeed the meaningful contexts within which the relevant morphological adjustments are supposed to be made (e.g. *'Es tut mir leid, aber ich (können) morgen nicht zu meinem Freund gehen'* – 'I'm sorry but I (to be able) go to my friend's tomorrow'). Translating into the target language also comprises an element of incidental lexical acquisition, in the sense that in striving to render the English text accurately into German, learners would have been very likely to retain some of the expressions they deployed, even in the absence of any attempt at conscious memorization. One final opportunity for incidental vocabulary learning is furnished by the text of the song at the end of the chapter.

With regard to atomistic lexical learning, the most obvious way in which the chapter addresses this dimension of learners' coming to grips with German vocabulary is through the provision of a glossary referring to the text, the contents of which are intended to be learned by heart, for example

> *der Bodensee (kein Pl.* [no pl.]), Lake Constance
>
> :
>
> *die Eisenbahn (en)*, railway
>
> :
>
> *abfahren, fährt ab*, leave
>
> :
>
> *hoch, höher*, high, higher etc.

Notable in this connection is, on the one hand, the presence of semantic information, which, as we have seen, appears to assist in the creation of durable memory codes for lexical items, and, on the other, a focus on morphological characteristics, which, again as we have seen, seems to be relevant to the kind of processing that results in lexical gains. The fact that the German words are placed alongside their English equivalents can also be seen as an encouragement to construct semantic–associative connections of the kind: *hoch* and *high* mean the same thing and both begin and end with *h*. Much the same can be said of the lexical revision section.

Grammatical exercises would also have led the learner to focus on specific lexical units in their various realizations. Moreover, since in many cases the focus on form was situated within a meaningful context, there would have been a semantic as well as a formal dimension to the attention which the learner was called upon to give to each item, which, as we saw in our discussion of verbal memory research, would have 'deepened' the processing and increased the chances of items being retained. Similarly with the text completion exercises which appear in the chapter.

All in all, the grammar-translation approach appears to have supplied plenty of opportunities for the operation of both incidental and specific item-focused lexical acquisition. The great drawback of this method was that it tended to be taught largely through the medium of the learners' mother tongue. This meant that exposure to the target language in the classroom was largely limited to the passages and exercises presented in the textbook. Another aspect of this limitation was that the target language input received by learners was principally in the written medium, which obviously restricted their chances of becoming fully familiar with the phonological shapes of words. Furthermore, although, as has been indicated, there was certainly a semantic dimension to such passages and to at least some of the exercises, the relevance of the meanings in question to the interests of learners would not always have been obvious. For example, the text of the song in Chapter 15 speaks of a man who can no longer march (*'ich kann nicht mehr marschieren'*) because he has lost his little pipe from his knapsack (*'Ich hab' verlor'n – mein Pfeiflein aus meinem Mantelsack'*).

Moving on to the audio-lingual method and the way in which it deals with vocabulary, this approach can be exemplified by an audio-visual course in French as a foreign language which was published by the Centre de Recherche et d'Étude pour la Diffusion du Français in 1972 under the title of *De Vive Voix* ('Live', 'In person'). Lesson 4 of this course opens with two filmstrips accompanied by audio-recorded dialogues, entitled in the *Livre du maître* ('Teacher's book') respectively *'Chez Mireille'* ('At Mireille's place') and *'Deux vieilles dames curieuses'* ('Two curious old ladies'). Each of these is then followed by a series of exercises in which the teacher is instructed to have the learners practise forms and constructions that crop up in the relevant dialogues. The lesson is also associated with a battery of *exercices de réemploi* ('exercises in re-use', i.e. structural drills) recorded on separately available audio-tapes and intended for use in a language laboratory.

Incidental lexical learning opportunities are obviously presented by the two dialogues and the accompanying visual aids. The dialogues in question tell a story, which is linked to a larger narrative theme which runs through the entire course (essentially the developing relationship, way of life and activities of the two principal characters, Pierre and Mireille). While the stories in question hardly constitute high drama, they contain enough of

interest – especially when listened to in the context of the attractively produced filmstrips – to motivate attention to their meaning. On the other
hand, they are short, taking up in total just two fairly generously spaced
pages of the *Livre du maître*.

As in the case of the grammar-translation method, further potential
learning opportunities are provided by the exercises associated with the
lesson – both those orchestrated by the teacher immediately after the dialogues and the further *exercices de réemploi* performed later by learners in
the language laboratory. An example of an exercise suggested by the *Livre
du maître* for the phase immediately following the presentation of the dialogue '*Chez Mireille*' is one involving personal pronouns and various ways
of expressing possession (*à* + X – literally, 'to + X', *de* + X – 'of + X' and
son/sa + X – 'his (or her) + X'). The suggestion is that these should be
elicited from learners by carefully devised questions referring to the
dialogue – thus:

| Question: | *À qui est ?* | ('Whose is ?') |
| Expected response: | *Elle (il) est à X* | ('It's X's') |

The exercises referring to the dialogues are thereby contextualized and
therefore have a clear semantic dimension; in contrast, the *exercices de
réemploi*, although involving sentences which in themselves have meaning,
do not connect with or into a larger meaningful context, and would appear
to be, for that reason, less facilitative of incidental lexical acquisition.

Finally with regard to incidental lexical learning opportunities in the
audio-lingual framework, it should be noted that all teaching conducted
under the auspices of this method had to proceed entirely in the target language, which means that, quite apart from the material in the dialogues and
exercises, learners were receiving additional second language input from the
teacher in the form of commentaries on the dialogue, explanations relating
to activities, instructions having to do with classroom management etc.
Obviously, learners would have had to attended closely to the meaning of
such input in order to keep abreast of what was happening and what they
were supposed to be doing, and in the process they would have been likely,
whether they wanted to or not (!), to acquire at least some of the terms that
recurred in classroom discourse.

As far as atomistic dimensions of lexical learning in the audio-lingual
lesson we have been examining are concerned, a first point, there are particular sections in the part of the *Livre du maître* devoted to Lesson 4 which are
headed '*Vocabulaire*' ('Vocabulary'). The vocabulary teaching recommended in association with the dialogue '*Chez Mireille*' is centred on polite-
ness formulas such as *Excusez-moi* ('Excuse me') and on words relating to
furniture and objects featuring in the film images – *étagère* ('set of shelves'),
livre ('book') etc. The vocabulary section relating to '*Deux vieilles dames
curieuses*', for its part, encourages the teacher to supply the expression that
is used to pluralize *un jeune homme* ('a young man') and to refer to *un jeune*

homme + *une jeune femme* ('a young man + a young woman') – namely, *des jeunes gens* (literally, 'young people').

In fact, however, many of the other activities recommended under the heading of '*Pratique*' ('Practice') are also lexical in nature. For example, among the elements recommended for practice in connection with '*Chez Mireille*' are the masculine and feminine forms of adjectives such as *petit* ('small'), *gentil* ('kind') and *bon* ('good') and different forms of the verb *avoir* ('to have'), and among the elements recommended for practice in connection with '*Deux vieilles dames curieuses*' are the pronoun complementation pattern of verbs such as *parler* ('to speak') and *dire* ('to say', 'to tell') – i.e. the use of *lui* ('to him/her') with these verbs – and the noun clause complementation pattern of the verb *dire*, e.g. *Il lui dit que...* ('He tells her that...'). Since, as was mentioned earlier, these activities relate to a meaningful context, they have a clear semantic as well as a formal dimension. On the other hand, the structural exercises intended for language laboratory use, which cover similar points, are not linked in to the dialogues and are, therefore less well supported in terms of meaning.

Thus, the audio-lingual approach seems to offer a set of conditions in which both incidental and particular item-focused lexical acquisition can readily occur. A point that has not been made so far but which perhaps needs to be, is that the lavish visual support supplied by the filmstrip might well have encouraged the construction of internal images in association with particular words on the part of learners, who might subsequently have reaped the earlier-discussed benefits of visualization in learning terms.

One drawback of the approach in this connection is that the range of vocabulary it makes available tends to be somewhat limited. Thus, for example, *De Vive Voix* draws the vocabulary it deploys from *Le Français Fondamental* ('Basic French'), a corpus of the most frequently occurring and most generally available expressions in French – as established by a research project conducted in the 1960s. The restrictedness of the vocabulary and the fact that the words in question have a high frequency and/or availability value gives the *De Vive Voix* materials a certain blandness. This is compounded by the fact that the primary purpose of the texts of the dialogues from the course-writers' point of view was to illustrate aspects of French grammar and the usage of basic vocabulary rather than to amuse or entertain. Although the texts were semantically coherent and, as has already been indicated, probably had enough of a story-line to hold learners' interest in some measure, they certainly did not have much of the savour of real-life conversations, and are unlikely to have engaged learners' interest to the point where they felt that the content of the dialogues actually mattered to them or had any connection with their own lives. All of this, as we have seen, would have had implications for depth of processing and durability of memory traces. It should be said that in the grammar-translation approach the texts used in textbooks were also often concocted by the textbook writers with the exemplification of grammar points in mind. However, in the grammar-translation case these artificial texts were typically supplemented with and progressively replaced by song-lyrics and literary texts which were 'authentic' in the sense of having originally been created with the entertainment or illumination of native speakers of the target language in mind. The problem in this latter case was that, as we have also seen, the choice of texts was not always inspired or inspiring from the learners' point of view.

A further point worth noting in relation to lexical acquisition in the audio-lingual framework is that the audio-lingual approach did not explicitly promote the making of connections between target language items and familiar mother-tongue expressions. Indeed, audio-lingual methodology set its face against any use of the learners' first language in the second language classroom whatsoever – even to gloss newly introduced words. While the use of the target language as a medium of instruction undoubtedly brought many benefits in terms of incidental learning, the complete interdiction on any use of the learners' mother tongue in class may have impoverished their more atomistic aspects of the vocabulary-learning process by failing to support the making of semantic–associative links between second and first language expressions. More seriously, it led to many misunderstandings regarding the meanings of the words encountered. According to numerous reports, explanations in the target language were often not fully understood and images were often misinterpreted.

A third disadvantage associated with the audio-lingual approach in respect of lexical acquisition was its emphasis on oral–aural aspects of the target language to the point where written language was totally excluded often until relatively late in the teaching programme. The idea behind this was to try to ensure that learners had a firm grasp of the spoken language before they had to cope with the complexities and inconsistencies of its orthographic system. The problem was that learners were already typically using written notes in other subject areas to help fix in their minds the material they were being taught. Naturally enough, they adopted the same strategy in second language classes, and since they were not being given access to the orthography of the second language, they invented their own (usually highly idiosyncratic) system of transcription, which meant that the orthographic entries they had for target language words in their mental lexicons often bore little resemblance to the actual orthographic forms of these words. Denying learners access to literacy skills in the target language over a substantial length of time also deprived them during that period of the opportunity to acquire target language lexis incidentally through reading.

Turning, finally, to the communicative approach, this is a rather difficult to define and describe because it is an extremely 'broad church' in methodological terms. All versions of the approach try to address the learner's needs, interests and expectations, and all deal with such needs, interests and expectations in terms of meaning in a social as well as a conceptual sense – in terms, for example, of giving and receiving various kinds of information, of expressing and understanding views, preferences etc., of participating in the organization of social interaction – inviting and being invited, requesting and being the recipient of requests etc. etc. However, there is variation among different versions of communicative language teaching when it comes to issues like the use of the learners' mother tongue, the explicit teaching of grammar and the ways in which the course objectives are presented (as general communicative functions, e.g. greeting, warning, expressing dislike, or in terms of communicative tasks, e.g. ordering food in a restaurant, shopping for clothes and food, speaking on the telephone).

The particular coursebook we shall consider as a source of illustration of the communicative approach – the third part of a course intended for Irish learners of French entitled *Salut!* ('Hi!'), first published in 1985 and still in use – takes a fairly relaxed attitude towards the classroom use of the mother tongue; is not averse to explicit grammatical instruction; and expresses learning objectives in terms of tasks. Unit 6 of this book, for instance, is referred to in the contents as follows:

> In this unit you can learn how to speak to friends on the telephone and to give and take phone messages.

It comprises:

- a summary of what learners might encounter or want to express in the context of telephone communication (e.g. answering the phone: *Allô! J'écoute* – literally 'Hello. I'm listening').
- four brief dialogues in French involving telephone conversations which are presented on audio-tape and incomplete versions of which are also presented in the book; learners are asked to fill in the gaps in the printed versions of the dialogues;
- four further dialogues in French involving telephone conversations presented on audio-tape and in print;
- an introduction in French describing the different ways one can telephone in France (from public telephone kiosks, from cafés etc.);
- a large number of short texts taken from French telephone directories and other French sources providing instructions about different aspects of telephone use (using a public telephone box, consulting the talking clock, reserving a wake-up call, telephoning different French regions, abroad etc.; visual support for these texts includes photographs, drawings, symbols, diagrams and maps (for example the instruction *mettez les pièces* – 'put in the coins' – is accompanied by a drawing of coins).
- some examples (in French) specifically relating to calling Ireland from France;
- some short audio-taped French dialogues involving telephone calls, each followed by a comprehension question or two in French;
- some examples of notes in French based on telephone messages;
- some exercises involving learners in simulating making telephone calls in or from France;

- a grammar section dealing with the present and imperfect tenses of the verbs *pouvoir* ('to be able to'), *vouloir* ('to want') and *devoir* ('to have to');
- some exercises asking learners to express particular meanings in French (e.g. 'You can't go to the cinema tonight, you have to do your homework');
- A page-long text (also available on the audio-tape) about the French rock-group Téléphone accompanied by a photograph of the group and followed by a comprehension question in French;
- a page-long text in French about a solar-powered house accompanied by a photograph and an annotated diagram of the house and followed by questions/exercises in French.

As can be seen from the above outline, the unit in question is extremely rich in both listening and reading material. The material is mostly related to the telephone theme and therefore connects broadly to an overarching context, and each dialogue or text also constitutes a meaningful whole at an individual level. Moreover, much of the material is in one way or other supported by appropriate visual aids. In keeping with the communicative philosophy of basing language courses on learners' needs, interests and expectations, the content of material relates to an activity (using the telephone in France) that learners probably think of as something that they might well have to cope with in the not very remote future (on holiday, on a school trip etc.) and to topics (rock music, the environment) in which many of them are likely to be interested. In addition, much of the textual material is authentic, in the sense noted earlier, and so brings the flavour of life beyond the school walls right into the classroom. All of these attributes are calculated to encourage learners to listen and read for meaning and to use the relevant contexts and visual supports to this end. The fact that possible future personal needs and personal interests are addressed by the material offers further encouragement towards treating what it says and how it says it with some attention. In short, the input supplied by the unit constitute a fairly favourable set of conditions for incidental lexical learning.

Other opportunities for incidental learning are furnished by the questions and exercises in French which relate to the various dialogues and texts, for example:

Quelle heure veulent-ils se lever?	('What time do they want to get up?')
Où se donnent-ils rendez-vous?	('Where do they agree to meet?')
Cherche les mots qui font penser au soleil.	('Look for the words that make you think of the sun.')

In addition, although the version of communicative language teaching adopted here allows for some use of the learners' mother tongue in class, the normal understanding would be that, as far as is practicable, the teacher will use French as the medium of instruction. Clearly, as in the case of the audio-lingual approach, this implies many further opportunities for incidental lexical learning.

With regard to opportunities for more atomistic types of lexical learning in the unit, one such is the text completion task associated with the first four dialogues, which bring particular expressions into focus (*ça va?* – 'how are things?', *désolé* – 'sorry' – etc.) within a meaningful context; another is the detailed treatment of various forms of the verbs *pouvoir*, *vouloir* and *devoir*, accompanied by commentary on their meanings and usage; and a third is the word-search exercise following the text about the solar-powered house. Also, the juxtaposition of English expressions with French expressions in the opening summary (e.g. Asking if you can take a *message*: *Voulez-vous laisser un message?*) may encourage the making of mnemonic connections between the expressions in question (e.g. the French word for 'message' is spelt exactly the same as the English word). Finally, as in the case of audio-lingual methodology, the provision of a visual material, often in close association with particular expressions, may not only assist comprehension but may well promote the creation of mental images in respect of such expressions.

There is obviously quite a lot to be said in favour of the communicative approach in terms of lexical learning. At least in the version exemplified above, it seems to combine the advantages of the grammar-translation method (rich textual input, association between target language and mother tongue forms, explicit focus on the grammatical profile of words, availability of written forms) with the advantages of the audio-lingual method (classroom discourse in the target language, visual support, provision of substantial oral–aural input). Furthermore, it addresses learners' needs, interests and expectations in a way that the other two methods do not, and thus in principle ought to deliver teaching and learning materials which have more personal significance for learners than what is delivered by the other methods. That is not to say, however, that everything in the garden is rosy as far as lexical learning in the communicative approach is concerned. Communicative materials have not always been as attentive as they might have been to the more atomistic aspects of vocabulary learning, with, for example, little or no encouragement being offered for the rehearsal of new target items, and with often all too few exercises being on offer which have a specifically and explicitly lexical focus. Another problem faced by communicative courses is that the authentic material by which they set such store dates extremely rapidly. Thus, for example, the long-distance and international dialling instructions set out in Unit 6 of the 1985 version of *Salut!* (3) have been out of date for years. Obviously, such built-in obsolescence is likely to undermine somewhat the claim of communicative language teaching to be in touch with learners' needs in respect of their use of the target language in the 'real world'.

One possible solution to the problem of obsolescence is to liberate communicative language teaching from the constraints of rarely updated textbooks and instead to equip teachers and indeed learners with strategies for 'didacticizing' – i.e. turning into usable teaching/learning material – *any* authentic sample of the target language – conversational, humorous, journalistic, literary, technical etc. – which is relevant to the language use objectives of the learners and therefore to the teaching/learning objectives of the course. There is nothing arcane about such didacticizing strategies; they include the provision of aids to comprehension of one kind or another (e.g. visual supports, explanations of particular expressions) and the devising of a range of exercises and tasks to exploit the target language sample in question to the maximum. In relation to vocabulary learning, the tasks and exercises might include not only diverse types of reading comprehension exercises but also tasks involving the extraction and grouping of words from the same lexical subsystem, the analysis of contextual meanings of words into denotational and/or connotational components, the gathering from texts of evidence about the collocational possibilities of particular words, and so on. Samples of the target language can be didacticized in this way not only by teachers for learners, but also, as has been mentioned, by learners for each other and for themselves. This last point brings us to the notion of learner autonomy.

In a way, a concern to 'autonomize' the learner is the logical conclusion of the learner-centredness of the communicative approach. If communicative language teaching is focused on the learner, then, logically, it has to be concerned with empowering learners to play as wide a role as possible in their own learning. The Dublin-based researcher David Little, who has spent the last 20 years exploring the idea of learner autonomy, defines it as 'a capacity... for detachment, critical reflection, decision-making and independent action'. The relevance of learner autonomy for vocabulary acquisition has to do with the earlier-made point about the effect on depth of processing of learners' seeing an activity as having personal significance for them. Where learners are allowed to make their own decisions about choice of target language reading matter, topics for discussion, project themes, exercises etc. and have been brought to the point where they can make such decisions both confidently and wisely, the interest and commitment that they then bring to the activities in question is bound to bear fruit in higher levels of retention of lexical (and other) material than where they are simply following a path pre-ordained for them from on high.

10.5   Lexical learning and other aspects of language learning

Since the message of this entire book has been that the lexicon is inextricably intertwined with language at large, the message of this last section of the present chapter – namely, that lexical acquisition is not sealed off from coping as a learner with other areas of language – need not be laboured. Let us simply look at some specific instances of procedures leading to lexical learning – in both incidental and atomistic mode – in the above perspective, and see what we find.

The following passage represents a typical case of an ideal opportunity to pick up a new word from reading for meaning. The word in question, *pygostile*, is embedded in a context which actually defines it:

> 'One of the fossils we heard about was a dinosaur in Mongolia that had a pygostile – the fused vertebrae that support a bird's tail feathers . . .'

Even in a straightforward case like this the interpenetration of lexis and other linguistic areas in the reader's dealings with the word is evident. The reader interprets *pygostile* as a noun, because it functions as the object of a verb (*had*), because it is preceded by an article (*a*), and because the phrase it is equated with is also a noun phrase (involving another article: *the*). Whether or not the reader has access to terminology such as *noun, verb, article* etc., he/she will know from this much evidence that *pygostile* may also be preceded by adjectives (e.g. *a small pygostile*) and prepositions (e.g. *beneath the pygostile*) and may function as the subject of a verb (e.g. *the pygostile was the final proof*). From the context it is also clear that *pygostile* keeps company with words referring to anatomical features (e.g. *vertebrae*) and to birds (e.g. *feathers*). From the wider context – an article in the *National Geographic Magazine* – and from the general look of the word it may also be inferred that *pygostile* is a learned item more likely to occur in scientific discourse than in casual conversation. The reader will also probably try out some possible pronunciations of *pygostile*. (Does *py* sound like *pie* or like the *pi* in pig? Is *stile* like *style, steel* or *still*?). If, after all this, the word *is* retained, it will undoubtedly be retained with its grammatical, collocational, stylistic and (intelligently guessed) phonological profile as well as its spelling and its meaning.

A number of examples of components of classroom activities leading to atomistic word-learning have already been cited. Let us return to the most traditional strategy – namely, rote-learning word-lists – as exemplified by the earlier discussed extracts from the German coursebook *Heute Abend!* (re-cited below).

der Bodensee (kein Pl. [no pl.]), Lake Constance

:

die Eisenbahn (en), railway

:

abfahren, fährt ab, leave

:

hoch, höher, high, higher etc.

As was noted when these lists were referred to in the previous section, they contain information not just about the orthography and meaning of the items in question, but also about different forms of the word associated with other grammatical environments (plural forms of nouns, third-person singular present forms of verbs etc.). The lists also indicate certain facts about the impact of particular words on other words with which they combine in sentences. For example, by supplying the appropriate nominative (subject case) form of the definite article alongside each noun included, they specify that the noun in question requires a particular set of forms of the elements which surround it such as definite and indefinite articles, quantifiers (*viel* – 'much', 'many', *mehrere* – 'several' etc.), demonstratives (*dieser* – 'this', *jener* – 'that'), adjectives etc.

Often, word-lists of the above type go so far as to indicate the kind of syntactic patterning that is associated with a particular word in a particular sense. For example, *Actualités Françaises* ('French Current Affairs'), an advanced French course for English-speakers, systematically includes, after each text it presents, a list of verbs which appear in the text together with their complementation patterns, for example:

résister à qch. [quelque chose]: to resist sth.

se rendre compte de qch.: to realise sth.

apprendre à faire qch.: to learn to do sth.

permettre à qqn. [quelqu'un] de faire qch.: to allow s.o. to do sth.

insister pour faire qch.: to insist on doing sth.

At the very least, then, word-lists of the traditional kind, i.e. designed to be learned off by heart, tend to contain morphological information as well as orthographic and semantic information, and they may well also contain syntactic information. Some lexically oriented pedagogical activities take such multidimensionality much further, as the following example – borrowed from a fairly well-known book on learning foreign languages from authentic texts – illustrates. The activity in question can be thought of as having both an incidental learning aspect and a more atomistic aspect.

> *Preparatory task relating to the reading of a German text on an accident involving a car originally believed stolen*: sort a jumble of nouns and verbs (e.g. *Polizei* – 'police' – *Wagen* – 'car' – *stehlen* – 'to steal' – *melden* – 'to report') into categories according to meaning; create a story from combinations of nouns and verbs; re-order a set of sentences containing the above words into a coherent accident report; use this report to edit the story created; read the authentic text (which contains all the words in the original jumbles).

This task demands attention to form and meaning, to morphology and syntax, and to collocation patterns and context. As far as context is concerned, for example, the task requires a coming to grips with the fact that the word *Wagen*, which in other contexts may mean 'cart' or '(railway) carriage', means 'car' when used of a motor vehicle.

In the light of the discussion in the previous section, and indeed in the light of discussion in the rest of the book, the more dimensions lexical learning tasks can incorporate, the more effective they are likely to be, not only in terms of addressing the fact that lexical knowledge has to be multidimensional in order to be of any use, but also in terms of promoting the deeper kinds of processing that are likely to result in lexical knowledge actually being added to in a durable manner. There is a lesson here too for lexical testing. Too often lexical tests have focused solely on words in isolation. Not only has this kind of testing failed to tap into aspects of lexical knowledge which are absolutely vital to its functioning in language use, but the 'washback effect' of such tests on classroom practice – that is the consequence of teachers' teaching towards such tests – has frequently been a severe impoverishment of the lexical components of language instruction. If lexical tests are to be valid measures of the kind of lexical knowledge that can be deployed to some purpose, and if they are to encourage teaching and learning activities that lead to the construction of such knowledge, they must – whether individually or collectively – demand a great more of the testee than simply the decontextualized recognition or regurgitation of isolated items.

10.6 Summary

This chapter has looked at two ways in which support has been offered to lexical knowledge and its advancement: the making of dictionaries and the promotion of lexical learning in the classroom. It has provided a brief history of lexicography – with particular reference to the evolution of English dictionaries – and has demonstrated some of the challenges for the lexicographer that arise from the multifaceted nature of the lexicon. In this latter connection it has suggested that a full and imaginative use of the new technologies may solve some (though not all) of the problems that dictionary-makers have traditionally had to face. The chapter has gone on to provide an overview of different approaches to the lexicon in the classroom, including an exploration of how lexical learning has been approached in three important methodologies used in the teaching of second languages. The message of this section of the chapter has been that, whatever the teaching approach used, lexical learning in the classroom has had both an incidental and an atomistic dimension, and that both dimensions can be shown to have a valuable contribution to make to the process. Finally, the chapter has looked at some specific lexical learning opportunities and procedures and has demonstrated that in all cases they are characterized by a certain multidimensionality – reflecting the fact that the knowledge aimed at is itself multidimensional.

Sources and suggestions for further reading

See 10.2. General sources for this section were Chapter 1 of K. Whittaker's book *Dictionaries* (London: Clive Bingley, 1966), N. E. Osselton's article,

'On the history of dictionaries' (in R. R. K. Hartmann (ed.), *Lexicography: principles and practice*, London: Academic Press, 1983) and A. Walker-Read's article, 'The history of lexicography' (in R. Ilson (ed.), *Lexicography: an emerging international profession*, Manchester: Manchester University Press, 1986). The examples from the *Glosses of Reichenau* are selected from those cited by P. Studer and E. G. R. Waters in their edited volume *Historical French reader: medieval period* (Oxford: Clarendon, 1924, 14–19).

Treatments of Sumerian–Akkadian glossaries and grammars are to be found in J. A. Black's article, 'The Babylonian grammatical tradition: the first grammars of Sumerian' (*Transactions of the Philological Society* 87, 1989, 75–89) and T. Jacobsen's article, 'Very ancient linguistics: Babylonian grammatical texts' (in D. Hymes (ed.), *Studies in the history of linguistics: traditions and paradigms*, Bloomington: Indiana University Press, 1974). The thesaurus examples are from *The Oxford Thesaurus: an A–Z dictionary of synonyms* (Oxford: Oxford University Press, 1991), compiled by L. Urdang. *The Oxford Dictionary of Slang* was compiled by J. Ayto (Oxford: Oxford University Press, 1998). The comments on alphabetization in early dictionaries are based on Chapter 12 of N. E. Osselton's *Chosen words: past and present problems for dictionary makers* (Exeter: University of Exeter Press, 1995). The relationship between the first European vernacular dictionaries and the Renaissance is discussed by, e.g. R. Harris and T. J. Taylor in *Landmarks in linguistic thought I: the western tradition from Socrates to Saussure* (second edition, London: Routledge, 1997, 94). The O examples from Cawdrey's dictionary are borrowed from p. 16 of N. E. Osselton's article 'On the history of dictionaries' (cited above). The brief discussion of the moves towards the inclusion of everyday words in English dictionaries has its source in Chapter 3 of N. E. Osselton's *Chosen words: past and present problems for dictionary makers* (see above); the quotation from John Kersey's Preface is to be found on p. 26 of this chapter. The discussion of *The Oxford English Dictionary* is largely based on H. Aarsleff's article 'The original plan for the OED and its background' (*Transactions of the Philological Society* 88, 1990, 151–61). The quotation from H. G. Liddell and R. Scott's Preface is cited on p. 160 of Aarsleff's above-mentioned article. The discussion of the use of electronic corpora in dictionary making is informed by J. Sinclair's edited volume *Looking up: an account of the COBUILD Project in lexical computing* (London and Glasgow: Collins, 1987), the same author's book *Corpus, concordance, collocation* (Oxford: Oxford University Press, 1991), and by Chapter 6 of R. Carter's book *Vocabulary: applied linguistic perspectives* (second edition, London: Routledge).

Information about and links to online dictionaries are available from Internet sites such as:

- http://www.facstaff.bucknell.edu/rbeard/diction.html
- http://clicnet.swarthmore.edu/dictionnaires.html
- http://www.encyberpedia.com/glossary.htm
- http://cctc.commnet.edu/libroot/dictionaries.htm

See 10.3. The source of information about Chinese spelling reform and its non-acceptance outside the People's Republic of China is L-J. Calvet's *Histoire de l'écriture* (Paris: Plon, 1996, 101). The *Dictionnaire Encyclopédique Général* was compiled by J-P. Mével, V. Chape and A. Mercier (second edition, Paris: Hachette, 1996). The definitions of *kip* are taken from p. 651 of the *Concise Oxford Dictionary* (eighth edition, see above). The discussion of the grammatical coding system used in the third edition of the *Oxford Advanced Learner's Dictionary* and the associated examples are based on pp 155–7 of R. Carter's book *Vocabulary: applied linguistic perspectives* (second edition, London: Routledge, 1998). The account of the grammatical coding system of the fifth edition of the *Oxford Advanced Learner's Dictionary*, edited by J. Crowther (Oxford: Oxford University Press, 1995), is drawn from pp B1–B8 of the dictionary (especially p. B4) and also refers to the dictionary's entries for *give* (pp 499f.) and *drop* (pp 357f.). The entries from the *Hugo Pocket Dictionary: Dutch–English, English–Dutch* (London: Hugo's Language Books Ltd, 1969) are cited, respectfully, from pp 37 and 107; the 'Explanation of the Imitated Pronunciation' (guide to symbols used in representations of Dutch pronunciation) is to be found on p. xi of this dictionary. The brief account of the *Oxford Dictionary of Current Idiomatic English* (Oxford: Oxford University Press) is based on pp. 160ff. of R. Carter's book *Vocabulary: applied linguistic perspectives* (see above). The dictionary appears in two volumes, the first of which was edited by A. P. Cowie and R. Mackin and published in 1975, and the second of which was edited by A. P. Cowie, R. Mackin and I. R. McCaig and published in 1983.

See 10.4. The source of the point about explicit and implicit definitions in teacher input (and the related illustrations) is E. Hatch and C. Brown's book, *Vocabulary, semantics and language education* (Cambridge: Cambridge University Press, 1995, 401). The discussion of incidental vocabulary acquisition is largely based on W. Nagy's article 'On the role of context in first- and second-language vocabulary learning' (in N. Schmitt and M. McCarthy (eds), *Vocabulary description, acquisition and pedagogy*, Cambridge: Cambridge University Press, 1997), and on the relevant section of Chapter 4 of my own book, *Exploring the second language mental lexicon* (Cambridge: Cambridge University Press, 1999). The research on combining context-based with word-focused activities is reported in T. Paribakht and M. Wesche's article 'Vocabulary enhancement activities and reading for meaning in second language vocabulary acquisition' (in J. Coady and T. Huckin (eds), *Second language vocabulary acquisition: a rationale for pedagogy*. Cambridge: Cambridge University Press, 1997). Studies dealing with the role of rehearsal in the construction of memory codes for newly encountered words include: A. Baddeley, C. Papagno and G. Vallar, 'When long-term learning depends on short-term storage' (*Journal of Memory and Language* 27, 1988, 586–95); S. Gathercole and A. Baddeley, 'Evaluation of the role of phonological STM in the development of vocabulary in children:

a longitudinal study' (*Journal of Memory and Language* 28, 1989, 200–13); C. Papagno, T. Valentine and A. Baddeley, 'Phonological short-term memory and foreign-language vocabulary learning' (*Journal of Memory and Language* 30, 1991, 331–47); E. Service, 'Phonology, working memory and foreign-language learning' (*Quarterly Journal of Experimental Psychology* 45A, 1992, 21–50; E. Service 'Phonological and semantic aspects of memory for foreign language' (in J. Chapelle and M-T. Claes (eds), *Actes: 1er Congrès International: Mémoire et Mémorisation dans l'Acquisition et l'Apprentissage des Langues/Proceedings: 1st International Congress: Memory and Memorization in Acquiring and Learning Languages.* Louvain-la-Neuve: CLL, 1993). A widely cited study on associative strategies in second language vocabulary learning is: A. Cohen and E. Aphek, 'Retention of second-language vocabulary over time: investigating the role of mnemonic associations' (*System* 8, 1980, 221–35). The quotations concerning the findings of verbal memory research regarding rehearsal and extensive processing are taken from A. Wingfield and D. Byrnes's book, *The psychology of human memory* (New York: Academic Press, 1981, 290), and the quotation concerning deep processing is taken from R.M. Gagné's book, *The conditions of learning* (third edition, New York: Holt Rinehart & Winston, 1977, 197). The quotation about the recallability of statements with personal significance is from p. 251 of A. Ellis and G. Beattie's book, *The psychology of language and communication* (London: Weidenfeld & Nicolson, 1986). The keyword technique example is borrowed from p. 166 of I. S. P. Nation's book, *Teaching and learning vocabulary* (Boston, MA: Heinle & Heinle, 1990); the effectiveness of the technique is noted by, among others, N. Ellis and A. Beaton in their article, 'Psycholinguistic determinants of foreign language vocabulary learning' (in B. Harley (ed.), *Lexical issues in language learning*, Ann Arbor/Amsterdam/Philadelphia: Language Learning/John Benjamins, 1995). The more general research on visualization is reported by B. Tomlinson in his article, 'Helping L2 readers to see' (in T. Hickey and J. Williams (eds) *Language, education and society in a changing world*, Clevedon: IRAAL/Multilingual Matters Ltd., 1996). *Heute Abend* was written by M. Kelber and was published in London by Ginn and Company in 1938. *De vive voix* was written by M.-T. Moget with the assistance of J. Boudot and was published in Paris by Didier in 1972. *Salut!* (3) was prepared by participants in the Institiúid Teangeolaíochta Éireann (Linguistics Institute of Ireland) Modern Languages Project under the leadership of J. Sheils and S. McDermott; it was published in Dublin by the Educational Company in 1985. A variety of ideas relative to didacticizing authentic materials are to be found in D. Little, S. Devitt and D. Singleton's book, *Learning foreign languages from authentic texts: theory and practice* (Dublin: Authentik Language Learning Resources, 1989). The D. Little quotation on autonomy is taken from p. 4 of his book, *Learner autonomy 1: definitions, issues and problems* (Dublin: Authentik Language Learning Resources, 1991).

See 10.5. The quotations from the *National Geographic Magazine* are both from Vol. 196, No. 5 (1999); the first appears in a piece entitled 'Feathered dinosaurs' on a unnumbered page in the preambulatory section headed 'On assignment', and the second appears on p. 44 (in an article written by Johan Reinhard entitled 'Frozen in time'). The French verb-list is quoted from p. 32 of the second volume of *Actualités Françaises* (written by D. O. Nott and J. E. Trickey, London: The English Universities Press, 1971). The final example of a lexical task cited in 10.5 is from pp 51–3 of D. Little, S. Devitt and D. Singleton's book, *Learning foreign languages from authentic texts: theory and practice* (Dublin: Authentik Language Learning Resources, 1989).

Good treatments of the evolution of lexicography (in addition to those in publications already mentioned) are to be found in:

J. Green, *Chasing the sun: dictionary-makers and the dictionaries they made* (London: J. Cape, 1996);

T. McArthur, *Worlds of reference: lexicography, learning and language from the clay tablet to the computer* (Cambridge: Cambridge University Press, 1986).

Shorter introductions to this topic (with particular reference to English) are provided by a number of the articles in the *Oxford companion to the English language* (ed. T. McArthur, Oxford: Oxford University Press, 1992).

Other recommended publications on lexicography are:

H. Béjoint, *Tradition and innovation in modern English dictionaries* (Oxford: Clarendon Press, 1994);

M. Benson, E. Benson and R. F. Ilson, *Lexicographic description of English* (Amsterdam: John Benjamins, 1986);

R. R. K. Hartmann and G. James, *Dictionary of lexicography* (London: Routledge, 1998);

F. J. Hausman, O. Reichmann, H. E Wiegand and L. Zgusta (eds), *Wörterbücher/dictionaries/dictionnaires. An international encyclopedia of lexicography* (Berlin: De Gruyter, 1989–91);

D. A. Walker, A. Zampolli and N. Calzolari (eds), *Automating the lexicon; research and practice in a multilingual environment* (Oxford: Oxford University Press, 1995);

L. Zgusta, 'Problems of the bilingual dictionary' (*Lexicographica International Annual* 2, 1–161).

With regard to lexical learning in the classroom, the kinds of issues discussed in 10.4 and 10.5 are explored at greater length and from various points of view in:

R. Carter and M. McCarthy (eds), *Vocabulary and language teaching* (London: Longman, 1988);

J. Coady and T. Huckin, *Second language vocabulary acquisition: a rationale for pedagogy* (Cambridge: Cambridge University Press, 1997);

E. Hatch and C. Brown, *Vocabulary, semantics and language education* (Cambridge: Cambridge University Press, 1995);

N. Schmitt and M. McCarthy (eds), *Vocabulary: description, acquisition and pedagogy* (Cambridge: Cambridge University Press, 1997).

Books dealing with concrete strategies for dealing with lexis in a formal instructional setting (apart from the Nation volume and the Little, Devitt and Singleton volume mentioned above) include:

R. Gairns and S. Redman, *Working with words: a guide to teaching and learning vocabulary* (Cambridge: Cambridge University Press, 1986);

M. Lewis, *The lexical approach: the state of ELT and a way forward* (Hove: Language Teaching Publications, 1993);

M. Lewis, *Implementing the lexical approach: putting theory into practice* (Hove: Language Teaching Publications, 1997);

M. Wallace, *Teaching vocabulary* (London: Heinemann, 1982);

M-C. Tréville and L. Duquette, *Enseigner le vocabulaire en classe de langue* (Vanves: Hachette, 1996).

Focusing questions/topics for discussion

1. Try to think of some different sets of circumstances in which the authority of a dictionary is used to settle disputes about language.

2. List the major advantages an electronic dictionary has over a traditional printed dictionary, and try to think of some advantages a traditional printed dictionary may have over an electronic dictionary.

3. Examine the way in which any dictionary with which you are familiar deals with multiple meaning. Try to come to some conclusions about the principles underlying the approach in question, and suggest some possible improvements to the approach, giving reasons for your proposals.

4. Devise a connected sequence of classroom activities (for use in the context of a mother tongue or a second language teaching programme) which contains opportunities for both incidental and atomistic learning of lexis.

5. Try to create a lexical learning activity (for use in the context of a mother tongue or a second language teaching programme) which includes a stylistic dimension alongside other dimensions.

Conclusion

Given the range of topics covered in this volume, and given the fact that a concluding summary is provided at the end of each chapter, it does not seem sensible to refer to all the elements of the book's content in these concluding remarks. Instead, the focus here is on the general theme that has run through every chapter – namely, the very considerable extent to which the lexicon interacts with dimensions of language which have traditionally been regarded as relatively separate from it. Indeed, in the light of all that has been said the question that poses itself at this point is whether we are justified as treating the lexicon as, on the one hand, having any kind of existence which is distinct from the rest of language and, on the other, forms a component which can be seen as cohesive and unitary.

In relation to the issue of whether it is possible to separate out the lexicon from language at large, it is not that linguists have changed their fundamental view that the lexicon is that part of language which deals with 'idiosyncratic information', but rather that their research and reflections on such research have led them to the conclusion that very much more of the functioning of language than they had previously imagined *is* idiosyncratic. The response to such findings has been, essentially, to 'slim down' the generalizing elements in linguistic models and to assign more and more responsibility to the lexicon. It appears at times as if this process is at some stage soon going to reach the point where the notions of lexicon and of language will become interchangeable.

The usual line of argument offered in favour of continuing to see the lexicon as distinguishable from other dimensions of language is that, however many aspects of language can be addressed in lexical terms, it is nevertheless still possible to identify linguistic phenomena which can be described without reference to lexical particularities. For example, all human languages are characterized by what is sometimes known as *double articulation*. That is to say, as we saw in Chapter 6, they are organized into two levels. At one level, meaning*less* units (phonemes, letters) combine to form meaning*ful* units (inflections, affixes, words etc.), and at a higher level small meaningful units (morphemes, words etc.) combine into larger meaningful units (phrases, sentences etc.). General design features of language such as this, although certainly rich in implications for the lexicon, clearly do not depend on the lexical specificities of any particular language.

There are other features of linguistic organization which are more specific in nature – insofar as they relate to particular domains of language (syntax, phonology etc.) – but which operate universally, irrespective of the lexical attributes of the units involved. Structure-dependency is one such feature. This is the principle, common to the syntax of all languages, according to which the ways in which sentences relate to each other have structural dimensions. For example, in English, in order to produce an 'interrogative version' of a statement, we have to take account not just of how the words are sequenced but also of how they cluster into constituents and how those constituents are organized and hierarchized in respect of each other. Let us consider in this connection the following two sets of sentences, the third member of each is ill-formed.

The tall chap is one of the men she has been seeing.

Is the tall chap one of the men she has been seeing?

*Has the tall chap is one of the men she been seeing

The tall chap who kissed her is one of the men she has been seeing.

Is the tall chap who kissed her one of the men she has been seeing?

*Kissed the tall chap who her is one of the men she has been seeing

Whereas the first set of sentences might lead us to believe that making a question out of a statement might be simply a matter of putting the first verb in the sentence to the front, the second set shows that this 'linear' rule does not work, and that in moving elements around in such cases we have to take account of – among other things – which words in the sentence constitute the main clause (*The tall chap is one of the men*) and which constitute subordinate clauses (*she has been seeing, who kissed her*).

It is true that, as we have noted, many linguistic phenomena which were previously viewed as independent of lexical considerations are now widely acknowledged to be essentially lexical in nature, and that, on this basis, there is always the possibility of further shifts of perspective in a lexical direction in the future. However, it still seems plausible to suppose that, whether or not one accepts the Chomskyan notion of Universal Grammar, there will always remain aspects of language that have to be seen as standing outside the lexical specificities of individual languages.

With regard to the question of whether the various facets of the multifaceted lexicon can be genuinely be seen as cohering into a unitary level of linguistic reality, numerous voices have been raised against this notion in recent years. Interestingly, the voices in question come largely from the realm of psychology and psycholinguistics, and, even more interestingly, they come from two schools of thought which in most other respects are in sharp disagreement with each other – namely, on the one hand, advocates of the Fodorian version of the modularity hypothesis and, on the other, advocates of connectionism.

As we saw in Chapter 9, two defining features of Fodor's conception of the language module are *informational encapsulation* (the notion that language processing mechanisms are, as it were, blinkered with regard to data other than the specifically linguistic data on which they are designed to operate) and *shallowness of intramodular processing* (the idea that language processing within the language module is an essentially formal matter, with no semantic analysis taking place 'inside' the items being processed). We noted in Chapter 9 that the advantage for modularists of limiting their conception of the language module to that of a formal processor with no semantic role is that it does not confront them with the problem of where to draw the line between linguistic and non-linguistic meaning. The implication of this point of view is that, since the formal lexicon falls within the informationally encapsulated lexicon and that the semantic lexicon falls outside of it, lexical knowledge of a semantic kind has no role in the processing of lexical form.

This position would seem to gain some support from the fact that the lexicon appears to be organized both along formal lines and along semantic lines – as evidenced, for example, by the fact that slips of the tongue sometimes involve the substitution of a word which is phonologically close to the target item, for example *antiquities* for *iniquities,* and sometimes the substitution of a semantically related word, for example, *finger* for *hand* (meronym– holonym), *asleep* for *awake* (complementaries) etc. On the other hand it departs from the classic view of modern linguistics – strongly enunciated by its founder, Ferdinand de Saussure – that the formal and semantic aspects of a linguistic sign are as intimately connected as the two sides of a piece of paper. It also falls foul, as the discussion in Chapter 9 indicates, of evidence of 'online' context effects in the processing of words.

Regarding the connectionist perspective, as again we saw in Chapter 9, this represents knowledge in terms of connection strength rather than in terms of patterns. According to this approach it is not the patterns that are stored – not even the patterns of features that make up what we know as words, morphemes and phonemes – but rather the connection strengths between elements at a much lower level that allow these patterns to be recreated. What this obviously implies is that there is no level at which even words have a stable psycholinguistic existence as symbols, still less a level at which collections of words have such an existence.

It may be worth mentioning in this context the way in which natural scientists are constantly on their guard against reductionism, recognizing that the fact that a particular phenomenon can be reduced to component parts does not necessarily mean that such a reduction constitutes a complete or useful account of the phenomenon in question. The illustrative example that is sometimes deployed in this context is that of a sign made up of coloured light bulbs – AMUSEMENTS, BAR, CIRCUS, DANCING, SOUTH PIER etc. Analysing such signs as simply a number of individual light bulbs would provide an account of such phenomena at only one level. A complete account would require the recognition of both higher levels of analysis, for example, the shape of the configuration at letter-level, the shape of the configuration at word-level, the meaning of the configuration etc., and lower levels, such as the component parts of each light bulb, the chemical elements of each of these components etc. To return to connectionism and the lexicon, the fact that it is possible to analyse lexical knowledge in terms of connection-strengths at a micro level does not exclude the notion that there may be other possible levels of analysis.

Both the modularist and the connectionist approach to the lexicon would appear to be called into question by the fact that, as we noted in Chapter 1, the word – in all its complexity – is so widely perceived as the basic ingredient of language. It is difficult not to see this perception as strongly suggesting that a high degree of psychological reality attaches to the idea of a multidimensional but coherent lexical level of analysis. This should surely give some pause to those inclined to consign the lexicon concept to fragmentation and the four winds.

Nevertheless, despite arguments such those put in the foregoing few pages in favour of continuing to demarcate an area of language under the heading of lexicon and of treating that area as some kind of coherent reality, we have to acknowledge that it may eventually prove that the lexical construct is neither theoretically nor empirically dissociable from other linguistic or psycholinguistic domains. Given the exciting advances in technologies that now allow the direct observation of brain functioning, the clinching arguments may in the end come not from linguistic theory or psycholinguistic experiments but from neuroscience.

In the meantime it seems very likely that research and publications on and around the lexicon will remain a 'growth industry' within all the many mansions of linguistics. After decades upon decades of being treated by most language specialists as the least interesting aspect of language, words have returned to the very centre of linguists' field of vision. And not before time. In support of this last remark I offer as my parting shot a quotation not from a linguist but from a writer of science fiction. Here is what one of the characters in the Dan Simmons's novel *Hyperion* (London: Hodder, 1989) has to say on the topic of words:

> It might be argued that the Siamese-twin infants of word/idea are the only contribution the species can, will or should make to the reveling cosmos. (Yes, our DNA is unique but so is a salamander's. Yes, we construct artefacts but so have species ranging from beavers to . . . ants . . . Yes, we weave real-fabric things from the dream-stuff of mathematics, but the universe is hardwired with arithmetic. Scratch a circle and π peeps out . . . But *where* has the universe hidden a *word* under its outer layer of biology, geometry or insensate rock?)

Index

Printed in the United Kingdom
by Lightning Source UK Ltd.
133693UK00002B/42/A

9 780340 731741